a collection of

Madness
in BLOOM

Meanjin, Australia

ISBN 978-0-6453392-0-8 (paperback)
ISBN 978-0-6453392-1-5 (eBook)

Cover design by Alexander Coolican
Typeset by Wallea Eaglehawk

First published in 2021

Revolutionary University Press is an initiative of Revolutionaries to publish the work of emerging and established creatives and thinkers from university places and spaces. One press for all universities.

Moonrise
Meanjin, Australia
www.moonrise.revolutionaries.com.au

RELATED TITLES FROM MOONRISE

a record of my remnants by Katie Hulme

Through the darkness, I will love myself edited by Wallea Eaglehawk, Nikola Champlin & Padya Paramita

FOREWORD

Madness in Bloom is an asylum of new voices calling out from within dreams, reality and reverie. This collection of 62 works by emerging Australian writers is an eclectic mix of short fiction and creative non-fiction, poetry, flash fiction, personal reflections, and experimental works that leap across genre borders in at times thrilling, sometimes sad and often hopeful ways. But forever enthralling. From phantasms of the mind to the epiphany of waking, this weighty anthology is a glut of creative explorations into the euphoria of love, the torment of loss, the yearning for truth, the whimsy of daydreams, and the reckoning of nightmares. We invite you to turn the page and come join us, as we witness madness in full bloom...

—R.W. & J.L.

daydreams — nightmares — hallucination — phantasms
— in/corporeality — in/tangiblity — reflection — truth —
lies — ambition — the unfulfilled — being — euphoria
— whimsy — serendipity — epiphany — yearning —
reckoning — hope

CONTENTS

HORRIFYING REALITY

Seanna Burnett

A jagged, bloody cut ran from June's left ear to the corner of her mouth. Sticky goo dripped from it and from a gash on her forehead, painting her pale skin red. The flesh around her white eyes was sickly and black bile had oozed out of her mouth, coating her chin. The 18-year-old looked like she had been attacked, blinded and poisoned at the same time. But physically, June felt fine.

She plucked strands of blonde hair out of two, otherwise perfect, space buns on her head and teased each piece with a brush. Once she was happy her hairstyle made her look dishevelled and crazy, she reached for her white nurses' cap. The cap with the red cross in the centre was stained with crimson paint and looked like it had survived a war having never been washed. The rest of her outfit was the same. The collared, button-up dress was recognisable as that of a nurse from the past, though June could never pick what era a real nurse would have worn it. The scary nurse was simply a common illusion that people willingly fell for in video games, horror movies and scary attractions like this one.

A middle-aged man with greasy hair in a tight man-bun poked his head into the dressing room. 'Hurry up, Juney. Some idiot just punched Gazza in the face again,' said Jonas.

'Again?' June groaned. 'That guy is going to end up with the scariest crooked nose by the time he's 18.'

Jonas shrugged. 'He'll learn to dodge that shit eventually. I've got Lucy putting on his hazmat suit for the rest of her shift, so I need you in there now to take her usual place in one of the back rooms.'

'Will I get paid for the extra half an hour this time?' June asked.

'Grab yourself a free drink at the end of the night,' Jonas said with a smile. His teeth were yellow, and June knew that wasn't because of any makeup. Her boss must have noticed her unimpressed expression because his smile turned to one of pity.

'Look, I'll even throw in one of those small bags of lollies. This is a tough weekend for everyone. Especially for you,' the man said.

June gave him a smile and said a half-hearted thank you. Jonas wasn't a terrible person, just a terrible manager. His mostly teenage staff were overworked and underpaid, but he knew he had them hooked with the occasional bribe of free food and the bragging rights of working at the 'coolest' place in town. Club Fear was famous for being the best entertainment centre around before the incident dominated the front page of all the local papers.

June slammed the dressing room door behind her and turned towards the other side of the building. Club Fear's bowling alley took up the bulk of the establishment and was permanently decorated as if it were Halloween. June gritted her teeth against the urge to speed walk through the crowd of teenagers already buzzing on soft drink, fried food and lollies. Instead, she focused on the familiar movements of her character. Jonas was big on his staff always staying in character when around guests. Which, for June's crazy nurse attire, meant smiling widely, staring too long and walking slowly with her arms pinned to her sides. After three years, the act was automatic. Fake spiderwebs clung to the bowling alley walls with plastic spiders hot glued onto them. June passed Mrs and Mr Femur, the fake skeletons having tea in the cafeteria, and Uncle Jimmy, the wax zombie who stood by the pair of old arcade machines. His 1970s suit looked old and dusty, but not as bad as Captain's pirate hat. The pirate skeleton lounged on a loveseat near the bathrooms, his hat over his face and an empty bottle glued into one bony hand.

A young girl with pink hair and too much pink lipstick stepped in front of June, holding up her phone. 'Let's get a picture with the creepy nurse!' she said, turning to address a group of girls behind her. They all looked 15 years old but were probably only 12. June struggled to tell most of the time and as she smiled at the pink girl's phone, she was too busy thinking about Club Fear's skeletons to care. A year ago, two more hung from nooses near the back wall. A friend from school mentioned to June once that the child-sized skeleton twins hanging on either side of the bowling lanes weren't appropriate for the target audience of the entertainment centre. At the time, June had laughed.

On the opposite side of the bowling alley was the zombie-themed mini golf course and beyond that, the hallway to the party rooms; one of which was still locked and taped off since the incident. The police said business could go back to normal months ago, but Jonas liked the look of the crime scene tape covering the door to the windowless room. All things considered, the incident was good publicity for a place like Club Fear. June stared intently at her destination as she passed. She knew if she looked at the door, it might zap the courage she needed.

The entrance to the haunted hospital maze was covered in a brick-like wallpaper and metal light fixtures jutted out of it. The lights glowed a harsh white and flickered in time with crackling sound effects from several hidden speakers. A ticket booth stood to one side where patrons could exchange their $12 ticket for an ink stamp on their wrist that they'd be sure to show off to their friends the next morning. June knocked twice on the semi-concealed side door of the ticket booth

'Hey, it's June. I'm here for my shift,' she said, though half of her words were cut off by a pre-recorded scream erupting from inside the haunted hospital. The door to the booth swung open, and a large, pimple-faced teen stared at her. He sat on a stool behind a high bench holding a bag of frozen chips against his nose.

'Ouch, Gary. Why haven't you gone home?' June stepped inside, shutting the door behind her.

Gary, the 17-year-old with shoulders broad enough and legs thick enough to carry two of her, looked at June sheepishly. 'Jonas said he needed someone to cover the booth. I don't exactly make a good actor when I can't stop my nose from bleeding.'

June shook her head. 'Jonas always says we're short-staffed. He's picking on you 'cause you're new.' She reached for one of the small torches lined up along the bench. 'If your face hurts, grab someone from the cafeteria to cover you and go home. Trust me, this place isn't worth the pain.'

The staff passages that ran alongside the guests' section of the maze were dark and cramped, barely a metre wide in some places. Fluorescent paint on the walls and floor lit the way under the UV reactive torch. An eerie mix of horror music and pre-recorded screaming filled the enclosed space. Occasionally there was a sudden bang as one of the actors hit a wall or prop, often followed by a real scream.

June hardly needed the torch. Right turn, left, right, right, left. The secret door she would emerge from was hidden behind a thick curtain. She checked there were no guests inside, through a peephole next to the door, before entering. It was her favourite room, though one of the smallest in the maze. The infirmary-themed space was full of old hospital beds, some of them just rusty frames, others with fake corpses on top and bloodied blankets drooping over the side. A lonely metal chair stood in the centre of the room. June would often sit in it with her head lowered until a guest walked in, then she'd lunge at them, laughing and grinning maniacally.

'Am I wrong or are you starting a little early today?' said a voice behind June.

There was something so calming about hearing his voice. Even in a haunted hospital attraction. She smiled. 'Didn't you hear? Gary got punched again.'

'Probably by some stupid guy trying to show off to a girl.'

'More than likely.' June turned to face the voice. 'How are you, Ben?'

Ben was the same height as June, and she looked him in the eyes briefly. Like the white contact lenses she wore, his blue eyes were unnaturally dead and marked with detailed red lines that made them appear to bulge out of his head. His face was pale and a rough, wine-coloured bruise traced a line across his throat. The bruise was purple in patches and the skin around it a puke-yellow colour. Dried blood stained the corner of Ben's mouth. His short, dark hair was greasy and wild. June had been horrified when she first saw him like this, but eventually had grown as accustomed to it as to her own gory makeup.

He wore a simple grey t-shirt and white pants, looking like a ghostly victim of June's nurse character. They had always been a good team here.

Ben shrugged and sat on one of the empty hospital beds. He opened his mouth to reply, but a shriek in a nearby room cut him off.

'Incoming,' June said. They smiled at each other. Ben put his head in his hands and began muttering nonsense to himself while June took a bloodied saw from a steel medical trolley. She grinned too widely and examined the teeth of the blade intensely. A group of teenagers entered the room, bunched up like penguins in winter. Two girls clung to each other behind a skinny boy.

June looked up at the teens. She began to laugh, softly at first but growing louder as they stepped further into the room. When the boy was within two metres she screamed and lunged at him while waving the fake saw in the air. He shrieked and skittered towards the exit with the girls following close behind.

'Nice scream,' said Ben once the teens disappeared.

'Thanks, babe,' June said.

As guests entered the room in small groups, she and Ben played with different ways of scaring each one. When a teenage couple walked in with arms linked, June snuck up behind them. They didn't notice her until she tapped the girl on the shoulder with a large syringe full of dried red paint. The girl ran out of the room, leaving her laughing boyfriend hurrying to catch up. Between scaring guests, Ben and June talked and laughed together. June's shift seemed to fly by. She always enjoyed time spent acting. That was why she applied for the performing arts scholarship, though she hadn't really expected to get it. Her boyfriend, however, knew she would. He'd known she was a talented actor from their first shift together at Club Fear.

June checked her watch and sighed. 'Ben, we need to talk.'

'About?' Ben said.

'I'm leaving.'

June watched him carefully. They'd had this conversation once before, in a brighter room a year earlier.

Ben and June had been enjoying a sunny Saturday together. They had wandered around a local market and shared an overpriced slushie in the back of Ben's old sedan. Ben had seemed withdrawn all week but while relaxing in June's bedroom that afternoon she thought he was finally in a good mood. June sat beside him on her bed, fingering the fountain pen her school had gifted her the day she graduated.

'I got accepted for that scholarship I was telling you about. At Griffith,' she said.

Ben smiled. 'That's great, babe,' he said. 'You're still going to ANU though, right?'

June stared at the pen, clicking it twice. Then twice more before looking at him. 'I know it's closer ...'

Ben's smile disappeared. 'But?'

'The degree Griffith is offering—those courses ... I think it's a better option for me.'

Ben checked his phone as if looking for a distraction. An image of them in their work costumes smiled back at him. June remembered posing for the photo a week earlier. 'You know I can't leave town.' There was a note of panic in Ben's voice when he spoke, 'I'm stuck here until I finish the apprenticeship.'

June put a hand on his arm and smiled reassuringly. 'I know, babe. That's fine. We can just do long distance for a while.'

'That shit doesn't work.'

June put the pen aside and picked up her boyfriend's hand. 'Maybe it will. We can only try,' she said.

'Or you could just go to ANU.' Ben squeezed her hand tightly.

June could see the emotional freefall this conversation was starting in him and hoped his new medication would be a strong enough parachute. 'I want to go to Griffith.'

'You're leaving me.'

'No!' June tried to squeeze Ben's hand back, but he stood abruptly.

'You're planning to move to a completely different state,' he said.

'Ben, you're overthinking it. This isn't—'

His shaky voice drowned hers out, 'You don't love me like I love you. You never have.'

'That's not true. Ben, you're being ridiculous.'

'Ridiculous! I'm not the one moving away for an acting degree. Newsflash, June, a haunted house actor is the best you'll ever manage with that.'

June stood. Guilt, anger and hurt boiled inside her. 'You're such a moron. I've been there for you through every breakdown. Every time you can't handle the world and lock yourself in your room like a whining child.' From her bed she picked up a stuffed bear he had bought for her and threw it to the ground. 'If you can't support me then I'm done. I'm over it, Ben!'

Anger flared in Ben's eyes for a fraction of a second, then his entire body seemed to deflate. 'If I'm such an inconvenience, I'll leave you alone,' he said, and strode out of the room.

June didn't turn as he passed her. She felt like a teacup full of liquid emotion, afraid to move in case it spilled and stained things further. It was the rattling sound of Ben's car speeding away that finally cracked the teacup and June collapsed onto her bed.

Lost in her memories, June didn't notice the two boys entering the room until one of them tripped over a fake corpse's leg. She turned around quickly, baring her teeth, and half growled, half screamed until they hurried out of the room. Their nervous chatter mixed with the eerie horror sounds being played throughout the haunted hospital. This wasn't the place for a serious conversation, but it had to be done.

She turned back to Ben, and her eyes fell on the bruising around his neck.

'You said you were leaving,' he reminded her.

June nodded, forcing herself to look away. 'When you didn't contact me for a week after our fight, I thought it was for the best,' she said.

'Babe, that was months ago—'

'Exactly a year,' June said.

'Oh.' Ben massaged one hand with his other. June recognised the nervous habit and wished for a moment that she could hug him.

'Your foster mum said you hadn't been going to work, but I told her we'd broken up. I told her you would be fine.'

Ben reached for June's arm.

She stepped away, shaking her head. 'I wasn't there for you when you needed me.'

'Babe, you didn't know I was off my meds. It made it hard to do stuff. We're ok now, though,' Ben said. He smiled as if trying to calm a skittish animal, but all June could see was the dried blood in the corner of his mouth.

'I was the one who found your body,' she said. Warm tears dripped down her cheek and June knew they would destroy her makeup.

Ben opened his mouth to speak, but nothing came out.

'I blamed myself for so long. That's why I couldn't leave.' June took a deep breath, trying to ease the sobs that shook her body. 'When I found you again, I thought I was dreaming. I deferred my degree because I couldn't stand the idea of not being there for you,' she said.

Ben frowned. 'What do you mean? You said you changed your mind.'

June shook her head.

There was no sound as Ben sat heavily on one of the hospital beds.

A mother and a young girl walked into the room. This time June let her appearance do the work for her. A bloodied nurse, staring at an empty hospital bed and sobbing uncontrollably. They eyed the fake blood splattered around the dark room and took in the cold, tense atmosphere of the space. Then they moved on.

June wiped her nose on the sleeve of her dress, grateful for the excuse to gather her thoughts. 'It wasn't okay, Ben. But now I know it wasn't my fault.' She smiled through her tears. 'I think I'm ready to face reality.'

June's boyfriend stood silently. No. This wasn't her Ben. The real Ben had left that night a year earlier when the stress of life and the demons in his head pushed him to copy the skeleton twins. She closed her eyes and imagined him as he had been. Tanned skin, ocean eyes and that lopsided grin she once loved.

'Goodbye, Ben,' she said.

LITTLE DEATHS

Clare McGhee

Your eyes burn into mine
The way my cigarettes melt holes in my clothes
Blurring the blank space between us
I've been chasing sweetness, no matter how fleeting
So, I fold into you when the sun goes down
And the moon boasts above us, swimming in light
My name dances on your tongue
And my gut churns, begging to hear it again

Whispers of love tease the air
While we knead ourselves together
A tangle of golden limbs, you sigh into me
And nudge into my neck
As unconsciousness pulls us under
The roar of your breath wraps me up

Time melts, in flux

I feel something growing inside me

Pitter pat—the bathroom tap is loose
           The two lines bold and unmistakable

Find myself at the house on top of the hill
Splitting at the seams, syncopated heartbeats
A bird piles petals, building her nest on a wounded fence post
I try to sing along, but she's always changing the melody

The curtain rod just won't hold
That lilac linen you've wrestled for the last hour
In the corner room, where lemon sun seeps in
And the storm of your gaze draws me into its whirlwind

Time washes over me, caressing me on the shore then crashing
me into the cliffs
Up
         and
                                up
               down
                                        and

                                                down
A girl beside me clicks her pen under sterile light
Her doll's eyes darting over the office
The home of my body, hollow and still
Gasps like an empty train station
In the dead air where no one exists, even just for a moment

The kettle dings
I pull the teabag from the mug you hand me
It splits open and the weary leaves bleed over the corkboard
motel floor
We crumble together again and again
Your tempest eyes burn into mine
And room service will do fine

Time stops dancing
                        We sigh together, a finale
The Sunday sun peers over the hill
You cradle me and a coffee in bed
And the new day holds clarity
I'm neither here nor there
Empty or full, alone or in love
As the weight of you
                        and all that we could be
Rinses off my skin and escapes my lungs
I sneak out the side door to the rhythm of your roar
As it washes over me, la petite mort

LIFE, DEATH
AND PICKLEBALL

Jen Francis

The smell of liniment burned Peggy's nostrils. She looked up into the glow of the court lights reflected back at her from a thousand spectacles, a veritable swarm of hungry flies hovering, anticipating carnage. Like a wounded gladiator, she hobbled to the service line, swinging her bat, feeling its welcome weight in her hand. In the corner of her eye, the glint of the trophy. And on the other side of the net, the only thing still standing between her and that holy grail—Ted bloody Vickers.

He faced her from the other end, doing his ridiculous jig, bat at the ready. Peggy wasn't fooled. His lips pulled back over gritted teeth and sweat poured from his forehead. She could see the darkened material around his collar and under his arms. She was glad. Let him fear.

She raised her arm and served, relishing the echoing *thock* as the ball hit the sweet spot and flew true—an orange harbinger of doom.

The day Peggy got the don't-call-us-we'll-call-you letter from the State Lawn Tennis Association, she'd packed up her dreams and her racquet bag and stowed it under the stairs of her parents' house. She was tired of being the 'nearly' girl. Nearly finished school. Nearly won *Miss Haymaker* two years in a row. Nearly got that big break into the pro-am tour that would have taken her away, once and for all, from the flat, square grid of the country town where she was born.

She'd lost count of the number of times her mother had sighed and said, 'It's all for the best. God works in mysterious ways.' Too mysterious for Peggy. She decided that a deity who had made her not quite smart enough, not quite pretty enough, and not quite fast enough, was actually not quite good enough for her unquestioning faith.

Her mother was scandalised. 'But what will people think if you don't come to church?' she choked, with the very same chest-clutching dramatics she'd shown when Kennedy was shot. But Peggy just couldn't bring herself to go. To smile, to give thanks, to pray, to ask for the things she truly wanted. It was time she grew up, faced who she was and stopped wanting more.

For a long time it worked. She trotted through the motions of life and wasn't unhappy. She worked in an office and was known as reliable, always-pleasant Peggy. She married Bob, who worked for the local electricity board, and together they built a very respectable home with hydrangeas in the front yard, filling it with three pleasant children and a series of medium-sized dogs. When Peggy's parents passed and the old house was sold, she'd allowed the bag of dreams to be tossed away with all the other unwanted trash.

One by one the children flew the nest, and when Bob died quietly one sombre April day, Peggy wondered whether it was worth going on. She sat alone in her tidy kitchen a month after the funeral, breathing, when there was a knock at the door.

'I've brought a lasagne, Peg.' Noelene let herself in. She eyed Peggy and took a deep breath. 'Now, I know I've asked you a thousand times, Peg, and you always say no—'

'I don't want to join the golf group, Noelene.'

'I know, I know. It's not that. I thought—'

'I don't want to come to the ladies church group, Noelene.'

'Gawd, Peg, I know better than to suggest that. It's not that. I just—'

'Whatever it is, Noelene, the answer is thank you, but no.' Peggy folded her hands in her lap and looked at a breadcrumb on the floor.

There was silence. Suddenly Peggy felt strong hands close like a vice upon her arm and she was hoisted to her feet.

'That's it, Peggy Broughton,' Noelene growled into her face. 'I've seen that look before. I'm not going to stand by while you sit here and decay. You are coming with me.'

Noelene had been a ward nurse at the local base hospital for 40 years; Peggy was no match. As the hydrangeas watched in surprise, she was gently but firmly manhandled out of her own front door, marched along the path, and bundled into Noelene's car like a misbehaving child. Not a further word passed between them as Noelene drove to the local basketball stadium, parked the car and got out. She strode around the car to wrench the passenger door open.

'Get out,' she ordered.

Peggy didn't move.

'Get out or I'll make you get out.'

Inside the stadium was a hum of activity. People in activewear sauntered about, greeting each other cheerfully, unzipping bags, putting up nets. Peggy blinked in the glare of the stadium lights, the smell of stale sweat pervading her senses.

'Pickleball,' said Noelene. She picked up what looked like an oversized ping pong paddle from a nearby table. 'It's like a cross between badminton and tennis. It's the new thing. And you are going to be my partner.'

Peggy's head swam. She felt sick. She looked around desperately, searching for escape.

'Shoes. Bat. Ball. Hurry up,' said Noelene, pushing the items into her hands.

'I can't,' Peggy said faintly. 'I can't. I'm old. I'm eighty years old, Noelene.'

'Take a look around,' scoffed Noelene. 'We're all old, Peg. That's why we gotta hurry up.'

Peggy found herself on the court. The bat felt strangely familiar in her hand, like the voice of an old friend long absent. We belong, it said.

'Get ready,' said Noelene.

The woman at the other end of the court served straight at Peggy. The orange ball hit the floor and bounced up into her stomach. Peggy hadn't moved. Her heart hammered; her hands shook.

'Give it a rest, Barb. She wasn't ready,' called Noelene. 'Go again.' Noelene walked over and looked Peggy square in the eye. 'You can do this, Peg.'

Peggy's throat was dry. Barb lined up again and sent another serve over the net. Rusty synapses sparked and Peggy's arm moved; her bat connected, and the ball went straight into the net. It was a terrible start. But something was happening. Something big. Something electric. Peggy felt a flush, a surge of energy flow through her body, to the ends of her fingertips and out. It was terrifying.

It was wonderful.

And so Pickleball became a twice-weekly event on her schedule. She played with Noelene against the other ladies' pairs. Soon the other players learned to fear them; with a smile, they systematically demolished every pair. During court rotation, she and Noelene began to find themselves without an opponent, leaving them no option but to play against the men.

'We can't have that,' said Ted Vickers, the club president. 'That's just not done. It's not fair on the ladies.'

'Put a sock in it, Ted,' said Noelene.

So Ted put them up against Len and Bill, 89 and 85 respectively. The girls delivered them a lesson in Pickleball, walking away 11–4 winners.

From then on, they were a major attraction. The ladies' pairs rushed through their games to grab coffees and sit in the bleachers to watch Peggy and Noelene work their way through the men. The day it came to the last untried pairing, Ted Vickers' sciatica suddenly sent him to the bleachers early. There was muttering in the crowd.

Noelene saw the writing on the wall. 'I'm holding you back, Peg,' she said one Tuesday. 'My arthritis is giving me hell today. You gotta go it alone.'

'Yes, yes, singles!' chorused the other ladies, and chinked their cappuccinos.

Noelene joined the ladies in the bleachers. 'I got her playing,' she boasted, as they watched Peggy smashing, slicing, dinking, making mincemeat of her opponents. The women cheered. The men suddenly remembered they had sore joints and physio-prescribed rest. Ted Vickers watched from the corner, arms crossed.

Peggy herself was addicted. Sixty years of repression poured out of her every Tuesday and Thursday, giving her wings on her feet and iron in her arms. Never mind the days in between of puffy knees, Radox baths and anti-inflammatories. It was worth it. She noticed that people in town began to look at her differently, and inside Peggy felt a change—a stirring of something both familiar and foreign that she wasn't quite able to identify.

When the word went out about the regional tournament, Noelene began to run a book, giving short odds on Peggy to win the whole damn thing. Barb organised a cheer squad. But there were the sceptics; after all, Peggy had never versed Ted Vickers, who was widely acknowledged to be the best men's pickleballer in the district. Ted himself played humble. 'Of course she's a very good ladies' player,' he said. 'But. Well, *you* know.'

The day of the tournament saw a record crowd at the stadium. When the bleachers were full, people brought in camp chairs and set up around the edges of the courts. Noelene shortened the odds. As the day progressed, it was clear that the crowd were gradually forming into two camps—on one side, the association traditionalists, who tut-tutted over the inclusion of a mixed competition. On the other, the new guard, who swung into full voice during Peggy's matches and took their toilet breaks in between.

For Peggy, the day passed like a dream. She couldn't put a ball wrong and barely dropped a point during the rounds. The quarters and semis pushed her harder, and she felt her strength beginning to ebb. Noelene dosed her up on red frogs and anti-inflammatories, massaged her sore knees with heat rub and sent her back onto the court.

Finally, there were only two names left on the board, and she watched Ted approach, swinging his arms and jigging around on his toes like a 20-year-old McEnroe.

'Good luck, Ted,' said Peggy, as they touched bats over the net.

'Likewise,' said Ted, without a smile.

Ted's first serve flew fast and low, tipping Peggy's bat and skewing off to the right.

'Ooooohhh,' said the crowd.

It was clear that Ted meant business. He used his height and strength to send three balls directly at Peggy's head and she was quickly 4–0 down. His fifth smash went wide and Peggy was on the board.

'Aaaahhhh,' said the crowd.

She walked to the service line, ignoring the twinge in her right knee. She took a deep breath. She gripped her bat. And for the first time in nearly 60 years, she asked for what she truly wanted.

'Please,' she whispered.

Her serve dropped neatly in and spun wide, away from Ted's outstretched arm.

'That was long,' said Ted, pointing at a spot on the court.

'Booooooo,' said the crowd.

Ted began to sweat. 'Maybe it was in,' he conceded.

At 4–all, Ted asked for a towel to wipe his forehead.

At 5–all, he began to grunt.

At 7–all, he closed on a loose ball and smashed it into the back corner. Peggy smiled and raised her bat in acknowledgement of the good shot.

'Mind games,' muttered Ted.

At 9–all, Ted sent up a lob. Peggy backed up and as the lob landed long, she stumbled, dropping her bat with a cry of pain and clutching her knee. Noelene was there in a moment, gently pressing the swelling flesh.

'I think you've gotta call it, Peg. You've blown your knee.'

'I've got to play,' said Peggy.

'No one will think any worse of you. We are all so proud. You nearly beat the old bastard.'

'I've been waiting for this my whole life, Noelene,' said Peggy, squeezing her friend's caring hands. 'I'm going to play. And I'm going to win.'

The smell of the liniment burned Peggy's nostrils as, like a wounded gladiator, she hobbled to the service line for match point.

As soon as the ball left her bat, Peggy knew it was the one. Her signature serve, spinning away to Ted's left, out of reach. She was vaguely aware of the roar of the crowd, of Ted groaning in dismay and collapsing to his knees as spectators rushed onto the court, but it was far away, drowned by the roar in her head. Finally—finally—she had done it and she feasted on the roar and the rush and the sweet, sweet nectar of victory. She was not the nearly girl anymore. She was going all the way.

When the paramedics arrived, they shook their heads and said nothing could be done. Ted had died of a massive heart attack and most likely been a goner before he even hit the floor. Later, the association declared the game a dead rubber—no pun intended—and named both Peggy and Ted as joint winners of the tournament. But in the hubbub immediately following Ted's collapse nobody gave a thought for Peggy, and by the time they did she was gone, and the Grand Pickleball trophy along with her. When Noelene called over the next day, the curtains were drawn, the house was locked and the car was gone, and only the hydrangeas stood waving in the winter's sun, waiting to bloom in the spring.

COLD HEART

Jessica McColl

L ike charred bone, a lamppost stood silhouetted before the street, flickering eerily yet its luminosity was inviting. Children in ragged clothing ran past playing hoop and stick while the thunder of hooves split their laughter. A stallion pulling along a brougham advanced from a glorious mansion, trotting towards the city lights.

Watching from the mansion's window, Thana waited as the brougham finally disappeared. After having married her wealthy Lord, her new neighbourhood was far different from the surplus of chimneys that preposterously stuck out on every house. She fidgeted with the golden locket around her neck, until it unfastened, revealing a little girl with striking curls of strawberry blonde and blue eyes. A small tear travelled down Thana's cheek. She knew this sacrifice would haunt her.

Abandoning the thoughts, Thana restlessly drifted from the window to acquire the used candle from the nightstand, the wax pooled into the holder as she proceeded down the immense staircase. As she passed the floor-length mirror, she caught a glimpse of a child's bloody hand in her peripheral vision. Thana's countenance was dishevelled, her breath sharpening as she spun towards the mirror. Nothing seemed out of the ordinary. Her thoughts drifted to the smell of fresh bread, distracting her from her painful memory.

Following the scent into the kitchen, she found the fresh bread cooling atop the galley countertop. Letting her locket rest on her chest, she lazily resigned to the drawing room with a slice. Seated by the magnificent fire that mimicked the warmth of day, she finished the slice before proceeding to groom her burgundy curls. As the last ringlet fell from her shell comb, silence caressed her. No familiar creaks or groans of the mansion. No crackles from the fire. Thana's own breath seemed to die as she exhaled.

Suddenly, the sound of a child's laughter drifted through the window with the breeze, eerie, yet recognisable. A vivid memory of her child running in a flowery meadow burned behind her eyes. Goosebumps erupted along her arms as the breeze drifted around her.

Once the breeze ceased, tapping from the entrance erupted through the mansion. Thana looked at the grandfather clock next to the fire, noticing it was quarter to seven. Curiously, she approached the front door and unbolted the hefty lock to reveal a little girl with striking strawberry blonde curls and blue eyes on the terrace.

'Can I come in? It's cold out 'ere ma'am,' asked the little girl.

'Where are your parents, child?' Thana questioned.

'Ma'am, it's cold out 'ere, can I come in?' she asked again.

With an exhale, Thana moved aside, permitting the child indoors and led her to the drawing room with the crackling fire. In hypnotised joy, the girl ran towards the fire and held her hands over the burning logs.

'Where do you live, child?' Thana asked.

The girl didn't answer.

'Where do you live, child?' she asked again, slowly approaching her.

The girl let her arms drop to her sides.

'I don't ... know.'

Thana approached the girl and pulled her into a hug. 'I'm sorry ... to hear this.'

The girl embraced the hug, sobbing into Thana's dress. 'I've been going 'ouse to 'ouse looking ...' She sobbed harder.

'I'm sorry to hear this,' Thana repeated.

While embraced, Thana could feel the skeletal structure of the girl. Her hand caressing the child's bony spine, feeling each vertebra shifting under her fingers. Yet something felt unnatural. When Thana tried pulling away, her hands seemed to melt into the skin.

'I live 'ere now,' was all Thana heard.

'You're confused ... I live here,' she replied, trying to release their grip.

'Oh, Ma ... how could you forget me so easily?'

The girl's body convulsed underneath her grasp. Frantic, Thana tried harder to pull herself away. Then, like the drop of a coin, the spasms stopped. Thana was able to let go.

She looked at the girl with a sceptical face, the child's body remained normal, however her eyes had slightly changed. Her once blue eyes were enveloped with clouds of inky black; Thana could only see her reflection in the void within.

'Are you ok? Do you need a doctor?' she hastily questioned the girl.

The child's lips quirked upwards, revealing jagged teeth. Eyes wide with horror, Thana's mouth felt rigid, fists clenched as her nails dug deep into her skin, her palms becoming bloody from the force. In the blink of an eye, the girl's smile returned to normal—showing off what was left of her decayed teeth.

'Lila ... ?' Thana said weakly.

Lila's hands reached out and tightened onto Thana's wrists, white-knuckled and resilient. Thana's eyes enlarged as her nape hairs prickled along her skin.

'Let's play a game ... Ma.'

A croak was all that escaped from Thana's dry throat as Lila attempted to drag her closer to the fireplace. The little girl fished a sharp-pointed, staff-life metal sceptre out the sweltering fire. Fear curled inside Thana as the girl twisted around, gripping onto the metal.

'We're going to play a game,' Lila uttered, 'if you get these que'tions right, I'll let you go—deal?'

Thana nodded, eyeing the rod.

'One, why did you choose to remarry?'

'I ... how? ... the home was ... abusive.'

'Interesting. What was "abusive" with your old fam'ly?'

'My husband.'

Lila froze. 'You're wrong.'

Thana paused. 'No. My ex-husband was abusive towards me and my child.'

'~Wrong~' Lila sang.

Lila smiled for Thana to see her sharp teeth.

'Three, why wo'ld you leave your child with your sup'osed "abusive" ex-husband?'

Thana paused, staring into Lila's black voids of eyes. Her mind blank, she could only tell the feeblest of lies.

'I don't ... know.'

Screeching, Lila grabbed her by the hair and dragged her closer to the fire, bringing the metal down to Thana's face.

'Why don't you know!?'

Tears welled in Thana's eyes. 'I fell in love with another man,' she blurted out.

Before Thana could move, the sceptre penetrated her abdomen. Her flesh sizzled, blood boiling as she was cooked inside out. Screaming erupted from her parched throat, her eyes widened, her pulse accelerated. Crying, she was desperate, terrified ... human. She breathed in small spurts, hot and hysterical.

'Wrong, wrong, wrong. How dare you say he was abusive,' Lila growled through her lips.

'He ... was!' Thana sputtered between heavy breaths.

'Wrong!' the screech filled her ears.

Thana's eyes widened as the hot metal pierced deeper, puncturing her intestine. Lila laughed malevolently as she propelled deeper. Blood gushed in a bubbling crimson wave, splattering to the floor as the baying laughs of the demonic child echoed throughout the mansion. With one last cackle, the sceptre was ripped from her stomach—pulling out her intestine in one big squelch. Thana's screams liquefied into the night. Then silence. Nature waited for the malevolent presence to leave, the natural sounds of the world waiting with quiet fear. The mansion stood dark and brooding once more. The locket, resting in a pool of warm blood, gaped open with gore staining the photo of the beaming black-eyed child.

THE KEY, THE BLOCK, AND THE GREAT STONE DOOR

Maddison Woods

I understand that the circumstances that led to my current state of institutional confinement may seem preposterous in the least. And yet, I am bound by my confidence that my tale is true, however obscure it may seem. Those around me are determined to seek other means of the truth, and suspect that I perhaps indulge too much in the partaking of wine, or have carelessly stumbled and received a blow to the head—a case I am sure I would have remembered, were it the truth. No, my stubbornness in my account of events holds fast, no matter how tightly they bind me in the cotton jacket. Surely, my unwavering recollection is a justification of my sanity?

Two months ago, on the eve of winter, I found the night too cold to find any hope of sleep, and instead situated myself in front of the large fireplace within my family's drawing room. My father's glass chessboard lay on a small table; the battle against my brother splayed across the board in disarray with no clear signs of a winner. The temptation to move a piece was inviting, but rejected. My mother's half-finished embroidery hung over the arm of her chair, with small purple lilacs blooming across the fabric. It matched the rug that covered most of the drawing room floor, and made one think they had stepped into a garden, with a brilliant display of every flower you could think of. It succeeded in making one feel quite small.

With a blanket, I settled down in front of the flames, armed with a copy of *Alice's Adventures in Wonderland*, and set about reading until drowsiness attempted to consume me. Drowning within the pages of the book, I could not help but wish for myself some kind of strange happenstance that would force me on the path of the most incredible adventure. My sheltered life afforded me little in the way of mystery and society, and I had to rely on imagination to entertain me. All manner of stories I had written in my journal, exciting dreams and adventures that I hoped to release into the world, although never completed. Yet, I do not believe I could have imagined what happened next.

The small clock upon the mantlepiece gently alerted me to the fact that it was two o'clock in the morning, and I pondered whether I should attempt to sleep within my own bed, or if the journey back would return me to my active state. However, as I deliberated on my next move, without a whisp or a whistle of wind, the glow of the fireplace was snuffed out and the room plunged into darkness.

On my hands and knees, I searched for the matches, previously seen on top of a small side table about two metres to my right. I crawled, too disorientated to stand, as the rug felt thicker and deeper around my wrists. After much searching, I came to the table, bumping my head on its side as I reached for the matches. Following the scent of charcoal, I shuffled through the rug, shook open the matchbox and struck one alight.

By the faint glow of its light, I was met with the unusual sight of one's fireplace having grown two times larger than it had been. Vines and flowers erupted from the surrounding structure and wove a floral tapestry through the walls. I dropped the match into the fireplace, igniting in an instant to reveal to me that beyond the fire was a great stone door. One flame reached out and grabbed my wrist. I still nurse the singed mark.

'It's looking for the key,' an eerie voice spoke from behind me. A scream almost escaped my throat as I turned and came face to face with a large glass horse dragging itself towards me. A heavy knock came from the other side of the fireplace, and my heartbeat quickened with a sense of urgency.

'Wh-what key?' I stammered.

'The one in the book.'

I picked up my book and shook it. Sure enough, a large black key fell out of its pages. I snatched up the key, stepped over vines that spread across the length of the drawing room and found that the stone door did indeed have a keyhole, safely out of reach from the fire. Without hesitation, I slipped the key inside and turned it, then scurried back to hide behind the glass horse. The fire died down and the stones began to shake, until the door burst open and a large gathering of figures tumbled into the room.

It was at this moment that a sensible amount of fear coursed through my blood and I sprinted to the door, where I would then wake my parents and my brother and they could enforce the required disciplines necessary for removing these curious fellows from the house. The door of the drawing room, however, was locked, and I was left to deal with the debacle myself. If it were not for the perspiration on my skin, or the pain around my wrist, I would have dismissed it all as a dream.

A towering figure in black armour stepped forward, silent, with no creak nor twang of metal, and knelt before me. 'Are you the one who opened the stone door?'

'She is,' the glass horse interjected. 'She is one of the masters of this room.'

A small man, two feet in height and with bright red eyes clapped his hands together rapidly. 'Let's eat her hands.'

A stone frog leapt up onto my chest, knocking me back, where it nestled upon my stomach, significantly heavier than it looked. 'Stay where you are.'

'I can't breathe,' I gasped.

The glass horse shuffled forward. 'Enough. You know the rules.'

'Rules?' I croaked. 'What rules?'

A young woman stepped forward, who at first appeared perfectly normal, until her body sporadically shook and faded in and out, and her voice came out muffled. 'You must play a small game with each of us. If you win all eight games, we leave you alone.'

'And if I lose?'

A boy of about eight stepped out from behind the woman, his eyes sunken and black, with no whites or coloured irises. 'We get to eat your brain.'

'And your hands!' the small man chimed in.

The peculiarity of wanting to eat my hands and brain did not escape me, but as a writer, they were great assets that must be protected. From my position on the ground, I could only see six figures.

The glass horse hazarded a guess as to what I was thinking. 'The other two will reveal themselves in due time. Do take comfort in knowing that we cannot interfere with each other's games. Those are the rules.'

The blurred woman removed the frog from my stomach, allowing me to sit up.

'I am guessing I don't have much of a choice?' I asked.

The black knight, with a surprising degree of gentility for one who had just burst into someone's home uninvited, helped me to my feet. 'Unfortunately, my lady, this circumstance now binds us all together, and we must each do our part, whether we wish to or not.' He gestured towards the mantle clock. 'We have four hours. All games must be played before sunrise, unless you fail early. Choose your first game.'

The quizzical party situated themselves around the room, and the flames in the fireplace grew to a full roar. I knew not what games they would play. I, who had little experience with games, already felt an overwhelming sense of defeat. But my mind was at stake, and I needed to make sure they never got their hands on it.

Won over by his manners, likened to a romantic hero, I pointed towards the knight. 'I'll play your game first.'

The knight bowed. 'Thank you, my lady.' From within his breastplate, he extracted two bundles of knotted twine. 'Unravel this twine and create a single line. Fastest wins.'

I was shocked at the simplicity of the game. With my small hands against his armoured ones, surely, I was at a greater advantage? But a niggling in the back of my head reminded me that while dexterity may be on my side, this was the knight's game, which he had undoubtedly played many times.

The glass horse counted us in, and the knight and I got to working on the amalgamation of knots and loops. The knots held firm, any attempt to dishevel them only making them tighter. Frequently, I looked over at the knight and saw he struggled too, and found a small amount of comfort in the fairness of the match. I tugged on a single loop, found it moved more freely than the others, and continued to pull. To my surprise, a small piece of twine the length of my hand separated from the bundle. How could this be? The knight had said 'a single line'. Had I been set up for failure? I looked over at the knight just as he too extracted a disconnected piece of twine.

I had to think outside of the box.

I rushed over to my mother's chair. Nestled underneath her embroidery was her pair of fabric scissors. I cut at the bundle, right in the middle, and quickly pulled apart all the exposed threads.

'That's cheating!' the small man cried.

'Quiet,' snapped the glass horse. 'You know very well it is not.'

The knots came apart easily, and soon I was surrounded by a multitude of strings. The knight looked over at me with what I imagine was enamoured curiosity, and without thinking, I handed him the scissors. I had every confidence that I would be able to tie together all the strings before he could. After tying the ends for twenty minutes, a single line of twine wrapped around the edges of the room.

The black knight bowed and handed back the scissors. 'I accept my defeat.'

A small sense of relief eased the strain on my heart, but I still had seven more games to play. I only prayed that they would all be as easy. For the next game, I chose the frog, who produced from his mouth multiple pebbles used to form a circle on the largest table in the drawing room. With the circle constructed, two snails slid out of the frog's mouth, and after marking one as my own, they were placed in the centre and made to race. A game based entirely on luck, which on that night was in my favour, as my snail headed straight for the stone circle.

Next, I challenged the little boy, who proposed the most spine-chilling game of hide and seek. From his pocket he extracted an hourglass and a long scrap of black cloth.

'You have until the hourglass runs out to steer clear of my roaming hands. You may move, but just know that I have excellent hearing.' Without warning, or time to prepare, he tied the cloth over his eyes and began his search. I crouched down and swiftly made my way to a spot between the woman and the small man, only for the man to call out, 'She's here!' I heard the frog kick the small man in the stomach as I scurried over to the corner closest to the fireplace. I turned, and clamped my hand over my mouth as the little boy loomed over me. His fingertips grazed the wall a foot above my head. My hands shook with fear, and I hoped he could not hear my ragged breathing against my palm. His hands roamed lower, then stopped just inches above my head, while I tucked my feet closer to my body, just in case. The sickening thought of being caught by him made my eyes swell, but I held my breath as he stalked to the other side of the room, pouncing on his companions. The hourglass finally ran out.

For my next game, I chose the small man; purely out of revenge for interfering in the previous game, which was supposed to be against the rules. His interference had not gone unnoticed by the glass horse and the small man was forced to play his game of tag on one leg. This proved to be a significant disadvantage for him, and the game was over as soon as it had begun. The small man threatened that the game would have gone differently if he had both his legs. I did not doubt him. He spent the rest of the games sulking in the corner, mumbling about how he wouldn't get to eat my hands.

'I wish to face one of those who have not yet presented themselves,' I told the glass horse.

'Very well. You must be brave, and think quickly on your feet.'

The black knight stood to attention and the scabbard at his side quivered. Before I could register what was happening, his sword freed itself from its sheath and aimed right at my chest. I dodged its advance just in time, grabbing the closest book to shield myself.

'What do I do?' I asked the glass horse.

'*Whatever you want.*'

I needed a weapon, one to match up to the strength of the sword that made continual strikes at my head. But there was very little in the drawing room that could be considered great defence against a sword.

Whatever you want.

Once again, I was forced to think outside of the box, and this time I would also have to think outside of any logic or sensibility that my mind clung to. My fireplace had turned into a door. Eight beings wanted to eat my brain.

Reason be hanged.

I parried the sword's next swing with the book then sprung over to my mother's chair. With a silent apology, I pulled the needle from her embroidery. As I pulled, it grew larger and larger, until it was equal in size to the sword. I spun to face the angry sword a second too late and it struck the top of my shoulder, tearing my nightgown.

My inexperienced hands fumbled with the needle, and I caught a glimpse of the small man's face break into a smile at the possibility of me losing the game. So, I swung the needle about in a chaotic manner, until I heard the sound of metal strike metal.

We sparred in the most curious manner, for I had never fought against anything, let alone a sword, and clearly the sword had never fought a needle before. With a final swing, I knocked the sword off its course, and it retreated back to the knight's side.

Five down, three to go. Sunrise was approaching.

I chose the blurred woman, who initiated a game of charades, of which the knight was to guess and the glass horse to judge. It was a close game, as we both bent and shaped our bodies, and made complete fools of ourselves. But I was to be crowned the winner after the woman struggled to physically demonstrate an apple.

'I choose you,' I said to the glass horse, trying my best to disguise my exhaustion. 'What game will you have me play?'

'Mine is not a game, but a question.'

'A question?'

The glass horse shuffled closer. 'Are you asleep, or are you awake?'

I froze. Such a question seemed almost impossible to answer, and I was almost bound to choose the wrong one. I could not rely on luck and speed to figure this one out, but perhaps I could use imagination, for how was the glass horse to prove me wrong, no matter how I answered.

'I am awake,' I replied. 'In one's dreams, one is always awake, whether they are asleep, or merely daydreaming.'

The glass horse pondered a moment, his companions looking upon him eagerly for his verdict. Without a word, he shuffled back and I was awarded my win.

Sunrise was but moments away, and I had one more game to play. One more chance to keep my mind and my hands intact.

'Last game,' announced the glass horse. 'Defeat the block.'

A small black cube appeared before me and hovered level with my face. Without fear, without thought of what the cube could do, I snatched it out of the air and threw it into the fireplace.

Everything disappeared; the vines and flowers retracted back into the walls, the fireplace returned to its regular size, and all the puzzling folk who had filled the drawing room vanished as the first rays of sunlight poured through the window.

It is at this point that I should perhaps point out my error in deciding to tell my family of the events that transpired that night. Great ramblings beyond their comprehension became too much to bear, and I was sent to this god-awful place to join those who engaged in an equal share of rambling. However, once here, I kept to myself, and when allowed paper and pencil, wrote for hours and hours on end, completing multiple volumes of work. Attendants tried to coerce me with promises of finding a publisher for my work in exchange for admitting my incident was fiction. Many a time, the temptation almost got the better of me, but I remained solid in my belief of its occurrence.

So now I am in isolation; a curious case of madness, with no paper, no pencil, and my hands bound behind my back. I jump around, bouncing off the padded walls, waiting for some kind of delusion to take my mind far from here.

Nothing.

So, I bounce and bounce some more, until one day, a large black key slips out from underneath my straight jacket.

COUNTERFEIT

Georgia Beard

M y family doesn't want you here for the holidays.' Tristan squeezed the words through his teeth like they were giving him abdominal pain. Clinging to her duffel bag, Ainsley knew those words should've struck her in the abdomen too. She waited for that lingering ache, lowered her gaze when it didn't come, searched for an answer in the toiletries and half-folded clothes strewn across her mattress.

'I still need to return that book your mother gave me,' she said.

Silence stretched out.

Tristan sighed, slow and brassy over the phone. 'She won't miss it.'

'Are you sure? I was the one who asked for it.'

'Not worth the trip.'

'You could come and pick it up, at least.'

'I'm not driving all the way back into the city for a book.'

'Of course not, but maybe next time—'

'Forget it, Ainz. There's not gonna be a next time. My family doesn't want you here at all, and I don't—' He broke off, in pain again. He was probably standing in the cluttered bedroom he moved out of at 17, pressing his fingers into his side.

Ainsley wanted to hurt more than he did. She wanted to yell at him for thinking he was the casualty here, but she couldn't find a gash or an entry wound. 'I already paid for my train ticket,' she said softly.

'Stop. You're not allowed to do that, not when I can't tell if anything you say is real or just another pity grab. After last time—'

'I apologised for that.'

'You think that's all you had to do? You just checked it off your list like everything else? God, it's worse than I thought.'

And there it was. She knew this kind of pain, buried low and blistering. Hot ash on the floor of her stomach someone forgot to stamp out. 'Why did you really call me?'

'I—I've wanted to say this for months, ok? I can't—It's not something I—and my parents think it's for the best.'

Smoke rose in her throat. 'What is it?'

'I can't keep loving you,' Tristan blurted. 'You don't even know how it feels or what to do with it. I don't think you ever knew.'

She dropped the duffel bag, and the rest of her body ignited, tearing through flesh and muscle and bone, soothing her as it scorched every nerve ending.

She told him about watching his favourite movies. Eating all the shitty dinners he made for her when she stayed at his apartment. Following him through the gallery uptown and letting him analyse the overanalysed art just to keep him talking.

That was love, wasn't it?

When she had nothing left to say, she smouldered. She crossed the cramped space between her walls and waited for Tristan to apologise and tell her she was right and ask her to bring his mother's book when she visited.

Something shuffled on the other end of the line. 'You did all that because you wanted to keep me around,' Tristan muttered. 'I wanted you to see me. But when I looked at you, there was nothing there.'

Ainsley flinched. She ended the call and pushed her phone into her back pocket.

Nothing there.

Cold light fell into her room, striking last night's water glass, the empty bin, the hospital corners. She'd skipped breakfast, and now she didn't know if eating would make her satisfied or nauseous.

Nothing there.

He used to joke that he couldn't find anything behind those frigid grey eyes of hers.

She snatched her keys from the dresser. She would give him something to see.

On the sandstone stairs of the gallery, crowds hid in coats and turned their faces away from the street. They passed through security gates in currents, voices clambering on top of each other. This place always grew busy when the wind grew bitter.

Ainsley rubbed her bare arms and wove her way to the arched doors. As she entered the hall, she came up to her ears in laughing, touching, pulsing people. All their best emotions rose to the surface of their skin, loud and radiant. It was a state of being that frightened her, and one she could never reach.

She pulled her gaze to the walls instead, the canvases painted with lovers and garden parties and children holding hands. Oils and watercolours diluted their emotions.

Is that what people saw when they looked at art? The loose outline of a feeling they coloured in themselves? Is that what Tristan saw? He could stand in front of a portrait for 10 minutes and still find something in the arch of an eyebrow or the tilt of a head. He saw everything, even her.

She had to see these feelings for herself.

The hall spilled into smaller chambers, and she swept into a room where people were few and emotions were fewer. A sign stamped into the wall read: *Impressionist Works by Mary Cassatt.* She skirted the room, glancing at women wearing high-collar dresses and gentle frowns. She didn't know them. She didn't see anything in their eyes. She wanted desperately to give something back.

Then she saw it. In the corner, a pastel-drawn mother and child clung to each other, smearing at the edges as they coalesced. Pushing her lips against her son's cheek, the faceless mother seemed to push all her love into him too—warm, stubborn and uncontainable.

Ainsley had never felt warm before, but she couldn't mistake the feeling when it broke free from the canvas, took root behind her ribcage and unfurled. It was a belly laugh. It was closing her eyes against the sun. She didn't have to take it; it was given. She was the one holding onto the mother's neck and receiving the mother's kiss. She couldn't look away.

The warmth stayed wrapped around her ribs as she ran to the gift shop and asked the clerk for a reprint of *A Goodnight Hug*. As she pressed cash into his hand, she expected the feeling to grow cold like the rest of her. But it didn't, not even when she stepped out into the wind in her short sleeves. She didn't know what to do with it except hold on.

A Goodnight Hug went propped against the wall on her bedroom floor because the landlord wouldn't let her hang up pictures. After tossing bubble wrap and paper aside, she crossed her legs in front of it. The mother still cradled the child to her chest. The child still lifted his arms to grasp her. Ainsley imagined herself in the space between, where she could intercept this thing called love without the collateral damage it wreaked.

The coalescing. The kiss. The warmth.

Why didn't she feel warm anymore?

White-hot panic burgeoned in her stomach, and she reached out for the feeling. All she found was the cold weight of a memory.

Callum sat in the barren backyard, eyes red with tears and palms red with blood. Mum crouched and hoisted him into her lap. She checked over his hands like they were ceramic.

'Did you do this, Ainsley?' she asked.

'She pushed me,' Callum sobbed. 'I didn't do anything. I just wanted a hug.'

He burrowed his face into Mum's chest, and Ainsley couldn't understand why. She kicked at the dirt next to them.

'You know you can't do things like that,' Mum said, glancing up.

Her voice wasn't angry enough.

'Come here, love. He needs that hug.' She reached out and squeezed her elbow.

Her skin wasn't cold enough. This feeling Mum was trying to plant inside her—it didn't belong there.

'Stop touching me,' Ainsley shouted, slapping Mum's hand away. 'I don't care if I pushed him. He deserved it.'

As the memory shrank, Ainsley scrambled to her feet and kicked the painting down, burying the mother and child in white carpet. This wasn't what she wanted.

Fire rose from the floor of her stomach, licking at her lungs. She tugged on a jumper and strode into the apartment hallway. There would be another painting. Another feeling, one that wouldn't unravel. She just had to look again.

La Danse had an audience. At the back of the hall, bodies pressed in, murmurs swelled and phones reached up to take photos. The colours grabbed her first—clover green, lightning blue, a violent, overbright orange. Ainsley saw them in bursts between heads and shoulders as she moved closer.

She knew the moment when a light switched on in the dark rooms of her heart. On the canvas, naked figures swung in a turbulent circle, hands joined and heads bent as if praying. They created a circuit that surged with exhilarating love, fusing their skin together.

They were pulling her into the dance, heating up her filaments and making her glow. She laughed at the feeling, shrill and incredulous. She'd never laughed like that. With a coloured gleam in her frigid grey eyes, she didn't care about the startled looks of the crowd.

The vaulted halls, the gift shop, the concrete path to her apartment—all of it passed without her notice. She gazed at the reprint in her hands, caught in her own incandescent light and desperate to stay there. She was only halfway home when she burnt out.

The figures in the painting kept turning, turning—

Laura and Jasmine were turning in the kitchen, slow and lopsided. Laura was dry sobbing into the bony part of Jasmine's shoulder. Jasmine was rubbing circles on her back.

Ainsley slouched in her stool and held onto the bench separating her from her friends. Every time Laura's cry pealed out, her grip on the laminate tightened. She didn't know what to do. She wanted Laura to stop sobbing so she could stop wondering what to do.

As Jasmine shifted around, she met her gaze and nodded down at Laura. Come here, *she was saying.* Prove that you care.

Unease settled in Ainsley's stomach. She didn't move. She just stared at Laura's shaking frame and grimaced.

Jasmine stuck out her chin. 'Her parents just threw her out,' *she hissed.* 'You can't even stand next to her?'

Ainsley couldn't say that comforting a friend felt like moving around in the dark with arms outstretched to find the furniture. 'It doesn't look like you guys need me.'

Jasmine watched her for a moment. 'You might be right.'

Ainsley lurched out of the memory. The spiralling dancers spun her out of balance, and she braced herself on a brick wall. She tried to breathe, but there were shadows in her lungs and over her heart.

She wanted the light back. She wanted a feeling she didn't have. Something other than fear, frenzy and spite, the only emotions she could shelter and stir up in her stomach.

The reprint slid from her fingers. She wanted art that reached out and dragged her in without dragging up memories too.

Landscapes and portraits discarded in op-shops. Wall art displayed in homeware stores. Illustrations hidden in social media feeds. Ainsley overran her three-room apartment with all the pieces she could find. They ran the lengths of her walls and took up space on her furniture. They stood against the kitchen backsplash, slumped in the bath, sat on windowsills blocking the sun and the view of rooftops. A lot of the paintings had long since exhausted their reserves of emotion.

Each one started in Ainsley's heart and flared out, glorious and good. Enough to make her believe it had pushed everything else out—until it landed on a vision of her old life, of feelings that moved around her instead of picking her up in their currents.

She stayed in her apartment for days, eyes tracing brushstrokes for a glimpse of something she hadn't felt yet. The only time she opened her door was to collect a delivery—another canvas, another panel, another print. Meanwhile, her clothes collected sweat, and her meals became bare ingredients she could nick from the pantry.

When her savings ran low and the art stopped coming, she refreshed the website for the gallery uptown. Something jerked in her chest. They had opened a new exhibition: *Real Romanticism*.

She left the apartment with bedraggled hair and a stained hoodie, all smudged at the edges. At the gallery doors, the security guard stared at her a little too long before letting her pass.

The exhibition unfurled across the walls of a rotunda, drawing visitors to every Blake, Cabanel and Delacroix. Ainsley reeled around the room and felt nothing. Then, *The Roses of Heliogabalus* grabbed at her periphery. She sensed the pull and succumbed to it, jostling to the front of the crowd and seizing the roped barrier. As she gazed up at the canvas, her chest opened.

It was hedonistic. Rose petals plunged from the ceiling of a Roman villa in a languid rush. While an emperor looked on with dim amusement, his circle of dinner guests suffocated under the deluge. They sprawled and flailed, half-buried in pink and white—some more serene than others. But one figure turned his face to the roses, resigning himself to the crush and reeling from their touch at the same time.

That inexplicable contradiction swelled in Ainsley's chest, churning with all the things she ran from and all the things she wanted. She felt it then: a thick surge of love, slow and overwhelming. Congealing between her heart and her lungs, clogging up her throat.

She thought of Tristan. In the two years she spent with him, she hadn't felt that surge. She wanted to tell him before the emotion leached out.

He didn't answer the phone when she called.

'You were right about me,' she gasped after the tone, staring at the figure in the painting. 'And I'm sorry. But I love you now. I found a way.'

Then love shuddered out of her, more violent than any other emotion. Like someone had reached into her chest and wrenched out her organs, breaking arteries and tearing tissue. They left another memory behind.

The dining table bore candles and homecooked casserole. Tristan's family grinned at each other like school kids. He sat on her left, covering his rosy face with a free hand while the other held her own. His skin felt like sandpaper, wearing her down with every caress.

Tristan's mother asked her what she loved about him.

Ainsley couldn't think of anything.

By the end of the night, she'd come up with seven things. But his mother wasn't listening anymore and his father was scraping plates in the sink and his younger sisters had been sent to bed early. Tristan hid his hands in his pockets as he saw Ainsley out the door. She wanted him to hold her and wear her down one last time.

Ainsley dug her nails into the rope, shoulders hunched and quivering. She pulled in a breath and looked up at the painting again, where the figure reached out from the roses with one hand. A beckoning. She stepped over the rope and crossed the empty space between. Voices behind her stopped and simmered. Somewhere, a security guard cried out.

When she touched the figure's hand, it was nothing more than skin on dried acrylic. Then the tether fastened, and she felt everything. The flesh-like curl of petals. The coarse grasp of fingers. Heat, inside her and everywhere.

She fell into the feeling.

Later, when handlers came to collect *The Roses of Heliogabalus*, visitors would talk for months of the woman who walked into the canvas. Only they would remember how the figure disappeared from under the petals and left another in his place: bedraggled hair, a stained hoodie and paralysed eyes—once a frigid grey, now burning with kaleidoscopic colour.

THESE VIS/CERAL GALAXIES

Adam Brannigan

She says her favourite way to *you know*, to fuck, is to ...

Is to what? you ask, looking into her charcoal eyes, to make it clear you might be able to fuck her just like she wants, after this fifth? sixth? glass of wine, after you take a seed of mull cake back from her mouth, after running the bath, dipping your finger, going deep in the water, the wine, then her honey.

Blood.

You ask her again, is to what?

This. Just like this, she pronoun/cis into the templed air of the bathroom; arms outstretched. Bone. Sinew. Here in the dark water, while ... you know, she answers, undressing, gesturing to the background of lactic tiles, as she steps into the inviolate water and you notice the milky way the light catches the scars on her belly.

You blush and turn away, not realising what was hidden until now. Yes, she says, her ancient ritual of voice, yes, my scars. These vis/ceral galaxies. I gave birth to the whole world, why should it matter? What are you thinking, daughter, because ...?

I'm not thinking, you answer in your head, not thinking straight. Where did you meet her, again? Why doesn't she finish her sentences?

Lighted candles. Drip wax.

Thick. Black.

Her pubic hair.

There are forms in the water. On the slick walls are shadows. And you take hours to turn back your head through atmospheres of honey, wine, water. And you see a greater shadow behind her. Folded. And she says, in echoed syllables, do you like least my ancient scars or my ancient wings, daughter of butchery, because when it is time, I will show you, well, you *already* know ...

No, I don't know. How could I know? You never finish your sentences, are the last words drowning in your head.

The whole world slips away while she laughs. And then she says, but I never finish my sentences.

N/ever.

LOVERS' ODYSSEY

Sheridan Burdon

She casts a spell on you as your lips
collide, kissing you slowly as your hips
dance together to choreograph a routine.
The bed is your stage, spotlight on you.
Perform like no-one is watching.
She is the serpent of seduction as
her tongue entangles yours,
poisoning you with passion.
Strip her bare.
Peel the layers from her chalk-white skin,
to let your mouth travel across the dips
and valleys of her body,
craving more as you savour her taste.
Start a fire within her.
Watch the sparks fly as you trail
your fingertips like a match across her skin.
Bite her neck and surrender to
the scent of her pheromones
as they flood your airways,
intoxicating you like a drug.
Gently circle her supple pink buds and
feel them blossom under your tongue.

Tease her.
Beauty of a rose, she possesses
infectious thorns that claw you
as she begs for more.
The searing pain builds with
each scratch, awakening the
desire within you to devour her.
Soft and silky like petals, her
skin seems delicate,
fragile; it flushes red
as you grip her tighter.
Pull her closer.
The flames engulf her as you
venture through her garden,
the tendrils of her venom
afflicting your being.
Listen to the cadence of her moans,
as the Siren's song guides you
on your journey.
Let it enchant you,
lure you,
ensnare you,
in the depths down below.
Her poison is ravenous;
you have no choice but to
succumb to the adrenaline
rushing through your veins.
Skin on skin, goosebumps
are rising,
hearts thumping,

pulses racing,
eyes fixated on her glistening
pink flesh.
Ripe and dripping—
Persephone's bounty awaits your
tender touch.
Feast on the fruit and the seeds
will explode on your tongue,
flavour pooling,
cascading,
enslaving you both to the ecstasy.
Hips rocking,
tongue swirling,
thighs tensing,
moans fill the air—her thorns
leave marks of passion as
her grip constricts you.
Crescendo reaching its peak,
her back arches as her climax
takes control and Cupid shoots her
with his arrow, diffusing her venom,
as she submits to the release.
Ride the wave as her honey fills your
mouth, the rush of euphoria threatening
to drown you.
The Siren's song dissipates as she releases
you from the trance.
The blaze is extinguished
as your limbs intertwine
like serpents once again,

two hearts thumping rhythmically
as she basks in her reverie.
Cool fingertips trace the goosebumps
that remain, and your lips curve into a smile,
knowing you've tamed the temptress
and satisfied her insatiable hunger.
Just the beginning of your lovers' odyssey.

THE FIRST AND LAST DAY OF US

Ronni Snook

Poppy – The Last Day

He's back on the couch, eyes glued to the footy playing on the screen. A row of beers line the length of the coffee table, bleeding watermarks into the wood. He never bothers to use the coasters that sit in taunting proximity to the bottles. It's enough to make her want to scream—again. It's the small things that bother Poppy the most. Her best friend's words ring in the back of her head. Four years ago Kat heralded a warning—

don't expect much, she had said, and it fell on Poppy's deaf ears. She bought the coffee table from a woodworker a year ago; it was once a beautiful mango wood that had cost her more than she's willing to confess and it sits tainted by the water rings of cans. She stares at him, long enough that the words of their argument sit like bile in the back of her throat. She swallows them. His eyes roll at her appearance, at the dress which flowed in pleated layers and synched in at her waist.

'It's not my fault things never work out for you, Leo. Just figure something, anything out and get off my fucking couch.' She spat those words at him in the midst of their argument, twisting that knife in defense. He hates how she buys things he can't afford. It made him vicious. In the beginning his ugliness felt like a form that would take over who he truly was. Now, the charming side of Leo is a secondary character to the man she lives with, whose bitter form is custom made. Their fights, although the topic changes, at the core they are always the same. His self-enforced inferiority in comparison to her, a woman who, despite being six years his junior, is earning double him. He is emasculated by success and she can't bring herself to offer him any more pity.

When they started, they were absorbed in each other, obsessive even. She fueled that; he wasn't lazy, he was *relaxed*, he wasn't abrasive, he was *upfront*. She pulled new adjectives for him every chance she got. She's twenty-three now, no longer the eighteen-year-old girl that pulled the twenty-four-year-old she met at the party. She had grown, albeit slightly, and he had remained happily situated. Happily situated on her couch.

She went to the first party alone; this will be no different. *It's going to be okay, Kat will jump in at any mention of Leo's name because her intuition will pick it.* She still hesitates. They will all understand, but that doesn't remove the biting humiliation of it. Leo has a way of making people dislike him when he wants, when he allows the charm to slip away and what remains is a distortion. Her stomach twists, thinking of their judgement of the man she loves. Despite coming alone before, this is fundamentally different. She's older, yes, but lingering at the door, the anxiety rippling through her, she feels eighteen again.

Leo – The First Day

Leo noticed her the moment she appeared at Kat's side. She was a short thing, meek, timid like a mouse. Her eyes darted to every corner of the garden and her arm looped with Kat's. He was captivated by the blonde. Leo hadn't learnt yet that he had a type, but he knew he liked girls a certain way. Quiet and passive, often younger than him. His friends gave him shit for it but nothing that counted, it amused them really. And she was just that, his type, he could tell all that from the moment she entered his threshold. It was in the way she walked, how she pulled at the hem of her dress, the sensible flats that she had worn. He had seen it before, liked it before.

Sat on the steps of the pool, Evan by his side, he was comfortable. Kat's garden had become a fixture in his life, he'd been close with her brother Evan for years. Around them, the party pulsed with music and the thrum of conversation. The sun's beat was relentless, its burn gleamed from the pool's surface, reflecting through his sunglasses. Beneath its sweltering heat, an uncomfortable layer of sweat had coated the upper half of his body that wasn't submerged.

Kat had been quick to ditch her friend at the bar, without introduction to anyone. She was out of place, as she shifted on a bar stool, sipping from a tall glass filled with an offensively pink liquid. Nobody had tried to talk to her, even as she smiled at people that walked by. Something about it knotted his stomach with sympathy.

'You're joking,' Evan muttered, pulling Leo's attention to him. 'Poppy. Really?' Evan nodded toward her, having caught him out. Poppy—he hung the name in his mind. Poppy, like a flower.

Leo shrugged off his words, turning back to the girl in the yellow summer dress. She was closer there, close enough to see the tattoo on her forearm, he was yet to make out the image.

'She's hot,' Evan said, trying to sound uninterested but Leo could see straight through it. Leo pulled off his sunglasses to get a better look at her, the blonde hair reached her mid back, flowing in waves. Her face was fox-like. He could see the angled and sharp features through the distance. He couldn't make out much more detail than that. He thought she was pretty, 'hot' might have been a stretch on Evan's part. But he wasn't about to confess that.

'I'm going to go talk to her.'

Poppy – The Last Day

Crossing into the house, she is met straight away by Evan and her stomach twists. She awkwardly shifts beneath the fixture of his gaze. The change began after a holiday Evan and Leo took a couple years ago—since then, Evan met her with the same approach, as if he was constantly on the verge of saying something before deciding otherwise, and Evan and Leo no longer spoke, making their disdain for one another transparent. It was about her, that much she knew, but whatever it is she didn't want to know.

Kat peps in her spot, pulls Poppy into a hug with a tight squeeze, whispering a welcome into her ear. The rest of the crowd greets her with the same familiarity they usually do. She can't receive it in the same way, it acts as a reminder of all that she has missed in the last year. The tears prick at her ducts and she does all she can to hide them behind a perfectly woven smile. When the attention shifts from her to the centre of the party, Kat and her twenty-third birthday, she wanders over to the pool. The conversations of the party blend with the music until becoming one faded hum of noise behind her.

'You coming home soon?' The text pops up on her lock screen, lighting her face. She hadn't expected to hear from him, perhaps he knew the things that were milling through her. The sickening nausea that comes over in waves. An opposite to how he used to make her feel, light and pathetically fluffy. She shoves her phone into her purse and dumps it on a lounge chair, hikes up the bottom of her dress and sits on the edge of the pool.

The water laps at her legs, relieving her body from its flushed warmth. The cool surface chills the back of her thighs, she eases, and her posture slackens. She shifts her gaze to the skies above—most stars drowned out by the light of the city. The few that remain blink back at her with their shimmering opals—the infinite reality of the universe could swallow her and she still won't find any fight left in her. She indulges the part of her that clings to hope. The part that dreams of Leo's entrance, where he finds her at the pool edge they met on years before. Leo's apology would be muttered with his honey tone, sweet and sticky. In the dream he smells of their coconut body wash and wears the button-up shirt she bought him for Christmas. But that's all it is—a dream, a hopeless and desperate escape from what is clearly unravelling between them. Leo isn't coming, and she isn't going home.

Behind her, the screeching noise of the pool gate pulls her out of her mind. There it is, the familiar pulse, happiness, love—whatever it is, it has always been reserved for Leo.

Leo – The First Day

She didn't see him approach and if she did, she didn't look up from her glass. Perhaps she had grown tired of smiling at strangers. He grabbed two beers and leant against the bar, his worst attempt at appearing casual. Normally he was good at this, cool and collected, but when her eyes remained absorbed by the drink she swirled with a straw, his game slipped.

'Do you want a drink?'

She startled at his voice. He held the beer out, despite the drink already in her hand. When she glanced up at him, he finally got a better look at her, the freckles that scattered her nose and her hair wasn't as blonde as he thought it was—it had a hint of red that was golden in the sun. Her eyes trailed to his topless state. Perhaps it was the heat of the summer day, but he could have sworn her cheeks reddened. Her blush deepened his interest.

'I've got one,' she smiled, it was wound tight with no teeth in sight, dismissive and entirely fake. He could tell she was nervous from the way she kept glancing from him to around the party, as if she was afraid of keeping her attention fixed on him for too long, or searching for Kat.

'You seem like the type of girl who'd prefer a beer and some company.' He offered the beer once again and this time she placed her glass on the edge of the bar and took the can. Her fingers brushed over his. His grin pulled at the right corner of his mouth, and she returned it this time, a real smile, rows of white pearls topped by two dimples on her cheek. As she brought the drink to her lips, he watched her slight grimace but chose against teasing.

'Much better.' She grinned, squinting up at him. Her smile had widened, both dimples on display. Leo's heart jumped at the sight of them—little betrayer, he thought.

'I'm Leo.' He sat on the stool beside her. Their thighs brush one another, skin yearning to stick in the sweltering temperature, offering her his hand which she took with a slight shake.

'Poppy.' He felt the warmth of their bodies mold together in the grasp.

Hours passed, and he liked her more than he would've liked to admit. After a few drinks her shyness was washed down with them, and she was hanging off every word he said. He spoke about travel and how he had just gotten back from Vietnam, and she leant forward in her seat, their knees brushing one another with the proximity. He took the time to listen to her, at first it was out of obligation but that changed. She was smart, funny in a naïve sort of way but he found that cute. By the end of the night, with alcohol fogging any inhibitions in her mind, his hand was on her thigh, his thumb tracing along the soft flesh of her skin. Leo didn't consider himself romantic, but submerged in the bath of her attention, he couldn't help imagining that he stood on the precipice of something. He just wasn't sure what.

Poppy – The Last Day

It vanishes when she turns, and seeing the flash of red silk alerts her to who. It isn't often that she finds herself disappointed at the sight of Kat.

'Pop, I've been looking everywhere for you.' Kat smiles down at her, two cocktail glasses in hand. Poppy musters up a smile in return. Her feet kick out in the water and its coolness sifts between her toes. Kat sits beside her and hands over the glass of pink liquid. They are silent for a few minutes until Kat shifts her body towards Poppy.

'Let me say this, and you can tell me to piss off if you want. He makes you miserable, he's hollowing you out and I wouldn't say anything if I—' She pauses a moment, recalculating her words and continues 'If I could bear to watch it, but I can't. You deserve so much more. I hope you know that.'

'I know.' Poppy swallows the lump that has become situated in her throat. 'I'm going to end it.' She tries to convey as much sureness as she can, but it falls short. She can't be certain of it, she never could be, but she has to be okay with it because they were done. They had been done for longer than either of them knew.

Kat peers over at Poppy, her face set with a frown. Poppy hadn't expected her to be shocked at the news—Kat had a way of knowing these things, sometimes before she knew herself.

'Are you okay?' she asks.

It takes all of Poppy's will not to recoil at the question. 'Yeah, I think so,' she says. It's a lie which manages to sound like one. She fixates on the orbs of light dancing on the pool's surface. She relaxes into the touch of Kat's body pressed into hers. Her eyes shutter on the world, her head finds Kat's shoulder and the waft of Kat's citrus perfume fills her senses.

She wants to be angry, to tell Leo all the reasons he is the villain, but for every reason she can find against him she finds one against herself. It isn't a lack of love, she knows that. Complacency can be blamed, but to find one catalyst in four years of fuck-ups is a deleterious task. The matter of it is too complex, yet somehow, there is a simple truth to it—they don't fit in their life together anymore. The dreams they had conjured over the last four years would remain fantasies: the beach wedding, the two kids they had spoken about, all would die here. Poppy feels no humiliation about it, after all. She has no shame in wanting to wait for Leo—that's who she is: hopeful till the bitter end. And this is the end.

To expect change from him is the greatest falsehood. She knows him, better than he knows himself and no matter if he wants to, he won't attempt to fix their morphed reality. And she isn't going to submit, not this time. That leaves her here, waiting, hoping for a dream, anything over this ache. The slip feels physical—in her hands that are aching, her throat which has been scraped by the sharpness of the words she screamed at him, and in her chest that's so tight it causes a shortness of breath. She can no longer stand it, the iron grip.

Breathing in the humid night air, the stars and Kat the only witnesses, she allows herself to loosen her grip and watches them as they float away. Paper boats of words both said and those not said, dreams broken and those fulfilled. Poppy can see their glory as they go.

And god, they are beautiful.

PICTURE PERFECT

Amy Jarrett

Marriage can be such a complex thing. It has unrealistic idealisations and never-ending expectations. It's an everlasting daydream where you tell everyone lies about how happy you are. A phony *happily ever after* ending that young girls and boys are told to look forward to when many parents are unhappy themselves. But most times, it's a nightmare ending in divorce.

I'd witnessed both of my parents remarry multiple times, and yet here I was with a diamond ring on my previously unbranded finger.

I sighed as I reached for the open lipstick tube on the bed beside me and applied another layer. Wine red, *his* favourite colour. A gift he gave me two days ago, together with the red roses that were slowly wilting in the vase on the bedside table. I suppose I should've been happy. He had only ever treated me well, but I guess that's why I was concerned. I was well aware that this ... *honeymoon phase* wouldn't last forever.

I held up my hand and watched the teardrop diamond glitter in the sunlight coming through the window. Too fast. We'd only known each other for three months, got married a week ago and then just moved in together two days ago. It was all going way too fast.

I glanced at the wilting flowers, beautiful, brief, destined to die. Just like marriage. They made me think: why did I say yes? Maybe it was all the gifts and affection he praised me with. Or maybe it was his flowery words or the portraits he'd painted of me covering the walls of his home. He made me feel beautiful. Wanted. Desired. I *couldn't* say no. But now, he felt different. Distant. I hastily glossed my lips with more lipstick, accidentally smearing some on my fingers, as I recalled his words after I'd asked to see his studio.

'You may be my muse, but you're not picture perfect yet.'

Even though I knew he was a perfectionist, I wondered what his version of perfect was and why I was not perfect to him. Why was his studio locked? Was there another woman—

My phone buzzed on the bed beside me, dragging me away from my contemplative thoughts. I looked at the screen to find he was calling me. I shivered, remembering the time I didn't answer his call. Shattered vases on his

75

living room floor and my favourite portrait, torn beyond
recognition all over his rug. My disfigured face forever
burned into my memory. I picked up the phone and
answered the call.

'Hey, honey, is everything ok?'

'Yes, sweetheart, just letting you know I won't be home
tonight. Something has come up at work.'

My branded hand dropped the lipstick as I mindlessly
traced over the embroidered pattern of the duvet, faintly
staining the fabric red from the pigment smeared on my
fingers. 'Oh? Is everything ok?'

'Yes, I have to go now, but I'll be home early tomorrow
morning. Good night.'

'I love you—'

I climbed off our bed as he abruptly hung up, one hand
holding my phone and the other holding the lipstick. How
dare he leave me alone? I walked out of the room and
down the stairs, passing by my portraits decorating the
walls. *Nothing* could be more important than coming home
to me. In the three months we'd known each other, he
had always spent his evenings in his studio, working on a
portrait of me or doing something else for work. I stopped
in front of his studio, hesitating once I noticed the door was
partially open. It was unusual to see it unlocked and even
more so to see it left open. Something was different about
my husband. Why had he changed recently? Not only had
his pedantic behaviour changed, but his romantic actions,
his kind words and even his gifts had dwindled. *You're not
picture perfect yet.* I took a deep breath as I opened the door,
my hands shaking in anticipation and anxiousness.

The light was already on. I walked into the lingering smell of paint and setting spray and saw several figures lining the walls of the bright room. Each marble bust had been carved with the precision and meticulousness I recognised in my husband's artwork. I walked across the room, examining each sculpture. Each statue looked different, but all were of the figures of very beautiful women. Next to the door was a long workbench. A medium-sized black box rested on the bench next to a collection of paints, brushes, canvases and carving tools organised perfectly by colour and size. The two words engraved on the front of the box caught my attention. I placed my phone and lipstick beside the box and reached my hand out to trace the engraving, my vision blurring with tears. Would this give me answers as to why he had changed?

My masterpieces.

I opened the lid of the box, and the beating of my heart skyrocketed as I looked at the contents.

'What the hell is going on?' I said, my voice echoing throughout the studio. The box contained dividers, numbered 1 to 22, each appearing to contain only one photograph. With shaking hands, I pulled out all the contents and placed them in order on the bench. Section after section. Photo after photo. Woman after woman. My hands hesitated as they reached the final two sections, empty but named. My fingers traced the name on the first section. My name. I looked at the name on the second; the name seemed familiar. *Very strange.* I looked at the photos in front of me. They were very similar; the only difference was the woman in the pictures.

I gathered the photos and turned to look at the sculptures, noticing the busts were in the same order as the pictures. However, there were two more at the end of the line. I looked back at the box and realised the sculptures could only be of myself and the other female. I put the photos in my pocket and picked up my lipstick, carefully smearing on layer after layer as I picked up a carving hammer from the bench and approached the last sculpture. I stopped in front of it and put the lipstick in my pocket before resting my empty hand on the pretty woman's marble cheek. I recognised her face. My husband's assistant attended our wedding after all.

Is she with him right now? I laughed as I smashed the hammer into her sculpture, forcing the fractured figure off the edge of the pedestal. I revelled in watching her beautiful face shatter. Such beauty is only temporary. She will never be picture perfect now. I turned to face the other pedestals and smiled as I gripped the hammer tighter. My laugh echoed around the room as I destroyed each woman's beautiful sculpture. The marble was scattered across the floor like shattered glass—every single statue was now ruined. I loosened my grip on the hammer as I admired the view before me. Only my perfect sculpture remained, resting on its pedestal above the mutilated figures of the other women. I turned away and walked back to the workbench, and gently placed the hammer back in its rightful position.

I grabbed my phone and smiled at the broken figures as I exited the studio, turning off the light and closing the door behind me. I walked down the hall, stopped in front of the floor-length mirror near the kitchen entrance and examined my appearance. My hair was untidy, with pieces of hair stuck in the heavy, waxy layers of lipstick smeared across my lips and teeth. I breathed in deeply as I gently removed the strands and tidied my hair, cringing at the sickly-sweet scent of the makeup. I rubbed my lipstick-stained teeth with my fingers in an attempt to clean them before licking my index finger and rubbing the smudged makeup around my lips. I stared into the mirror and smiled widely, the unrelenting stain on the edge of my lips making them look fuller than normal. *Perfect.* I wanted to be the first thing he saw when he got home.

I turned away, still smiling as I thought about the masterpiece I had left for my husband in his studio. As I passed the kitchen doorway, I switched the light on and grabbed the apron that hung on the hook beside the door. I eyed my reflection in the kitchen window then gazed into the dark hallway as I took a seat at the table, waiting for him to come home.

The sun was starting to rise as his footsteps echoed through the house, much louder than usual. I applied a fresh coat of lipstick before walking to the counter. As he entered, I reached for a cutting board and an onion, like I had been to preparing to make food. A hand grabbed my shoulder and pulled me into a chest.

'Found you, sweetheart.' His arms wrapped around my shoulders and gripped tightly. 'I missed you.'

I thought of the photos in my pocket, *the other women*, as I picked up the knife and started chopping up the onions, my hands shaking slightly. In the photos I had kept, a teardrop diamond adorned the left hand of each woman. Their beautiful faces had been highlighted by their wine-red lips, their hand positioned as if caressing their neck. The same ring for them, and the same ring for me. His arms released my shoulders, and instead, he placed his hands on them and *squeezed*.

'Did you go into my studio?'

I fumbled with the knife but stayed silent.

'I asked you a question. Answer me.'

I bit my tongue, noticing his game, and refused to make a sound. His hands slowly dragged from my shoulders to circle my neck, firmly squeezing and slowly cutting off my airway.

He was enjoying this, I realised. The *thrill* of hunting his prey.

My hands stopped shaking as I gripped the knife tighter and twisted my body around, shoving the sharp blade between his ribs towards his heart. His eyes widened in disbelief and he gasped, reaching for the object in his chest. Before he could touch it, I ripped the knife from his chest and pushed him backwards. His knees collapsed from shock, and he crumpled to the ground.

I dropped the knife as I kneeled beside him before removing the bloody diamond ring from my hand and sliding it onto his finger. I shushed him as he weakly tried to push me away and delicately brushed his hair from his face. I positioned his newly ornamented hand over his neck, just like he did to the others. As I pulled away, I admired the crimson liquid on my freshly unbranded hand, the deep colour reminding me of the wine-red lipstick he had gifted us all.

'Well, would you look at that,' I whispered as I brought my bloody hand to his face and smeared the crimson onto his lips. 'Picture perfect, just like you always dreamed.'

HE DOES THIS ALL THE TIME

Brianna McLeary

This isn't the first time I've gotten myself into a situation like this. Walking along streets I only kind of know from the driver's seat. The distant sounds of nightlife my only company as I walk through the darkness. Stumbling on my mission to get away. Far away from the mess I just made, the mistakes I can't take back and the words that fell out of my mouth as quickly as if ... oh god.

Heave

Blurgh

Splat

Yeah, that.

Another night of ruining a stranger's front lawn with second-hand rum and whatever small amount of food I remembered to scoff down during the festivities. I can't remember how long I've been walking now, or even how far away I am from somewhere I know. That's the goal—find a street that is familiar. It's harder than it sounds when the streets are swaying too much to really focus. There's no way I could find my way back to Brock's birthday party, not that I can go back there. I wouldn't want to if I could.

I feel my phone vibrating in my pocket, the buzz scrambling my nerves over and over and over with each message or worse, the phone call. The obnoxious repetitive quacking—why in the hell did I choose ducks as a ringtone?

'You should definitely have a go. That was awesome.' Shane steps back, angling the handlebars towards Eli.

Eli knows he shouldn't even touch it in his current state, hardly able to hold himself up straight, let alone control a motorbike. Yet there are his hands, slipping straight into position on the handlebars. His dad's words echo through his head: 'Don't let anyone drive anything of yours and don't you drive anything of anyone else's, just to be safe.'

Yet there are Eli's feet, sliding straight into position on the pedals. He pulls the throttle back. The bike thunders beneath him, the rumbles sending vibrations through his body and shaking up the contents of his stomach. Eli doesn't notice the sick feeling the bike is causing, only the thrill it brings. He can't hear his sister over the roar of the bike.

'DON'T DRIVE DRUNK. STUPID.'

To be fair, even if he could hear her, he never would have listened. Too distracted by the calls of encouragement from his drunken companions. Eli inches the bike forwards, revving the engine hard. He does it again and again, and finally, the tyres flick up mud. The back tyre slides in a snaking 'S' before the bike takes off, with Eli clutching desperately at the handlebars, face white.

Whoa, that's a bright light. Nice, now I'm blind too. Why do terrible things always happen to me? It was a new bike too. Was. Now it's proper broken. Exhaust, fucked. Handlebars, fucked. Body, scratched to shit. I shouldn't have been on it, shouldn't have gone near the thing. I knew how Brock would react—his precious and expensive new bike. It's a dirt bike, though, it's gonna get scratches, gonna get busted up a little. I guess a little is a whole lot less than what I did.

Where am I? I don't recognise this road or a single house that's on it. Where are the lights of the city? I just have to find Centro, and then I should know the way back to Bella's with my eyes closed. Oh, don't close your eyes. I may not be able to see the world spinning but I sure can feel it.

'Oi!'

Who the—? Who's yelling at me?

'Eli! Over here!'

Oh, awesome, Brock. Maybe if I'm lucky he'll make me feel like shit again.

'Oi! Mate, what the fuck are you doing?'

Yeah, right, like you care, Brock. 'I'm going home.' Whoa, I sound rough. Is it the yelling? The crying? Or just the burn of alcohol?

'Don't be dense. Get in the car.'

Yeah, I'll do just that, and you can clarify how terrible of a person I am.

'Come on, Eli, you can't just walk around all night. Do you even know where you're going?'

'Yeah, it's'—I point towards the distant light of the Centro—'there-ish, so just fuck off and leave me alone.' If I wanted your company, I wouldn't have left the party.

'Don't be a stubborn prick. We're just trying to get you off the side of the road.'

'So you can get mad at me?' Don't deny it. 'No thanks.'

'Fuck's sake, stop acting like a kid. We just don't want you getting run over, mate.'

Sure, like you actually care about me. You just want to look like the good guy.

'What, not talking to me now, Eli? Just get in the car, stop sulking.'

What a perfectly round rock. I wonder how far it will go if I kick it? Nope, can't feel my foot. I missed. Oh well.

'Come on, mate, stop being an idiot. Why don't you answer your phone for once?'

No. 'Cause screw you, that's why.'

'How are you going to get home?'

'Duh, I'm walking.' Away from you, take a hint. 'Leave me alone, Brock. I'm done talking to you or anyone. Just fuck off and leave me alone. How many times do I have to say it?' Don't rev your car at me, you self-righteous prick.

'Mate, you screwed up, not me.'

It was a fucking accident. It's not my fault.

'Just get in the car, and we can drive you home.'

'You shouldn't have had the bike out in the first place. How stupid do you have to be to bring your brand-new bike out at a party full of drunk idiots, anyway?'

'Hey, you're the one who decided to show off. You didn't have to ride it the way you did.'

'Fuck off.' I don't want to do this now. 'Fuck you, fuck off, leave me alone and get fucked.'

'Fine, be like that. We're telling Bella where to find you.'

Seriously, dude, you don't need to rev your car that hard, regardless of how mad you are that I ruined your bike.

The bike lays in the mud, Eli 10 metres in the opposite direction. Smoke rising from the bike and groans rising from Eli's throat. Pain. Sharp, shooting pain even the alcohol didn't numb. Down his right leg, up his right arm and thundering through his head. The crowd of drunken party guests converges over his injured body, murmuring their worry with slurring words.

'Are you kidding me!' Brock yells as he stands over his damaged bike. 'It's munted, you idiot!'

All heads turn towards Brock as he leans over his bike, hands tangled in his hair, eyes wide with horror. Feet shuffling through the disturbed dirt as the crowd shifts their attention away from the body in the mud, towards their distressed friend and his precious bike.

'My bike's properly broken, mate.' Brock turns his attention to the crowd, grasping for their sympathetic stares.

A grunting sound from Eli as he shifts ever so slightly in his futile mission to stand on his injured limbs. The crowd's attention does not shift as Brock continues to stress over the damage to his bike, listing off every curse he knows mixed with every insult he can summon, aimed directly at Eli.

'Fuck,' Eli moans as he feels the pain shoot from his knee.

Brock takes one last long look at the damage before focusing solely on the slowly moving form in the mud. 'You!' He moves towards Eli, the bodies of the crowd parting in tension. 'Stupid!' He stomps in the mud, the anticipation of the crowd building at the promise of a fight. 'Idiot!' He stands over Eli, shoulders squared and fists clenched.

'What?' Eli hisses between moans, every movement a chore.

'My bike! You fucked it.'

The crowd gathers, shadowing the pair in their mass.

I guess the good thing about being drunk right now is the walking isn't bothering me. I could walk all night. In fact, I have walked further than this a few times before, especially when drunk. It's calming, the cool, fresh breeze filling my lungs and soothing my warm skin. While the world swims, I keep breathing. Alone and content, each step taking me further and further away from the problems I've created and the mistakes I can never undo.

Ok, it's brighter now. Streetlights line the roads and illuminate the buildings surrounding me. Ok, store fronts now, that's a good sign. Gone are the manicured lawns and clipped hedges, replaced by cracked cement and leaking ... something. Am I even going to be able to read now? D-A-V-I-S E-L-E-C-T-R-O-N-I-C-S ... I guess it's slow going, but I can make out the letters well enough. I still don't even know where in the city this store is, but from the sounds of things, I must be getting close to the highway. Do I jump the fence?

I'm jumping the fence. No, wait. I'm vomiting on the fence. Ok, maybe it would be better to walk around. Yes, good, smart thinking, Eli. Don't want to hurt yourself. That would be a bad way to end the night, facedown in my own blood and found unconscious in the morning by some random passer-by. I've just got to follow the sound of cars, and I'll be walking by the highway before I know it. I'll know my way once I find the highway.

Whoa, cars move fast when you're watching from the outside. Zoom, one. Zoom, two. Do I have to try to get across the road? Oh god, I think I do. Fuck. Well, I think this might be how I die, squashed by a truck going just that little bit too much over the speed limit because why would he need to slow down? It's the highway late at night—who's going to be dumb enough to walk out in this darkness? Maybe I shouldn't. I could just walk back.

No. Me. That's who's dumb enough. Ha ha, damn. This isn't going to end well. Here goes, I guess. Fuck, stand straight. Move. Move. Move. Fuck. Cars are too fast; this can't be legal. Fuck. Walk. Walk. Run. Run. Fuck!

And I've fallen over, in the middle of the fucking highway. Yup, cool, my leg gives out the one time I need it to do the one thing it's supposed to. Just my luck. Lights—I think I know how deer feel now, staring at the brightness as it grows closer and closer. Fast, way too fast. God, please, not like this.

'Gwaaaaaah! Fuuuuuuuck.' My hands grasp at the bitumen, clawing my way desperately towards the side of the road, to the safety of the weeds. Fuck.

I squeeze my eyes shut. This is it. This is it. My eyes ache. It's going to hurt. It's going to hurt so bad. I never even said goodbye to anyone. When was the last time I said I loved anyone? They know, don't they? Surely, they would know. That I love them, that I'm sorry I'm too stubborn to accept a ride. I squeeze my eyes tighter. So tight I think I can feel my eyelids folding under my eyeballs. Tighter. Tighter. Hot tears burn.

The headlights are bright. So bright I can see it through my closed eyes, so bright I can't think of anything but how bright it is. So bright. White light.

I clench my hands tight; I should feel the pain soon. I crush them tighter, and I feel ... grass? How do I feel grass?

I feel wind rush past me, way too fast to be safe. I slowly open my eyes, greeted only by the darkness left behind. No lights, no cars, nothing but empty darkness. I slowly crawl towards the side of the road, limbs weak and breath ragged. My heart pounds in my chest as I pull myself off the road to sit on the grass. I can see the spot on the road where I lay only moments before, the pool of blood so red. A tyre mark spreading it a metre further down the road. I check myself over once, then twice, then even a third time. There are no new injuries mangling my body. That was too close. I should be dead. I should never have been crossing the road this drunk and this hurt. That's how people die, Eli. How did I not die?

I've been staring at the road for so long now, I can see the orange tinge of the sun rising. I should get up. I have to get up. I have to get home and maybe tell some people some things. I still don't understand what happened.

Oh, a chicken shop. I wish it was open. I could so go for a good chicken burger right now. I wonder how far I would have walked by now. I could only imagine how it would look if I walked in right now. I'd look like a psychopath stumbling in covered in blood, dirt and grass, eyes staring blankly into space. Slurring my order to a terrified server and then not being able to pay for it because I don't think I have two dollars to rub together. They'd call the police the second I walked through the door. I just need a bath and bed and maybe even a hug.

I mustn't have sat there for too long; the world still swims in my vision, and my feet step in a serpentine pattern.

One left. I always forget how steep that hill is.

A right. Two lefts. That stupid mailbox shaped like a bird—who does that? It's not even a bird someone would use for delivery. A pigeon, sure, maybe. But a rainbow lorikeet? Annoying.

Another right. So close now. I wonder if Bella is worrying about me.

Up, up and up the next hill. Not as steep as the last one, but still no walk in the park. My right knee kind of hurts. No, that's a lie. It really fucking hurts.

And a final left. I can see Bella's house now, the only one with multiple lights on.

I can hear Bella's voice now—not the actual words she is saying, but the general tone in which she speaks. Louder than she should be speaking this late at night if I can hear her all the way from where I am. Maybe I should hang outside for a couple hours? To be safe? No, I should probably face it. She'll be mad no matter when I get there.

'I'm going to get in the car and go find him.' I can hear Bella speak as her silhouette walks out of the house.

'No, you're not, Bella. Don't you dare get behind that wheel. You've had far too much to drink yourself.' She is followed closely by her dad. Great. Dressed in his finest 'spending the night getting wasted on the couch' clothes.

'I'm fine. I've only had a few drinks all night, and they were spaced. I ate too.' She reaches out for the car handle as her dad catches up to her.

'No, Bella. Think. You know that's not right. You definitely had more than that, and you don't even know how to space out drinks, and what did you eat?' Her dad makes some good points. Maybe I should say something before this causes a rift.

'I'm fine.' The words sound raw coming out of my mouth.

She doesn't hear me.

'Dad, I'm worried about him.' Tears start to well in her eyes as she speaks, and my heart aches.

'Bella! Babe, I'm fine.' Maybe I should clear my throat. I really do sound rough.

She still doesn't hear me.

Her dad pulls her into a hug, gently taking the keys from her shaking hands. I walk closer, reaching out to her.

'Bell, I'm here. I'm ok.' Why can't she hear me? I'm right here.

'What if something happened to him, Dad? What am I supposed to do?' She's really crying now, head buried in her dad's shoulder. He holds her tight. That should be me holding her.

'He'll be fine, Bell. He does this all the time, and he is always ok,' her dad says. A tender whisper of a lie.

My fingers gently brush her shoulder, and she doesn't react. The sobs continue to wrack her body as her father pats her back.

'I'm here, Bell, I'm right here and I'm ...' My hand reaches right through her. I pause. Frozen by dread.

'What if he is ...' She's unable to say the word. The fear runs through us both as the truth settles.

Dead.

RUSH AND REVERIE

Gemma Neuendorf

Jeremy's world was finally quiet. Walking through a landscape of piercing aquamarines and ivories, only surrounded by his thoughts. He felt freedom like he'd never felt before, pulsing through his veins as the vines and marble around him continued forever. He was enveloped by the swaying scenery. Looking at the sky in awe, he continued down the path. Lilacs and carnations covered the sky in delicate paint strokes, every single one creating an artist's dream. Jeremy was home.

A voice began to echo, calling to him. *Jeremy? Hello, can you hear me?*

He wondered if the heavens were speaking to him, if they could hear him, too. He took a few steps forward, ready to ask them about their intentions. Suddenly, the serenity of the world around him became uneasy. He felt his shoulder quake.

Jeremy? Jeremy? Wake up.

Wake up? he thought. He stumbled back, stunned. Was this not real? Was this just another figment of his overactive imagination? Was he never truly free?

He woke with a jolt, finding himself at the window seat of his Grade 12 geography class. His teacher stood over him, looking worried.

'Jeremy, I was hoping you could answer Question 7 for me, but you fell asleep again. Since this keeps happening, I'll see you after class.' She walked back to the front of the room. Laughter and murmurs of 'mute' and 'weirdo' from the students nearby followed her. Jeremy had always been considered weird. He had always been nervous around people, to the point where talking wasn't an option. No one understood him. It had always been him, his sketchbook and escaping this cruel world through dreaming.

The rest of class always seemed blurry to Jeremy. He could never focus on the whiteboard or his teachers. Even when on the rare occasion he could focus, he never had the words to answer. When the bell finally rang, he made his way towards the door, seizing the chance to escape.

'Jeremy,' his teacher interjected, as he paused in the doorway. 'Is everything going ok outside of class? You always seem to be falling asleep. I'm worried about your education, that's all.' Jeremy simply nodded, silent. 'Look,

I think it might do you some good to visit the guidance counsellor. Here's a referral slip, and I'll make you an appointment for this afternoon.' His teacher stood from her desk, walking to where he waited.

'I believe this will be beneficial for you, Jeremy. Anyway, you may leave. I hope the appointment goes well.'

Jeremy walked out of the classroom, feeling stupid. He wanted to say he had already been sent to the guidance counsellor, multiple times, by his other teachers, and he'd even been referred to a therapist, who he saw once a week. He wished people understood him. He wasn't just the mute boy who dreamed.

Lucia was the girl who never stopped to smell the roses. Her schedule ran on, sprinting at a pace that not even Usain Bolt could catch up to. Today was Thursday, meaning she had therapy at 3.30pm. She always arrived twenty minutes early, frantically trying to find her journal in her bag, digging past her soccer boots, her chess playbook, work uniform and debate notes. She consulted her thought journal to emotionally sort out what she was going to say to her therapist. The cover of the journal stared into her soul, accompanied by the sound of the office's clock. *Tick. Tock.*

'Lucia Montero.' Her therapist interrupted her thoughts. 'You can come in now.' Lucia entered the office room and sat on the dark green couch. 'So, Lucia. Did you do the homework I set you?' Lucia never liked going to therapy. The therapist continuously went on about how she needed to slow down, which always seemed like a silly concept. Especially when she could be using her time on more important things, like actual homework.

'Well, you see, nothing's changed. But there's an excellent reason why. It's because I can't let anyone down during such a busy time of year.'

'Lucia, you need to slow down. Because it seems like your extracurriculars are causing a lot of stress and spreading yourself thinly might cause you to burn out. Although, it is a very common thing, it is something we can prevent by taking some time to reflect and find something that makes you calm and happy. Because what you're doing at the moment doesn't seem to be working as well as it should be.'

Lucia wondered what would possibly make her happy.

Tick tock. Jeremy's heartbeat thumped as he ran. He knew he was late for his therapy appointment again. Usually, it was because he'd missed the bus, too caught up in his reveries.

This time, there was a legitimate reason. He'd met with Ms Janet, the guidance counsellor. Janet knew Jeremy well. He was always being sent there instead of the principal's office. She understood he was getting help elsewhere, so she always let him go early. It was a sweltering Thursday afternoon, and he checked his watch. 4.05pm. He stopped and prayed he wasn't wasting his therapist's time.

Walking in, he apologised for his tardiness and made his way over to the dark green couch. 'So, Jeremy. Tell me, has anything different happened in the last week? Please, take your time to talk. This is a safe space.'

'Well,' Jeremy said. It wasn't like he was mute; it usually took him more time to open up to new people. 'This week, Biff and Boof shoved me into my locker. Different from the bin they usually go with.'

'And how did that make you feel?'

Jeremy always thought that was a stupid question. The answer was always the same.

'It made me sad.' His therapist's pen scratched against the paper in her journal.

'Well, was there anything good that happened this week?'

'I had a great dream in my geography class.'

'Can you tell me about it?'

Jeremy described his dream in-depth, detailing all the gorgeous colours he'd seen. With the vines of aquamarine and ivory marble everywhere, crawling up the walls, surrounding him. He told her it was the place he wanted to visit, though he didn't know where it was.

'That sounds nice, Jeremy. Very peaceful and quiet. It's a pity you dreamed of it in the middle of class, isn't it?' Jeremy nodded, embarrassed. 'I think I know what you can focus on this week. Although it seems large, I want you to talk to someone. You might think it doesn't relate to your problem, but if you make some connections with people, you won't need to spend your time searching for that place in your mind.'

She was right. Jeremy needed to get out of his head. No matter how gorgeous the scenery was.

Lucia's mind was a jumbled mess.

You need to find something that makes you calm, her therapist's voice rang in her head. It was all she could think about. When she was working her shifts at the post office, playing chess, working on debate pitches and even while kicking goals at soccer practice.

You need to find something that makes you happy.

She kept wondering what that meant. She thought she knew what made her happy. Kicking butt at debate tournaments, orange slices with the soccer team after a victory. Winning. But the more she thought about it, the more it skipped through her mind like a broken NSYNC record. She'd reached the point where she was questioning every little decision she ever made.

'What if it isn't what makes me happy?' she asked herself, out loud. One of her friends turned to her as they all walked down the crowded school halls.

'What was that, Lucia?'

'Uh, nothing. Don't worry about it.' They went back to arguing, as per usual. But Lucia had nothing else on her mind. Her world felt strange. She could not answer the questions in class, like she usually could, or think clearly enough on her early morning runs. Maybe what she thought she loved didn't make her happy.

Maybe it was her perfectionism. Trying to reach her goals of attending a prestigious university. She was filling her mind to the brink with worries about everything she had to do to keep others happy. She needed to find herself. She needed to find what made her happy, or, at least, find something to slow her mind a little.

Jeremy floated back into the mystical world he once knew. Sprinkled with lavenders and roses, the sun shone upon him. Fields upon fields of flowers, and not an allergy in sight. Jeremy knew this could not be real, but he never wanted to leave. Birds chirped melodically over the pastures, and Jeremy had found inspiration for a new drawing. He heard a familiar voice echo.

Jeremy, wake up. The bell has just gone.

He knew it was time to leave. Although he didn't want to, he opened his eyes and returned to the real world.

'Jeremy.' The world blurred for a moment, his eyes filled with sleep and the light seeping in. 'You can't keep falling asleep in class. I'm going to have to send you to the principal's office. I can't keep sending you to the guidance counsellor.' His teacher looked around, leaning in as though to share a secret. 'But, if I send you to the office now, I'll have to miss the special staff luncheon. So, this is your final warning.' Jeremy hated that he was continuously getting in trouble for things beyond his control.

Head down, he walked through the crowded hallway. He tried to fly under the radar and avoid as many people as he could. He heard two people call out to him.

'Hey. Hey, you.' He recognised the voice. It belonged to Biff: one-half of the school's renowned stupidity bully duo.

'Mute boy,' said the other. 'I think you owe us lunch money. Don't you think?'

'I do.' Jeremy knew exactly what was about to happen. It was routine. He would turn around to Biff and Boof, pass them his bag, then they'd make mean remarks and shove him in a bin or locker.

But not today. In the last week, Jeremy had thought about what his therapist told him. About how he should stand up for himself, even just talk to someone, to get himself out of his head.

'No,' Jeremy answered. That was all he had to say. The swarm of passers-by gasped in shock. They had all stopped to watch the freakshow, nothing new.

'Well, look what we have 'ere, Boof. The mute freak can speak.'

'You know what that means, Biff? We get to hear him scream while we shove him into the bin.'

Jeremy felt a hit of adrenaline. He knew whatever he said next would be a stupid idea, but he said it anyway. 'No, you won't. Not today.' His voice was shaking from its lack of use. He handed them the money and walked away. Over his shoulder, he called, 'There's also no need for the rubbish bin business. It's time to think of something more original.' Gasps and laughter roared through the crowd. Biff and Boof looked confused. These two tall, bulky bullies had just been owned by the mute, weird kid who slept in his classes. And Jeremy walked off, with his head held high. He knew he had one hell of a story to tell his therapist.

Lucia was furious. Her therapist sat in front of her with her notepad and pen in hand.

'So, have you made any progress this week, Lucia?'

Lucia's blood boiled. She'd spent the last week in a whirlwind of existential crises and it was all her therapist's fault.

'It isn't going exactly to plan at the moment.'

'Can you tell me why?'

'Well, I thought about what you said, and I hate it. Before you came along, everything was fine. Now, I'm questioning everything. Nothing makes sense anymore and I hate it.'

'Lucia, I know this is hard for you. Change is a very difficult thing to handle, even when it's happening internally. But it only makes us stronger. It will take time.'

Lucia sighed. 'That actually makes some sense. I ...' Her voice trailed off. 'I'm sorry for yelling.'

'It's alright. It's all part of the process. It's why I'm here.' For once, the rest of the session was tolerable for Lucia. She left the session with a sense of relief.

But even with a little less stress, she was still running behind time. Her hands clasped her textbooks and she looked down at her watch. She hated the days she had to bring her extra books.

4.05pm. She was never going to make it to the bus stop—

Thump.

She was knocked to the ground. Lucia looked up in a daze. A hand thrust before her face, and she grabbed it. The boy tugged her to her feet, and she met his golden eyes. They reminded her of pools of honey, deep and almost glistening. His wild blond hair was windswept and artfully messy. He looked familiar, but she couldn't place his face.

'I am so sorry. I didn't mean to knock you over. I wasn't looking where I was going,' he said with a warm laugh. He picked up her books, passing them back to her one by one.

'It's all good. I wasn't paying attention, either.' Where did she know him from? 'I'm Lucia, by the way.'

'I'm Jeremy. Sorry, my voice sounds weird. I don't usually talk much.' It clicked. The final puzzle piece, falling into place. He was that weird, mute kid from her school. The one she usually saw getting shoved into lockers or rubbish bins.

'It's all good. I'm just a little shocked. I've seen you around, but I don't think I've ever heard you speak,' she said, flushing.

'Oh, you've seen that?'

'Yeah,' she sighed. 'I'm sorry about that. Everything you've had to go through, it sucks. I've always wanted to step in, but—everything is so busy, you know?' Her gaze disconnected from his, ashamed. She'd been so caught up in her issues she didn't even consider how bad others might have it. 'Sorry, I know you probably don't want to talk about it—'

'I get it. I don't really understand people. But they don't take the time to understand me either.'

Something deep inside her forced her to say, 'Well, how about we change that?' She stepped closer, hesitant, feeling a nervous flutter in her stomach. 'You seem nice, and in need of a friend. And my therapist thinks I need to take time for myself and branch out from my normal, 'fast-paced' activities. So ...'

'What were you thinking?'

'I don't know. But I do think we should hang out sometime.'

He was quiet.

Her thoughts began to spiral. *What if I misread the situation? What if this was all a mistake? What if I made a fool out of myself?*

Before her mind spiralled out of control, Jeremy chimed in. 'Yeah, I'd like that a lot. You seem nice, and I think you'd make a good friend. I mean, you've talked to me more in these last few minutes than anyone else at school ever has.' Her racing thoughts started to calm down.

'Is there any way I could contact you, outside of school?' She placed her bag on the floor, rummaging through it for her phone. When she finally found it, she held it out in invitation. 'What's your number?'

He entered his number and passed it back. 'Look, I'd love to keep talking here, but I'm running late for my session, like, really late. I hope I see you around, though.' He walked away, disappearing around the corner of the long, carpeted hallway.

'Bye ...' The word slipped from her mouth like a memory. Long gone. She hadn't even noticed how quiet her mind became in his presence. His windswept hair and honest demeanour caught her off-guard. Lucia's world had finally been quiet.

A YEAR IN DREAMS

Hayley Evans

Summer.
Beach dreams under burning Sky.
Sun—heat stinging my eyes
Sandy shoes block the doorway
I hear the crunch of sand under my feet as I walk
Melted ice cream drips down my arm & sizzles on the
pavement.
The world stops, the ceremonies & traditions begin.
Holidays, family, parties, food, drinks.
The season of excess, gluttony.
A gift for ourselves & others.
The spirit of Santa infuses the soul
Songs of love fill the still air, hugging the audience with a
comforting melody.
The morning of celebration under a tree filled with hope,
happiness, dreams.
A New Year awaits an eager world promising new beginnings
& forgiving sins.
One day that does so much for so many creates new
dreams, new wishes, new hopes.
Autumn.
A kite spins a web through the air

Bronzed leaves wither, embellishing the grass.
Cheapened by the name of Fall. They float, swarm, trickle,
tango.
Not one word can describe the elegance of the way they
descend.
The expired leaves decay & produce the essence of Tomorrow.
Happy puppies jump in piles of confetti leaves losing
themselves in endless joy
Grumpy old men rake the joy away only for Wind to bring it
back again
The Day feels like it is growing longer, stalling Tomorrow
Mother Nature's artistry is at play.
She paints her hues in dusty browns & gold,
reminding us that beauty encompasses all.
Her paintbrush is soaked, her imagination runs deep.
A camera captures the image of a sunset that has no beginning
or end.
Forever changing, preparing life for the cold times ahead.
Autumn is packing humanity's suitcase for a long & treacherous
trip into Winter.
Get ready & welcome the harvest.
Winter.
Cuddled in warm blankets
Snow ladled on the rooftops like marshmellows
Children's frozen noses glistening pink, touched with Winter's
chill
Jack Frost gliding his fingertips over a crystallised lake ready to
launch snowballs at life.
Glaciers appear in the forgotten places, entwined in a dance of
danger

Clashing, smashing, & breaking—raising the stakes.
Hot chocolate percolating in welcoming bellies,
That frosty breath seeping & steaming as we laugh & snuggle.
An open fire filled with embers throwing sparks at each other
like crackling naughty children.
Diving in hot tubs, bubbling away the grief & sorrow
Roast meat & gravy poured with generous ease like a fiery pool
of comfort.
Late night movies, microwave popcorn & icing sugar resting on
the edge of our lips.
Sleeping in—watching the rain saturate the thirsty grass
outside.
Droplets escape with glee down the glass windows finding a
puddle to call home.
Spring.
The birds tweet a rhythm filled with bass & harmonic beats,
Fluttering & darting through branches,
Strumming away at nature's sweet ukulele
'Springtime is here!'
A rhapsody of petals awakens to the day
Each bud pokes its head into the morning, filling the air with
perfume
Their faces turn to bask in Sun's light, gorging on her rays
Laughter echoes from swarms of playful children
Swinging in unison,
They feel the air brush their cheeks
Lambs nestle sweetly against their mothers' breast
Milk flows like nectar to welcome & nourish new life
A magical bunny brings chocolate & prepares for the hunt
Children with straw baskets, ready for possibilities

Every icicle has thawed to create new beginnings
The serendipity of Spring is euphoric
Gifting us with eternal breath.

BUBBLE BURST

Natalie Richy

Child hurried 'long the arid slope—
drawn toward the amber light.
Free as air balloon did float,
when dreaming came to sight.
The flowers smiled toward the sun—
a charge of mischief pure.
Whisper through the field she run,
in nature's wildling cure.
Picked a spray of blooms to thread.
Sang each step she painted down.
Upon every ledge her petals fed.
A golden trail
of daisies
strewn.

Held up at gate by Man irate, who spat

and yelled and cursed, 'You're LATE!'

Child's skip froze by fretful frown—'till

Bubble burst curled rubber melt-down.

Sudden dread—he stroked child's head,

'those daisies are BAD weeds,' he said.

'Suck, sponge, take from earth like sin.'

Settled finger pointed—toward the bin.

Child profess to be at ease,

          disguised 'hind mask of brave.

Bugged by beauty deemed disease,   retreated to her cave.

In solitude reverie did flow, splash sing-song saved her face.

Till   daisies   all   round   did   grow   in
        every   inch   of   space.

Free painted the enchantress, for in her dreams Child could create.

And never spoke of them out loud,

          her secret sealed her fate.

THE HAND I HOLD

Marlene Jennings

This is the hand I hold.
Fingers clenched tight,
A stolen touch,
Every fibre, holding back tears.
Crevassed lines map a journey,
Frail skin, worn through time
From the disease within
Fingers tremble uncontrolled.

This is the hand that held mine.
Warm to touch, velvet skin.
Child's fingers enveloped
In a secure grip.
This sense of comfort
Kept me safe.
Love and admiration
For the person in this space,
Never to imagine roles reversed.

This is the hand I held.

Cold to touch

Death-brushed pallor

Lost to life

No longer mine.

Never to hold again.

DEAR GRANDMA ...

Stephanie Freeman

Dear Grandma ...
I wish you could read this ... I wish these words could reach you ... I wish I could talk to you and you would just know—know what I'm saying, know how I'm feeling, know how to respond ... I just wish you were here.

I went to see you the other day. Pop was with you, where he always is, right by your side. Dad was there and so was Aunty Roz. You were asleep with your head resting upon Pop's shoulder. I wanted to talk to you about the bees that I saw outside, playing in the purple hedge flowers, but I couldn't—you wouldn't understand.

I sat there and watched you. In place of the healthy, well fed, formally dressed body, was a fragile, undernourished one smothered in baggy sweatpants. I wished you would open your eyes, Grandma, and notice me, but you were too tired, your body was focusing on surviving. Pop looked tired too. He misses you. We both know he's not the type to say it but its ever-present, flowing out of his pores, displayed in his melancholic features and dishevelled clothes.

Dad and Rozzy were talking to Pop about the usual paperwork and medical stuff. These types of conversations aren't new, they're regular occurrences. The topics focus on financials, health, mail, recent calls from the nursing home, and you.

Our visits have changed Grandma. Gone are the carefree, fun visits and in their place are businesslike meetings. We still get to have our fun but there's a more serious aspect to it now. I guess that's because Dad is now your power of attorney.

That once blonde, curly-haired baby now looks after you physically, medically and financially. Your baby boy grew up, Grandma, and now it's his turn to take care of you. It's a hard thing for any child to do, but Dad would do it a million times over. He loves you so much. You raised an amazing man, Grandma; you should be immensely proud.

You were still asleep when we started to leave. I gave you an awkward side hug and whispered, 'Bye, Grandma.'

Did you hear me?

Did you know it was me?

I craved for you to whisper back, 'Goodbye, Steph. I love you,' but I knew that wasn't a possibility. I can't even remember the last time my name or those words appeared on your lips.

With my mind aching for the past, we walked away from you and Pop, exiting the nursing home, into the world of the present.

I think about it all the time, Grandma ... what it would be like if you were still of sound mind—Alzheimer's-free.

Would you and Pop still be living on your own?

Would Dad, Anna and I still have our weeklong stays during the December/January holidays?

Would you have taught me more things to cook from scratch?

Would we have more Freeman family gatherings?

Would you and Pop still come and stay at our house every now and then?

Unfortunately, I don't know what it would be like because this isn't the alternative universe where my grandma is Alzheimer's-free.

I'm sorry, Grandma, that this is your reality.

I dream about what it would be like to have had you at my high school graduation, or at my wedding, or just simply there to guide me through life. I dream about hugging you. Your arms wrapped tightly around me, holding me with intention and unconditional love. Our hugs are now one sided. I've never hated the decaying of the human mind as much as I do when I clutch your frail body. Your arms limp, your inner warmth absent, your eyes confused. I cling on to those special moments when vacant blue eyes recognise my existence, reminding me you're still partially there. The occurrences when you return my smiles or giggle because you notice that I am, reveal the remnants of our relationship.

I like to think that you are still there, residing behind the veil of the Alzheimer's disease. Fully aware of everything surrounding you but lost to the incompetence of your body. Your soul still surviving, still loving, still hearing us tell you that we love you. Continuing to know us, continuing to care for us, continuing to be our mother and grandmother. I know this is a selfish speculation, but I can't help wanting you to still be there. Facing the other reality of you being gone hurts way too much. I'm not ready for that type of heartbreak, Grandma, especially since you can't be the one to help guide me through it.

I also like to think that you aren't still there, isolated and trapped inside your head. Instead replaced by a zombielike void doing the bare minimum to keep the shell alive. This helps me to cope. The reality of you imprisoned inside of yourself is more heartbreaking than you being gone. It would mean that for over five years you would've been living that way with the walls slowly confining you—alone and helpless whilst your body dominated your soul. The idea of that kind of torture happening to you ... I would rather you not be there to endure it.

Which reality is real—I will never know.

I wish I could ask you ... I wish you could respond ... Our one-way conversations don't tend to go too far ...

I miss your voice, Grandma. I miss you singing your favourite hymns and Christmas carols. I even miss you scolding Pop because he forgets to smile in photos.

What if I forget your voice, Grandma?

Can I even remember it now?

I get glimpses every so often in your mischievous giggles, your 'ooos' and your 'ahhs', but it's not the same. I yearn for your voice ... I yearn for you.

What I would give just to be a child again—a time when you were fully you. I could run to you in the early hours when the sun first makes its appearance and crawl under the covers. I could be sandwiched between you and Pop, wrapped up in your arms, talking for hours. When it was time to face the world beyond your bedroom walls, we could spend the day doing all the things we used to—making crafts, reading the daily devotions, knitting, cooking and drinking tea. We could even look through your unique teaspoon collection and you could tell me about all 56 of them. We would simply be together and enjoy each other's company.

I want *that* to be my reality.

I know my wishing can't change the present, Grandma, but I know that one day, in heaven, I'll see you again. When I do, I will run into your arms and you'll hug me back like you always used to. I will get to tell you, 'I love you, Grandma ... I've missed you, Grandma ... and I'm so thankful that you are my grandma, Grandma.' I will have so much to tell you and so many questions to ask. We will once again be grandmother and granddaughter. I long for this moment, I long for that version of life after death—an eternity spent with you.

Until that day, I must face my current reality of you slowing slipping away.

However, I will not dwell on the pain but instead focus on the fact that I still have you here. I can see you—you are physically present in my universe—I will not take that for granted. Your hand is still there, I can grasp it.

This disease has not won, you haven't lost me. The memories may not be there but I am. You aren't alone, Grandma; I hope you know that.

I write to you hoping that somehow, in some supernatural way, these words will reach you and you will hear them. If that's the case, and I pray that it is, here is what I truly would want to say:

Grandma, I love you so much, with everything inside of me, and I am so immensely thankful for your impact on my life. It is because of you that I am who I am; you are exactly who I aspire to be. If I could be even a quarter of the woman you are, I would be so happy. You are one of the most amazing people I know. I miss you, Grandma, so much and I can't wait to see you again.

I hope this letter reaches you in the format of one of your iconic handmade cards. This isn't goodbye, Grandma, this is a 'see you soon' because I know I will. There's a universe beyond this one and that is where we will meet.

With an immeasurable amount of love,
Your Steph x

LETTING GO

Kirsty Gregory

ENTRY #11 TUESDAY, 1.50AM

I'm hugging my dad again, or trying to. He does not hug me back. He barely acknowledges my presence. Letting go and turning to my mum, I cry. I scream. I ask what I did to deserve this. I yell, telling her I want to fix things between us. I blame her for dad being so broken—or whatever he is. There's no response. She just looks through me with a familiar, vague expression, but she's not really listening or reacting to my screams. I hate being forced into actually experiencing my feelings. They usually lay dormant. In moments like this, my mum's indifference towards me feels jarring, and I'm not sure if

I know how to explain. Do you know how crazy people—those detached from reality—have a vacant look in their eyes? Maybe the word isn't vacant. The better description might be that they seem inclined to accept alternative perspectives. My mum's eyes don't have the welcoming capacity for what others might know or think. Her gaze is staunch, pointed, unwavering. But that is only my perception. If my sisters or I were to ask our brothers to describe mum's eye contact, they'd wonder *what the hell do you mean?* They'd tell me they don't remember stuff like that. I wish my impression of her was less significant, less nightmare-inducing.

ENTRY #12 THURSDAY, 11.11PM
We're riding our bikes through the abandoned zoo, I look back and see my sister trying to catch me, so I speed up. The pale yellow pavement is bulged and cracked from tree roots straining to grow underneath the bricks. On every pathway there are piles of leaves. Every fence line has moss and vines competing for space. At the base of each hill, there's a creek or pond. The air smells like moss. I'm almost catching up to my brother, but he doesn't slow down to take the corners like I do. We reach the old, dried-up water slides and dare each other to climb the fence. In this moment, I'm grateful for some freedom. I appreciate the time with my siblings, even if it's not real. At home, I'm reminded of my unimportance. Here, I'm free to just be a kid. When I'm around my mum, my childhood is not important.

ENTRY #13 FRIDAY, 2.33AM

I love this beach. There are so many rock pools full of sea critters that were too slow to ride the ocean tide out. I tell my daughters that you can hear waves when you press a seashell to your ear, no matter how far from the beach you are. Reminiscing of when I believed in magic, there's a feeling of being free from cynicism. Now I wonder if I'd be able to summon that feeling anymore. I'm curious about when I let go of believing in magic. It was probably a gradual string of disheartening realisations. Or maybe it was a moment of personal triumph, realising I couldn't be so easily fooled anymore. Regardless, the whimsical deceits of mothers, in persuading children that magic is everywhere—is nice. I wish I could have experienced this more as a child. My mum preferred to tell cautionary tales about the evil in the world. It wasn't until I became a mother that I realised the extent of the uncomfortable deceits I had endured. The bleak memories I have of my mother are ignited at random; then they trickle down into my growing reservoir of contempt.

ENTRY #14 SUNDAY, 3.32AM

I lose control of the car while I'm driving again. This time is especially tense because my daughters are in the back seat. The car rolls down a ditch, it feels like slow motion. I turn and look at my girls, and they're fine, having fun like it's a game. So, I face the front again, grip the wheel harder and I wait. Am I a good enough mother if I can't even keep a car on the road? The sole responsibility to keep them safe—it's daunting, especially when doubting if I've been equipped for parenthood. My role models failed me. Seeing my girls unphased and enjoying their childhood is reassuring, both in real life and in my subconscious. The way I parent is governed by the principle of *what kind of mother I wish I had*. I remember the things I wish I had heard as a child: *I'm glad you exist, you make me happy, I love you.* So, now I say them all the time. I have to let go of my childhood trauma. Although I wasn't validated, hugged, or given the impression that I was anything other than insignificant. This chance to offer my girls the childhood I deserved turns my pain into an opportunity. Writing this dream journal is musing. It's like therapy, to unpack the trauma and let it go. In writing each entry, there's an epiphany. In these moments of reckoning, even when they're imagined, there's hope.

THE IMMORTALITY OF A MOTHER'S LOVE

Emily Demamiel

I reached across the hospice bed bars and grasped Mum's hand. The warmth of her skin sent a spark up my arm, reaching my heart. I stared out the window behind her bed. The warm sunlight bathed her frail body and the crisp white gown covering her. A hummingbird whistled, perched on the water fountain in the garden. Peonies, roses and gardenias surrounded the little cottage, their colours refracting on the surface of the fountain water and speckles of colour shone on the white walls of the bedroom. Mum lay in a bed covered in blankets made by each woman in the family, including myself and my daughter, each blanket with an array of bright colours and designs. The one we made her was covered in flowers in every colour of the rainbow. The blankets helped make the hospital bed not to look so drab, but nothing could mask the fact that bed was the one she would take her final breath in.

I glanced over at Mum, eyes closed and humming a sweet, familiar tune.

'What song is that?' I asked.

'*Seven Wonders,*' she responded. I should have known. She had listened to Fleetwood Mac for as long as I could remember. Stevie Nicks was her idol. When she got sick, the music played louder and more often. When I was little, we would dance around my bedroom to the sound of *Second-hand News* on the record player after a breakfast of pancakes and orange juice. Mum's style even mimicked Stevie Nicks's in our house décor, and her wardrobe was full of sheer scarves and long, flowy skirts. A little bit of that style even rubbed off on my own closet, filled with floral pieces and jewellery collected from various farmers markets.

Mum brushed her thumb over the top of my hand, and I held her a little tighter. Leaning over in my chair, I laid my head gently on her chest. The rise and fall of her breathing lulled me to close my eyes, like when I was a child and I'd lay my head on her lap. Even with my eyes closed, the bright sunlit room still pierced an orange glow on my eyelids. I breathed in deep and held it for a second before letting it go. I felt a sudden urgency to savour every breath, a desperate attempt at pausing this moment in time.

'I love you,' I said.

'I know. And I you.'

Lifting my head, I opened my eyes to a tapping sound on the floor. A little bird padded into the bedroom through the folding glass doors that were open for the breeze. It craned its neck around, observing the room as if it had no idea how it arrived here. I watched its eyes dart around the room for a few seconds, its beady little eyes flickering open and closed like a lightbulb at the end of its life. Slowly, I rose from my chair and the bird's attention landed on me, its blue iridescent feathers gleaming in the light. It took a step forward. I took two steps towards it and it bounced towards me, curious and unafraid. I crouched down with an outstretched hand—I was within arm's length of it now. One hop and the bird leaped into my open palm. I slowly raised and turned to face Mum. She was watching me, smiling. Her expression was so carefree, perhaps the happiest than I had seen her in the past year. The bird seemed unbothered by my movements, and I walked back towards my chair, ensuring every step was smooth and slow to not frighten it. I held the bird towards Mum and beckoned to her to open her palm. She shakily lifted her hand off the bed and held it out. The bird reached its beak towards her hand, maybe expecting food to be there. When it realised there was none, it lifted its head to watch her.

'Aren't you delightful,' Mum whispered, smiling ear to ear. 'A Mountain Bluebird.'

A knock on the glass doors lifted our attention from the bird. The nurse was standing with lunch tray in hand, watching us. I smiled at her, welcoming her in. On her walk over to the bed she noticed the bird and her face lit up.

'Oh, how lovely! I often see these beauties bathing themselves in the fountain, but they always seem to fly away before I can get close enough to admire them.' She set the lunch tray down on the side table next to the bed and leaned over to watch the bird in Mum's hand. It danced around in circles, watching each of us. Curiosity emanated from its sparkling eyes, but then, as if it has suddenly had enough, it hopped down to the end of the bed, glanced back at us for a second, then took flight out into the sunny day.

Mum glanced at me and I saw a glint of happiness in her eyes that I hadn't seen in quite some time. It only lasted for a second before being replaced by the sad, longing expression I was all too familiar with. Feeling like it was time to distract Mum from her thoughts, I asked the nurse what she has brought for lunch.

'Today we have a spinach and leek quiche, with a cup of tea and some strawberries and cream for dessert.' She peered at my mother with a hesitant smile.

'My favourite,' Mum replied, offering the nurse an appreciative smile. The same one that always made me feel at home for as long as I could remember. She reached for the lunch tray so I got up and moved quickly to the other side of the bed to help. I placed the tray on her lap and began feeding her lunch.

Mum's illness took the whole family by surprise. One morning we were getting together for our weekend breakfast and that night she was in the hospital, hooked up to God knows how many tubes and machines. It was me who found her that morning. She had gone inside to take the breakfast plates in and get the kids some sweets. I wanted to talk to her in private about my daughter's first boyfriend, and so I followed her inside with the excuse of helping clean up, leaving the kids, their father and grandfather—my dad—to themselves. For a second, I didn't know where she had gone, the kitchen appeared empty from the entry. I noticed her hand on the floor, just peeking out from behind the kitchen island. I ran over and yelled out to my husband and from there on everything blurred.

We spent all day at the hospital waiting for answers, assurance that it was just a dizzy spell or something that meant she could come home. By night, the doctors said it could be a tumour—benign or cancerous, they didn't know—growing at the base of her brain. They had completed a biopsy and within a week the results were in. Mum had cancer.

All at once the weekend breakfasts stopped and were replaced with visits to the hospital for chemo. The doctors said it had developed in an undesirable spot and the risks of removal were too high. It progressed quite far by the time we knew what was happening and chemotherapy would only help to delay the inevitable. My husband became the friend my father needed at that time, and I never left my mother's side. Our daughter, Hailey, began catching a bus to the hospital after school, and she did her homework in her grandmother's company. My father often helped, having been a maths teacher in his younger years. Hailey liked it, having everyone together.

I once asked Hailey if it bothered her to be in such a place as a hospital every day.

'No,' she said. 'It doesn't feel like how you imagine a hospital to look like, not with all of us here at least.' She sat thinking for a minute, and I watched her consider the question. She finally said, 'I guess it just feels like another family breakfast, we're all here together talking, laughing, eating and there's flowers everywhere just like Grandma's garden so it's not all that different if you think about it.'

I knew then the impact my mother had on everyone's life and began to wonder what we were going to do in a world without her. The question of how I could create such a beautiful atmosphere for my children like my own mother did for me began to keep me awake at night.

The day Mum told us about her decision to choose when her life ended was full of tears and heated words. My father just walked out of the room, my brother following. My husband, who was sitting next to me, grabbed my hand. I asked her why, whilst Hailey sat by the window in shocked silence.

'Do you remember when you were five and your father and I had to take you to the doctors to get that really bad splinter out?' she asked me.

'Yeah, I do. But why does this matter now?'

'Because you made the choice not to have the anaesthetic, you wanted to get out of that situation with dignity—even if it was to just impress your brother. You were so afraid of appearing weak that you were willing to go through more pain. You didn't know what this meant when you were that age but it's a human trait to live with dignity.'

I had to turn away from her at this moment. I could tell in her eyes she knew that I knew why she wanted to end her life on her terms. She had always been a headstrong woman, always focused on everyone else before she would think about herself. This was the one time in her life she would be adamant in her decision, and for it to be her own—whether out of selfishness or to spare everyone from watching her wither away, we didn't know. I gazed at Hailey and she watched me with apprehension in her eyes; she knew what was going on but didn't know what to do or say. I beckoned her over with my outstretched hand and she came to stand next to me. Pulling her in even closer, knowing that she was looking up to me to help speak for her, I gathered strength for the both of us and returned my attention to my mother. She stared with a blank expression behind me, out the window. The bright blue sky and white clouds reflected in her eyes, lighting up her pale, greyish face.

'Mum ...' I said, my voice threatening to betray my calm exterior, 'we love you.' I felt a tear run down my cheek but paid it no attention. My lip quivered as I mustered the strength to say what was needed, without adding to the sadness blanketing the room. 'We will always love you. It takes a strong woman to choose this path, and I will never be able to explain to you how your strength has not only shaped me, but also my brother and my own daughter. We'll be with you through every step of the way, just like you have been for every step of our lives.'

My mother didn't have a response, except to reach her hand out for mine and offer that comforting smile that felt like a warm drink on a rainy day. With no idea about what the future held, instinct told me everything would be okay because her spirit would be there to guide us through life. She would be the sun after a shower, the tingle in fruity juices, the glee in our happiest moments and the knot in our hearts. She would live on in those moments, and she knew it, too.

The day my mother took her last breath, I laid next to her in that cold bed covered in bright colours. She held my hand as tightly as she could, until she couldn't anymore. I felt the rise and fall of her breathing, until I couldn't anymore. I listened to the birds in the fountain, until night fell. I watched the stars and the moon tell their story until the sun began to rise again. Only then did I rise from her side, walk out to the peonies in the garden, pluck one, walk back to her and place a single peony on her chest. At that moment, the morning sun rose from behind a cloud and the warmth of the spring light touched my outstretched arm. I turned around to see the fountain and witness the flickers of life awakening. I finally left that room, guided by the warmth of her hand in mine and that smile that would stay with me forever. When I reached the fountain, I looked towards the sun, but it was hidden by the silhouette of a bluebird. The same bird that had put one of the last smiles on her face. Only then did the wave rush over me and push me to my knees as my chest threatened to cave in as that image replayed in my head. I rested my head on the edge of the fountain, the cold concrete biting into my cheek as tears fell down my face and into the glistening water. Through the noise of the fountain and my raspy breathing, I heard the faint sounds of the nurses tending to her body in the room behind me. But I refused to look back. After all, she never had, not even once.

RECONCILIATION

Jack Carter

THE RED RIVER GUM

I had only parked my car on the street when Mum came flying out of our front door with something waving in her hand. My mum is an honest lady, and we live together in a miner's cottage she purchased when my parents broke up. It's beautiful, made from cream wooden walls with a slightly rusted tin roof. A green and cream picket fence with a colourful cottage garden bridged the gap between Mum and me. I opened my car door and stepped out onto the street; Mum had already made it to the front gate.

'I'm installing this seat belt right away.'

'What? What's wrong with the one I have?'

The thing is, my mum is amazing with her hands. Once the transformer for our street blew and the powerline company was too busy to come that night. So Mum climbed up and fixed it herself. Most of our neighbours bring stuff over for her to repair, and she never charges them. She says that being a funeral director pays enough money, as nothing pays out more to the heart than helping people.

'Honey, it's twice as strong as the one you have. Please let me install it. Please. It will make me feel better.'

She looked at me with the same eyes she used to pass bland food as fantastic and mind-altering. All that was missing was the 'mmmmm' to seal the deal. I assumed Mum had heard advice on the radio about car safety. I suppose she had a good reason after installing a turbo and tuning my car to be the fastest 1990 Rodeo in Australia.

'Alright, Mum.'

A smile tore across her cheeks. She held out the packaging containing the new seat belt. 'I'll be back with my tools. Hold on to this for me, honey.'

She nearly skipped back into the house. Watching Mum, the lumpy grey sky caught my eye. The day had been a winter's bright blue. Not often do we get that in Ballarat. But the blue had gone with the falling sun.

Mum sprung back with her toolbox in seconds. She jumped down the front steps and briskly walked back through our gate as if something must be done and Earth's survival depended on it. She swung my driver's side door wide open onto the street and dived right in. I held the end of the door, watching on like an apprentice on his first week. Moments later, she handed me my old seat belt and the packaging for the new belt had left my hands and returned empty.

'This is great, hun. I'm feeling better about you and this car already,' Mum said, head buried under the driver's seat.

The car turned dark—too fast to be from the oncoming night. The air smelt like rain. I looked up and saw a black cloud descending from what looked like a gathering storm.

'Done, and just in time,' Mum said, reacting to the loss of light.

I didn't answer. The black cloud kept descending as I heard thunder rumble towards me. A black mass broke off from the storm as lightning struck all around the outside of the cloud. Bang, bang. Two lightning bolts struck the ground at the base of Central Street's Red River Gumtree. Mum shot up beside me and stared, not saying a word. Three large objects began to protrude from the bottom of the dark cloud.

Mum wrapped her hand around my shoulder and said, 'They're here.'

A Shining Gum

The curtains were open; he could sense a presence outside. He sat up in bed, staring out into the black. The boy's hand paused on the lamp switch, trying to make himself hold for a few minutes longer before turning on the light. The boy waited. His breathing started to relax. His fingers released from the lamp switch, and his head rested back on the pillow.

The room turned a clean grey, not enough to wake a sleeping person but enough for a person awake to notice. He couldn't move his body out of fear, except for his fingers that pushed his blanket down enough for his eyes to see out the window, but not enough for an outsider to know he was awake and watching.

The boy could see the bare trunk of a Shining Gum standing alone in the backyard. The light shone a shade brighter, enough for his tv screen to show a dull reflection from the corner of the room. He could feel his chest thumping. A set of stairs extended down at a 45-degree angle to touch the ground. The boy's heart was close to jumping from his ribs. He wanted to run, but what if they saw him? His hand searched for the lamp switch. A foot stepped into view, followed by another, followed by a whole figure walking down the steps on two legs with two arms and a bald head.

The grey human-like figure stepped from the stairs and onto the grey grass. It walked up the Shining Gum's trunk and placed the palm of its hand on the tree's smooth skin. The boy's fingers found the dangling lamp switch. The figure's hand pushed back as another hand came out from within the tree. Then an arm and a leg followed, then a head and another arm and a leg. Both figures stood face to face with one another under the branches of the Shining Gum.

The boy's heart maintained galloping as he sat up in bed, rubbing his eyes for a better view. His vision refocused, and both figures stood looking at him. His hand triggered. The window became a mirror. His breathing stopped as he noticed the two grey figures stood on either side of his bed, looking back at him.

The Ghost Gums

Two men stood on a red hill together, one tall and proud and one with gathering tears in his eyes looking out on to Ghost Gum trees standing scattered over a vast red sea of dirt and rock. Behind them, engines roared, and wood dust flew.

'I had no idea, mate. I'm so sorry,' the man with tears said as his voice began to crack.

The man without tears said, 'It's ok to cry, mate, we've been crying for centuries.'

'I can hear their voices coming from the trees. They keep saying they forgive me. There is no forgiving what I've done,' the crying man said, as he crouched and put one hand on the red dirt and wiped his eyes with the other. Tears splattered over the man's R.M. Williams boots and the surrounding soil instantly dried. The crying man wiped his eyes dry, gathered himself, and stood up. He turned around, raising a hand to his throat in a sawing action.

The giant logging machine dropped the tree in its jaws and then shut down. The man turned to see the man he had been talking to, but he had gone. A cold streak brushed the hairs straight on his neck. Until he looked down and noticed a frilled-neck lizard staring up at him, its head cocked to one side. The man and lizard stared at one another.

'Hey, boss, are we stopping for smoko?'

The man turned to face his worker calling from the cab of his machine. 'Nah, mate. We're packing up and going home. When you've put that thing back on the trailer, we'll go around and pick up all the rubbish we've left lying around camp.' The man turned back to the lizard, but the reptile had vanished.

PLAY OF MIND

Marlene Jennings

My body is falling,
When will it stop?

Restless slumber.
Thoughts that drop
Into my dreams.
A molten core,
Unfettered emotions
Brought to the fore.
Painful memories of the past
Now lovingly restored,
Belie the truth, so in sleep distrust.
Images blur,
In this altered world.
As those once loved,
Are loved no more.
Connections broken,
Threads untied,

Only fleeting whispers
Eternally bind.
When awake,
Thoughts dissipate.
All that's retained,
A restless play of mind.

THE GHOST OF SOME OTHER RED CHAMBER

Adam Brannigan

I awake from a feeling of midnight's wine-intoxicant shroud of mull-seed cake, dreaming again I was my sis/ter, dreaming again I brought somebody else home to fuck. I finger the surgeon's trans scar and reach out for you, touch you in your sleep, but see the winged shadow shimmering in summer's dead air in the closed doorway. My groin is wet.

Piss.

Cum.

Blood.

Black wax.

It was no dream.

She hungers for the fouled world we have made today, or its corrupt seed is found in tomorrow's false dawn. I remember her from other lives lived. They say she is the truth uncovered in Baal-hazor. She is the wonder gone burning Bethlehem. The mystery who has conquered Babylon. Such is the ancient tw/i/light of her, that she rids even gods of their power.

A sound.

Bellowing as of ancient ectoplasm. She knows that men are no different from boys, their screams summon no sunday wife but summon her instead. Their secret places also flood, arise, ripen, wither, ready for her crystal scythe. Her sound of flies. Foreskin. They whisper mother into her dark, her chasm, her tide months of bleeding and breasts, such power of life and death.

Sacrifice.

In time, it will all make sense. But I have only moments, awakening in the middle of the night, mother's blood gurgling through me to seek the shape of her swirling, her desert tongue, as the dawn is breaking and she is beside me, now fading, now gone. And the last words on her lips are try harder, son of butchery, you have not won me. Yet.

Believe.

And I know that she has come to gather us all up in the cannibal nights of tomorrow. Feast upon hearts. But she is the ghost of some other red chamber. Harbinger of sorrow.

RICE BOWL

Beth Newton

I am so completely absorbed in studying my bowl of rice that I fail to register the chatter that is my dysfunctional family who are as normal as every other I've come across.

I am wondering why I don't fit in. Not here, not at school, not on the cricket team or even bloody handball at lunchtime. No one understands me and hell, I don't understand myself. I have so many desires, so many wants, so many dreams, but I don't know what any of my desires, dreams or wants are. I just have them. Or at least I know they are somewhere. Always unattainable. Within grasp but not.

I am particularly focused on a brown grain of rice. It is nestled like a lover; spooning a black rice grain and together they lay over three white grains. A blended family maybe? I wonder if they are happy, this mixed-up family of colour and texture. Of goodness versus not so good, but good enough to be together and form something supposedly healthy for teenage kids and grumpy fathers. Dads who don't understand their sons. My gaze deepens, blurs—I am zoning out—going into that dream state whilst still awake. It is great to escape reality whilst awake, letting my imagination take flight.

Suddenly I am a flying object, hurtling through space and time. I gaze about me in wonder. So free. The wind in my face and stars blinking like white cat's eyes that have been stunned by a torch light. The solitude of the darkness and the weightlessness of gravity lightens my soul and I start to feel like I might like it up here. This wondrous night universe where no one can look my way and make me feel another way; feelings I don't want to feel nor bother to process.

Without introduction, a blazing ball of fury is hurtling straight into my path. I rear up in fright and know within an instant that I am about to die a death I never dreamed of before. My death was always going to be lonely, that was never to be doubted; but by a meteorite? That was insane and new and maybe a little thrilling. I close my eyes as the heat engulfs me, the hairs on my arms singe and my tongue dries out like the beef jerky my sister hates. At the last possible moment, the blazing ball darts sideways and tracks like the fury of hounds on the scent, chasing some unseen object. I am stunned, sad, mad and disappointed. Where was my epic death going? Really? Could I not even conjure up this?

A clatter of metal hitting crockery and mutters and a slap from my mother's hand on the table and reality of life bursts through my foggy altered brain. I've dropped my fork and now rice is strewn all over me and the table and the cat is licking it off my shoes before I have a chance to kick it away. I glance at Mum who is tsking and declaring she doesn't understand where the hell I was and why can't I answer her questions and I am left wondering; do I care?

Dad gives a little grunt. More of a throat clearance to gain my attention. I sullenly look at him under hooded eyes, not willing to give him more than I have to. Bare minimum is a teenage motto and one I uphold at every possible chance. Give parents, teachers and coaches the chance to see 'something' and BAM! They push you to do more, be more, be something. Dad is staring at me so I stare back. He seems humorous. Like there's a joke to be told and I wait it out. But he just grins and pushes a black bean out of his mouth, nibbing it between his teeth like a stumpy cigarette. I have no idea where the bean has come from and I stare at it transfixed.

'Was it good, son?' his lips move and say but I don't register this fact other than that his lips moved and the bean nearly fell out.

He repeats himself when Mum moves away and raising my eyes to his I say, 'What?' I have found one-word answers best at preventing stupid conversation.

'Where you went. Was it good? Did the meteorite get you or what?'

Now he has my attention. He is grinning now, playing with the bean, making it stand up on its pointy ends, then flat, then suck it in, spit it nearly out only to spin it around and start the dance of the bean again. I stare hard at his face. Drill into his eyes and look for meaning. How would Dad know where I went? Did I talk out loud?

'Been there, son. If the meteorite missed you, that's a good thing,' he says.

I am sitting there, slouched in my chair, rice all over me and the cat now chewing on my laces, the voices of my sister and mum in the kitchen, reciting some stupid poem; and there is my dad, still boring his eyes into me with meaning I can't grasp.

'Why don't you go back and chase it? Can I join you?'

I risk a small nod, more a drop of the eyes and roll of the shoulders. Be damned if I'll say, 'Sure, Dad! Come tripping in my mind and soar above the galaxies,' but I play along. I'm probably going to be certified mad before the year is out anyway. And the year is nearly done.

I drop my eyes to the bowl of rice—what's left of it. I search for the little blended family that were spooning but I can't find them. Scattered to the winds or probably munched on by my cat and now sailing in pieces through the old mutt's intestines. They'll be cat shit by tomorrow. Truly a blended family again. I spy three white grains like soldiers clinging to the side of the bowl, right below the chip on the left-hand side. They look like soldiers alright. Standing there in unison, I swear I can see they have guns by their side and helmets on their heads.

My eyes blur and I am back in the galaxy and I am feeling the night breeze on my face again. Soaring and feeling free. I grin. Yes, I like it up here.

Just as I am settling in a force of air pushes on my back, making me stumble forward and an object whooshes past me. I am shocked and glance up, ready to get angry when the object morphs into my father. He is grinning again, looking at me over his shoulder. Get out of my head, Dad! He grins some more and spits the bean at me. It stings my nose before it ricochets off into oblivion.

'Catch me if you can!' Dad yells into the wind and in true superman style zooms off into the blackness. I am miffed. He can't be here. In my head. In my daydream. Although I don't want him in my head, the fact that he has disappeared has me scared. Do I want my dad tripping with me after all? And then all of a sudden he is back in my face, no longer grinning but staring at me, the wind making his hair look like the neighbour's dog after it got thrown from a car. 'Like I said, I've been here, son. Most of us have. It's okay. You got this. I got this. Together we got this. Now let's go!' and off he zooms again, beckoning with his hand to come on and hurry up.

I ball my hands into fists, exert a groan of frustration, lower my head and throw myself into a slipstream like a bullet destined for a target. My dad is the target. Where the bloody hell did he go? Suddenly he is beside me, grinning as the wind again whips his hair around his face.

'Come on, son! Let's go I said! Be free with me! Let's be wild, let's be so damned crazy we give crazy a new definition!' His enthusiasm is catching. I'm starting to feel bubbles of joy. Alright, old man, bring it on.

'Race ya!' I scream, trying my own version of superman but looking way better (of course) than my ageing dad can ever again be. And so we fly, dip down, and soar up. Together. So free.

I am laughing and Dad has his head thrown back. Is he howling? I want to howl too. And so I do. I howl and howl and howl and I push out all my frustrations and pent-up anger and wasted energy on negative thoughts and self-doubt. I howl for the frustrations of the unity of my family. I howl until my throat is raw and tears are coursing down my cheeks. Dad is grinning. I grin. I am about to soar off again when an almighty bang brings me back to reality.

I am back at the kitchen table. I quickly seek out Dad.

'Open your mouth, son,' he says and I realise there is something in it. Pushing it to the front of my teeth, I find a bloody bean I never put there. Dad pushes his back out to his teeth and says, 'I've got you, son.'

GRAN GIVES GOOD HUGS

Danyelle Woods

Every night, Laura was drawn to that *place*. The place between life and death, perhaps a gateway where time and the state of being is an irrelevant concept. Every night, her lids drew closed, her breath softened, the nape of her neck sunk into the embroidered fabric of her pillow. Her thoughts quietened down like a carousel after dark, the hymns of her mind softened into a blossoming silence. Laura's blankets cocooned around her body, leaving only her glistening pale face to be kissed by the looming moonlight. Down, down, down, her mind sunk.

She felt like she was flying, as if she had slipped off the edge of consciousness, was falling into a cold darkness that embraced her with possessive arms. Down, down, down, she fell past the dreams that provided comfort, and then finally, she hit the cold hard bottom. Every night she closed her eyes, and when she opened them again, she stood by the end of her bed.

Let me tell you about the first time.

It was her room. It was her peach wallpaper, her soft pink carpet under her feet, her Madonna posters plastered on the wall. It was her room, except, not quite. It could've been because she was standing at the foot of her bed yet staring right at a duplicate of herself curled up under the blankets. This girl, who looked like Laura, slept with a steady rhythm of breath. Her blonde locks caressed her cheeks, her limbs flayed out ungracefully in the turmoil of sheets.

This is me.

While Laura watched herself, she felt familiarity in the twilight. However, the cold and eerie atmosphere made Laura's heartbeat uneasy.

This was her room, but different. Laura's shoulders were heavy with lethargy, and her lean legs struggled to support her own weight. The moonlight travelled through the pulled curtains, illuminating just the outlines of furniture and the path to the door. When she yanked the door open, she was met with a palpable silence that blanketed her house. As she gradually, and cautiously, crept into the lounge, and into the open kitchen, her steps made no sound. The tiles offered no warmth, only stone-cold quietness to calm the erratic ticking of her heart.

'Mum?' Laura whispered, tiptoeing to her mum's room by muscle memory—sometimes bumping a shoulder into a wall. The wooden bedroom door emerged into her line of sight. She pushed it open, accompanied by a creaky tune from rusty hinges and a twang of musty air.

'Mum, are you awake?' asked Laura, voice quieter than her staggered heartbeat.

No answer.

She edged closer, tracing her fingers to the bottom of the itchy fleece duvet. Up, up, up. Laura's fingers clasped at the sheets in search of her mother, who didn't emerge under the blankets like she should've. Laura felt dread, contemplating the thought that her mother had run away.

'She said you would come here,' echoed a small but deep, masculine voice. It wasn't familiar. It came from over Laura's shoulder, perhaps in the corner of the room, which made her frigid with stifling fear. The voice reverberated in her mind, then she felt a heavy tug on her body. It wasn't just a small nudge on the shoulder, it was tugging on her whole soul with such aggression; she was swept up into the whirl of an unbreakable current and she could not think, feel, or do until it had reached its destination. She closed her eyes, her thoughts still lingering on the intense vibration of the voice that travelled through every vein.

Her lids opened.

The ceiling loomed over her, and the soft sheets clasped her neck in a chokehold. She was awake, but she wondered: *Was that a dream?*

The soft pitch of her alarm bounced off the walls, and the relieving and comforting hum from her mum returned from in the kitchen.

Night was lulled to sleep, and day shone through the window. Laura pondered on her dream continuously, sifting through piles of work nonchalantly. Before she knew it, Laura was weighed down under her sheets again. The moon kissed her a sweet goodnight as her lids drew closed.

Down, down, down. *It's happening*, Laura thought as she began to lose any control over her mind. Her eyes opened; she was standing by the foot of her bed and watching herself sleep.

Down, down, down. Again, and again. The next night, and the one after that. Laura never dared to venture outside of her room, where she remained captive with only herself as company. Laura could not differentiate if this was still a dream or not, as her peacefully sleeping self in her bed never seemed to breathe or stir.

Laura awoke, every time, with the hard tug on her soul. Feeling weighed down, lethargic, and empty, she trudged through the day, and then reluctantly crawled into the same bed every night. Down, down, down. Laura's mind sank to that place. It was the feeling of like being underwater that Laura loathed the most. The murky feeling that never left, even when she woke.

This time, like every other night, Laura opened her eyes to the foot of her bed. She saw herself sleep. Laura settled down in the corner of her room for the rest of the night to guard the door. From behind the door, a soft but deep voice taunted with mischievous laughter that ignited a fear inside of Laura. It was the kind of fear that ran cold over your neck and made your palms sweaty. The instinctual type of fear that sunk its claws into Laura, and kept her, far, far away from the door.

This night, there were three slow knocks. The sound of the knocking was like the sound of a heartbeat, strong and loud. First knock, Laura went stiff from head to toe, and her neck was riddled with chills. On the second knock, her chest was heavy with dread as a cold sickness clamped her to the ground. Third, she squeezed her eyes shut in anticipation as the doorknob rattled. The creak of the door hinge swept over Laura.

'I knew I would find you here,' sung a soft, light voice.

'Gran,' Laura replied with a swift, relieved breath. The outline of a short woman stood in the wideness of the open door. As she stepped forward into soft rays of moonlight, the creases of old age appeared alongside familiar sunken eyes. Laura shakily lifted herself from the floor, staggered forward and flung wobbly arms around the woman. 'I can't believe it's you, Gran.'

Gran laughed, tipping her silver head back. 'Dear, it has been a long time, hasn't it? My, you've become a beautiful young lady.'

'Are you real?' Laura asked with her head softly resting on Gran's arm. 'Surely I am dreaming.'

'I think I am real, Laura bear. They said I would find you here.'

'Who said that?'

'My friend, Jason. He might've scared you back to your body before, but he apologizes immensely,' soothed Gran. Laura never inquired further as to what that could mean, thoughts racing like a Grand Prix. They embraced each other for a few moments longer, each second making up for the years of separation. Gran was just as sluggish as when Laura last saw her. She still had wispy grey hair, sunken grey eyes, decades of creases that could each tell a tale from her fulfilling life. She was still dressed in the stiff fabric of a white nightgown that ended at her feet.

The last thing she ever wore.

Gran asked how schooling was, to which Laura told her she was in her final year. And Gran asked how little Ethan was, to which Laura told her little Ethan was not so little anymore. Then she inquired as to how Mum was, to which Laura told her how she and Dad were separating. Gran wore an exasperated look. 'That is sad. In times like that, Laura, a daughter always needs her mother—no matter how old you both are.'

And then she inquired how Grandpa was doing without her, to which Laura told her that he was doing great, but still missed Gran deeply.

They talked and laughed like old times. It was like those golden years, where Laura would bounce on Gran's lap, toil in the garden together, just a little girl in tow of her grandmother all the time. Gran's mouth tilted down in a sad manner and her tone was lonely, 'I wish I had a second chance at life again, Laura bear.'

Laura welled up, shoulders shaking. 'I wish I could still see you every day, too,' Laura whispered back.

Gran replied by placing a hand on Laura's knee. 'Perhaps one day.'

Laura told Gran that it was time to go. She felt that nudge in her chest. The inkling of departure now starting to caress her head to sleep. They embraced each other.

'When can we meet again, Gran?'

'I'll be here every time if you want to see me.' She gave Laura a warm smile.

Laura awoke to the ceiling looming above her. The comforting hum from her Mum rebounded from the kitchen. Again, Laura sifted through paperwork and school with her thoughts continually slipping away from her. This time she had a slight spring in her step as the sun began to fade out and close its curtains.

Down, down, down. She stood at the foot of her bed. Her Gran greeted her with a sweet smile that contrasted the darkness from the pulled curtains.

Down, down, down. She watched herself sleep, waiting for her Gran to knock three times. Gran would enter anyway, but Laura always said, 'Come in.'

Down, down, down, again. She met Gran's friend, welcoming them into the peachiness of her room. Jason was his name. Jason, short with wilting black hair, loved to talk to Laura.

'Is this you, Laura?' Jason inquired with a sense of curiosity. He pointed to the sleeping Laura, who was curled like a tightened ball of string under her pink duvet. 'Do you always come to this *place*?'

Laura said yes, and noticed Gran placed some distance between Laura and Jason with her body.

Down, down, down. And then again, down, down, down. Every night, Laura was drawn to that place. The place where time and being were an irrelevant concept, but the place where Laura could see an old familiar face. Every night, Laura emerged at the end of her bed, and every morning awoke with the soft hum from her Mum in the kitchen. And every night, Gran knocked three times.

Laura was telling Gran how today she put in her applications to universities. Gran went quiet, arm falling around Laura's shoulder, emitting a sombre aura.

'Laura, dear,' Gran interjected softly. 'Do you think Grandpa would want to see me again? Talk to me again?'

Laura, stunned by the sudden question, watched her Gran. 'I think he would do anything to see you again.' She placed her smooth youthful hands around Gran's cool knobbly ones. She hoped to offer comfort to Gran, who looked like she was ready to sink into the ground. The room however, ceased to a stillness.

'Do you mind if I join you two?' The deepness of Jason's voice startled Laura.

Silence circled the thick air like a predator and made Laura's stomach recoil with that instinctual fear. She watched Jason enter the room and idle closely to Laura for a while.

'I think I would do anything,' Gran said, removing her arm from Laura's shoulder and returning them to a tight clasp in her lap.

The tension was sickening enough to make Laura feel nauseous. 'That's great, Gran.' She flicked her eyes to the small sleeping Laura in bed, and then hesitantly back to her Gran, with the feeling of Jason looking at her. 'I think it will be a while until Grandpa will join you, though.'

Jason made a small comment, as he rested his hand on the leg of sleeping Laura. 'Don't we all want a second chance, Gran?'

Nothing more was exchanged. Laura let the nudge overtake her, felt the whirlwind intoxicate her until she awoke in the chokehold of her sheets. She was clammy and hot. Mum wasn't singing in the kitchen that morning.

Again, she trudged through the day. However, her mind pondered on Gran's and Jason's words. It was Gran's stillness that frightened Laura. The way the moonlight made her skin so pale, the way every hair hung without movement. The intention laced between, under, and around every word she uttered. It was the cold deepness in Jason's voice that made Laura shudder. It was the way he snaked his fingers around Laura's leg with a tight, malicious grasp.

Laura didn't want to return to that *place*, tonight. Or even perhaps, ever.

Down, down, down. Laura's mind sunk reluctantly into the void again. Her mind felt bogged with water, as she watched herself in bed.

Knock, knock, and knock. Laura didn't answer, her legs wobbly and heavy.

Knock. Knock. And knock. Each knock heavier than the last. 'Laura, are you there?' rang Gran's raspy voice. 'Can you let me in?'

She pressed herself so hard against her peachy walls that she thought she might melt into them. Laura didn't answer. She trudged through the day, and through the next, and the next. *Bang. Bang. Bang.* Gran knocked on the door, but Laura didn't answer nor let her in.

The next night, Laura's neck sunk into her embroidered pillow, a heavy darkness creeping up, up, up, into her mind until she fell. This time, Laura hit the bottom hard. She opened her eyes to the foot of her bed.

'I let myself in. I hope you don't mind.' Jason was sitting on the bed, legs pulled together, back straight, head lowered down at sleeping Laura. His presence was a surprise.

'I wish you would knock first,' retorted Laura in a small, frightened voice from the corner of the room.

Jason lifted his face to Laura, who was slowly drifting to her bedroom door. 'I'm basically family now, Laura. You know I don't need your permission. You've been avoiding Gran, haven't you? It's a bit tactless, you know.'

'I didn't mean to, Jason. I was feeling unwell, and I think I needed a break, that was all.' Laura, from the kindness of her heart, outstretched a hand to Jason, who continued to sit possessively beside Laura's unconscious body.

Jason lifted his eyes to Laura. 'If that's the case ... would you be able to do me a favour, Laura?'

'That depends.' There was hesitancy in Laura's voice.

Jason paused. 'Give me a second chance.'

Laura didn't respond—whether it was because she did understand or didn't want to—there was no way to tell.

'It would only be for a while, darling. A quick slip in, slip out. It would give me the opportunity to have *a second chance again.* To see my mother, and my wife.'

'I don't like the sound of that, though. How would I know it would only be for a while? Is it even possible?'

'Of course! All you would have to do is *let me in*.'

Laura, in an attempt to console herself, crossed her arms over. The walls felt like they were caving in on her. 'I don't think so.'

Jason's eyes lowered, and his brows furrowed. 'You're going to deny me the right to see my family, Laura?'

'I said I don't want to ...' she whispered.

Gran emerged from behind Laura, voice shaking with a seething anger as it shot across the room. 'Jason, get the hell out of my granddaughter's room.' Laura felt Gran's cold hands slowly grip both of Laura's shoulders.

Laura's eyes darted around the room. In this *Place*, there was no escape. Gran and Jason exchanged looks that seemed to telecommunicate a hidden message that Laura couldn't decode in those few seconds.

Jason clapped his hands together. 'I'll let you think on it, dear. I'll see you again.'

Laura jolted up to the sound of the alarm. It pulsed through her veins and her head, aching. She plodded through the day, like always. She heard from a university; she received a letter of acceptance. She ate lunch with friends, filled the day with contagious laughter and fought over the last slice of desert with Ethan.

Mum wished her a goodnight, to which Laura said she would see her in the morning. Her lids drew closed. Laura felt like she was flying, drifting through a calm, undisturbed void. Then, as if two knobbly hands latched on with a firm grasp, she slipped off the edge of consciousness. She fell into protective arms that cradled her awake.

Laura did not stand at the foot of her bed this time. *She* was in her bed, arms confined to her sides, her sheets tighter around her waist than a preying python.

The silver lining of Gran's eyes was lit up by the luminescence of night light. 'Sleep in my arms, sleep in my protective and loving arms, *my second chance*,' whispered Gran softly, lovingly, into Laura's ears.

Laura wondered; her gaze was stuck on her dark, pink ceiling. Fear was lodged down her throat and into her chest, feeling as if she was drowning and every breath was slowly evaporating under the weight of Gran's arms.

Why?

'Goodnight, Laura bear.'

Mum's soft hum echoed from the kitchen. Laura turned off her alarm, untangled her sweaty body from her sheets and proceeded to her door.

The sweet aroma of coffee and maple clouded the room. 'Good morning,' greeted mum who idled by the sink. She did not look up.

Laura gazed around, finally resting on the blonde boy who chewed on his breakfast and lounged next to the television.

'My, you have grown up, Little Ethan.'

THE AZREK

Nicole Jonsson

I
t came to me again last night, in my dreams. This time was different though. This time it touched me.

Familiar redwood pines towered above me as I walked along the moonlit path. The air was still and smelt of damp earth. As usual something lurked just beyond the edge of darkness, but I wasn't afraid, not with the distraction of twinkling fireflies dancing above me. As I entered the clearing, inhabitants of this otherworldly forest started manifesting to greet me. Rabbit-sized salamander creatures with iridescent wings gazed up at me with doe eyes and goofy grins. Something resembling a white Persian cat fluttered down on scaled wings, draping itself across my shoulders.

I idly petted my perched companion as I watched the stone archway ahead, awaiting the arrival of the mysterious creature that had been inhabiting my dreams for the past two months. Only ever appearing from within the swirling mauve liquid that filled the entryway and tonight was no exception. It stepped through the gateway, crouched to fit its eight-foot frame. Empty black eyes studied me. It was a mixture of so many recognisable animals, yet it was still something completely of its own creation.

At first, it feels warm and there's a tingle in the spot its hand just touched. The feeling spreads, until every cell in my body begins to vibrate.

Overwhelmed by the pain I finally wake. I can still feel the buzzing as I lie in my bed, paralysed and not entirely awake. My cheeks hurt, I must be smiling, but I can taste damp saltiness on my lips. I've never felt scared of my dream creature, never hated seeing it every night. Even though I can faintly remember the burning pain of last night's meeting, I'm still not afraid.

An hour passes, and finally I can move. My head, however, is filled with sand. Everything around me is slightly grainy. I stumble into the bathroom, gripping the sink with white knuckles as a wave of nausea washes across me. The rusty drain multiplies and spins as I sway side to side. Afraid the visual dizziness will send me over the edge, I squeeze my eyes closed. It offers momentary relief but immediately I flash back to the dream, and I can't help the grin that creeps onto my face as I slowly lose consciousness.

My gaze started at the set of twisted antlers, travelling down from a pair of large dog-like ears and a mane of scruffy black fur to a welcoming owl face. Veiny grey wings draped to the floor, attached to black bony arms, each hand equipped with inky talons. A row of transparent horns ran down its spine, and the legs belonged to a crow, although instead of feathers, more fur. It prowled toward me like an animal, yet its presence felt wise, felt familiar.

'Hello again, friend,' I said.

Its tan antlers tipped forward in greeting. This mysterious entity never responded with words, but I knew it understood me. I had recently learnt the creature's name, such a strange name. Old folklore calls it the Azrek, not much is written about it, only that it's a dream visitor.

The Azrek crept closer, closer than it had ever dared before. Normally it would watch from the distance for a couple of minutes and then I would wake up. I knew something was different when this didn't happen. I could almost reach out and touch it. Instead, a sinewy hand reached and gently tapped my forehead.

When I wake up the second time, I am on the bathroom floor, pain and dizziness free. I stand and look in the mirror, attempting to fix the mess my hair is in. That's when I see it, draping across my shoulders, the moth-cat from my dream. I reach up to pet it, not trusting that it's real. Sure enough, I feel its soft fur tickle my fingertips and it purrs in delight. A damp nose presses against my foot and I look down to see the salamander creature sniffing me. If one is real, the other must be as well. I catch a glimpse of light twinkling in the right-hand corner of my vision, a pixie is tight roping along my shower curtain. How is this real? Am I still dreaming?

My phone dings somewhere in my room. Dazed, I walk over to my bed and pick it up. *Hey, hun, are you still able to grab a coffee with me at Rosa's café? Say in about half an hour?* the text from my mum reads. I snap back into reality and reply *on my way Xx*, trying to ignore the mythical creatures running amuck in my bathroom. Particularly the one keeping my neck toasty warm. Remembering moth-cat, I gently push it off onto my bed.

'You can't stay there while I get ready, little friend, sorry,' I say to it. I sigh and turn to my closet. 'What to wear, what to wear.'

Fifteen minutes later I'm rushing down the busy streets of the city, weaving through the clusters of city-goers. I'd almost forgotten about my little encounter with the creatures in my bathroom in the rush to get out the door. But now as I watch faces fly past me, I realise some aren't as human as I thought them to be. I stare long and hard at a woman walking toward me on my left, she has a pair of pointy ears protruding from her long, blonde hair and her eyes don't have pupils. Eerie but also ethereal, I think to myself. On closer inspection, something short that I thought was a child turns out to be a goblin of some sort. His cheery eyes look up at me, he grins, flashing a row of bone white teeth. I wasn't expecting that.

This continues until I've seen every possible fantastical creature, including five more moth-cats. Even when I enter the café, the waitress who greets me has a tabby moth-cat sitting on her shoulder. I struggle not to stare as it preens its powdery wings. I sit down across from my mum, subtly checking her over for rogue creatures, nothing thankfully.

'Hi, Mum.'

'Hi, darling. How are you?'

'I'm alright, thanks.' I force a smile, like I do every time she asks me that.

'So, the new medication is helping?'

'Yeah, it's great, I'm feeling a lot more like myself now.'

'Any side-effects this time?'

'Nothing so far.'

'And you're taking it regularly? You know, like the doctor suggested?'

I suppress a long sigh; she's always asking too many questions. 'Yes, Mum,' I say through clenched teeth.

'Oh, darling, I'm so proud. Now, are you ready to order?' She smiles kindly, the soft crow's feet around her eyes crinkle. I can see the powder concealer she has on as the sunlight filters through the blinds, the delicate swipes of mascara on her eyelashes and the faint rouge upon her cheeks. She is always looking her best, my mum.

'I'm ready if you are.' This time my smile is real, but it falters when an orange pixie crawls up my mum's arm. I giggle when it starts to play with her earrings, swinging on the hoops like a child at a playground.

'What are you laughing at, honey?' Her giggle is of confusion. 'Is there something caught in my earrings?'

'No, no, sorry it's nothing. Just remembering a funny quote from a movie, that's all.'

She reaches up to check her earrings, the pixie that was using one as a swing vanishes as if it was never there. 'Oh ok,' she laughs, 'now how about that coffee?' We order our respective coffees and spend the next hour chatting and soaking up the warm, caffeine buzzed atmosphere. I enjoy watching the mischief the numerous pixies, faeries, and moth-cats I can see, get up to.

That night as I lie in bed, exhausted after a day of playing with my new moth-cat and salamander-fairy, I eagerly await my dream meeting with the Azrek. More excited than ever, I toss and turn, I can't wait to thank it for this gift. I slow my breaths, concentrating on the faint ticking of my clock, counting each tick. One ... two ... three ... fou—

I feel warm under the covers as sunlight pours in through the open curtains and washes over my bed. I can hear cars driving past and somewhere nearby, the sound of a bird warbling. It must be morning, but I sit up with a start. No dream, my first night without a dream, that's impossible.

On day five, I wake up to silence. No clock ticking, no bird's song, not even the sound of a car. I sit up, swinging my legs over the edge of the bed, rubbing my eyes. I grab the soft carpet with my toes while I stretch. Usually, by this time moth-cat has come over for some cuddles, demanding attention with its odd vibrational purr. Nothing, just more silence. I begin searching my small single storey rental house, every room, every cupboard and even every appliance big enough. Nothing. I haven't even seen salamander-fairy for two days. I think it ran away because of moth-cat's bullying. Now, however, I'm concerned.

I miss the Azrek; I can't explain why; I can't explain the happiness it brings me.

There is still no sign of moth-cat by the time I must leave for work, utterly heartbroken I close my front door and walk to the bus stop. The bus is just pulling in as I arrive, so I quickly hop on and find a seat. Hoping that a rogue pixie making mischief might cheer me up, I scan the bus for a twinkling light. Nothing. The bus is dull, everyone has their heads down scrolling on their phones, even the sun disappears behind a patch of ominously dark clouds.

I push and shove my way through the crowds of people in the city, looking at each face, checking each shoulder, but nothing. Something is wrong with everyone's expressions, they're all sullen, lifeless almost. The more faces I look at, the blurrier they become and then, the more similar. I start to jog, each face is the same, familiar yet a stranger. They're looking at me now as I run past, their eyes, there's something wrong with their eyes. Black, soulless, something reflects but I can't bear to look long enough to find out.

Eyes closed, I push my way through the bodies, running at full speed to escape this nightmare. When I finally stop to take in my surroundings, I see it. The same buildings as before, I haven't made any progress, not even in circles, just running on the spot. My head feels like it's filled with sand, everything starts to spin, and I can feel the vibration of the cells in my body. I scream, falling to my knees, ears ringing, eyes clamped shut.

Then I feel a furry whisper across my exposed neck. I slowly open my eyes and turn to look at my shoulder. Moth-cat's doe eyes meet mine and its tail bats the other side of my face. I look around, people are walking past, normal people, people with pixies dangling off their ears and salamander-fairies hitching rides on their shoes. Normal at last. I stand, clearing my throat and trying to casually brush the dirt off my white slacks. I continue to work and for the rest of the day it remains normal, like I hoped it would.

Next morning, I again awake to silence. No moth-cat, nothing.

'No, please no, not again,' I choke out, tears threatening to spill. I'm so on edge that when my phone rings, my heart nearly leaves my chest. I reach over and grab it off my nightstand and with the sound of my heart pounding in my ears I answer.

'Hi, sweetie, how are you? Oh, I hope I didn't wake you up, it is Saturday after all.' My mum's gentle voice drifts through the speaker and I relax instantly.

'No, it's alright, Mum, you didn't wake me up. I was just about to get up actually,' I say, struggling to keep the shake out of my voice. It doesn't work.

'What's wrong? Your voice, it sounds shaky or something, or maybe it's just my hearing going, you know how your father teases me.' She laughs at the end, and I want to laugh with her, but instead, her laughter makes me want to cry. She's so normal, how can I ever explain what I saw yesterday or what I've been seeing for nearly a week? She'd think I'm crazy.

'I'm fine, just a bad dream. Can't even remember it anymore really.'

'Well ok then. Anyway, I was just calling to see if you want to meet up for coffee, maybe some breakfast. How does that sound, sweetie?'

'That sounds great, Mum. See you in an hour then?'

'See you in an hour. Bye, honey.'

'Bye, Mum.' The call clicks and ends.

This time when I walk through the city my head is down, I watch my feet hit the sidewalk. I couldn't even bring myself to look for moth-cat this morning, too afraid of completely repeating my actions from yesterday. At the very least I make progress today, and soon I'm at the café. The little doorbell chimes as I enter; I'm hit with a wave of chocolatey goodness combined with the rich aroma of coffee. Heaven.

I find Mum and sit across from her, she's the first face I dare to look at. I wish I hadn't. Her eyes look like two chunks of coal, no soul, no life in them. Her face is expressionless, the more I stare the less she, it, looks like my mum.

'Mum?' I don't know why I bother asking. 'Mummy?' Tears start to gather, and my vision blurs. The lights in the café go out, the sun vanishes, it's pitch-black outside. I notice other patrons turn to stare at me, and all their faces look like my mum's. 'Stop staring at me. Stop it!' But they don't stop. Creatures crawl out from all the dark corners of the room. Moth-cat appears on my mum's shoulders. All their eyes are bottomless black holes. Red. Blood. Tears of blood drip from the eyes of every human and creature. It's like a nightmare. Like an accident I can't look away from. The wind picks up, howling, carrying a woman's screams. They're my own. My mum's mouth starts to stretch into a grin, unnaturally wide, it reveals a mouth of rotting, jagged teeth. I take back control of my hands and bury my face in them. My throat is raw from non-stop screaming, although I can't even hear myself over the wind to know if I am even making sound.

My body is on fire, each nerve ending buzzing, ripping apart from the inside. It's excruciating.

'—ney? Honey? What's wrong? Oh my goodness, what happened?' Slowly my mum's voice comes into focus. I peel my hands from my face and see her sitting across from me, horrified. It's not her though. It can't be.

'You're not my mum. You're not real. I'm still dreaming. This is a nightmare, that's what it is. I just need to wake up.' I rip at my hair, sweat pouring down my face.

'Wha—honey, stop. Slow down a second.'

'You're not real!' I run out of the café and back onto the busy sidewalk, stranger's faces flash past and I swear some morph right in front of me. Then, it's there. The Azrek. Standing next to the stone portal in the middle of the street. It reaches out a clawed hand and beckons me over. Relief floods all my senses and like I'm under hypnosis, I walk mesmerised right into the street.

I smile up at the Azrek, tears of joy washing away the sticky sweat. Wordlessly it points at the portal. I step up to the barrier of swirling liquid, tracing the patterns with my hand. Home. Safety. I turn and look back at the Azrek.

'I'm so happy to see you again, my friend.'

The Azrek creeps forward slowly, winged arms now dragging upon the bitumen. I stare at its gentle owl face and watch in horror as a disfigured almost human visage appears. Empty black eyes, dripping with blood and a wide sadistic grin. Something from beyond the portal grabs me with bony arms, attaching tightly to my wrists, ankles, and throat. I struggle against the grip, looking at the Azrek for help. Instead, I hear a deep growly voice in my mind.

'You were so easy.'

As I'm dragged into the flurry of mauve liquid, I see moth-cat float down to rest upon the Azrek's shoulders. A single tear trails down my cheek.

THE MIRROR'S REFLECTION

Darci Robbins

When Eva was nine her mother told her about the mirror. 'It's been in our family for generations ... your great-great-great grandfather apparently found it one day by Lake Saman and decided to take it back with him,' Mama had said. 'The mirror was beautiful back then, ornate gold and silver weaved into the base, and the glass would sparkle across the room projecting rainbows. He believed that it was a sign from beyond; a beautiful mirror sent by his beautiful wife, Hilda.' The pair had been reading in the library when curiosity got the better of Eva. 'I remember the first time your father told me about it. He said that Nico, your grandfather, had told him that there was another world living inside the mirror, a whole new species of humans living as if nothing was strange about it. Your father never believed it, but when Nico passed away and left the mirror for him, something changed.' Eva knew what she meant. Months before her conversation with Mama, her Papa had closed himself off from them, more often than not he could be found pacing the lengths of the library, hair a mess and glasses askew.

One night when Eva had been sick, she'd snuck inside the library seeking comfort from her Papa, only to find him frantically scribbling in his notebook, talking to himself like a madman.

'Papa?' Eva had said. He'd just kept working, looking at that godforsaken mirror until he'd heard the splash of vomit on the tiles and the small cry that came afterwards. That night after her father had sent for the maid to clean her up, he tucked her back in her bed and told her a story.

'There once was a land filled with joy. The townspeople sang in the courtyard and were always smiling, always laughing. Then one day the town started to fall asleep. One man fell asleep feeding his sheep, and the next thing the town knew everyone had fallen into a deep sleep except for one person: Freya. Freya had magic you see, and that magic kept her safe from spells and enchantments, so she knew that something really bad had happened. She tried everything to wake her people up, but she was only nine and hadn't been properly taught,' her Papa said, and Eva valiantly fought Mother Sleep, desperate to know what had happened to the girl.

'What happened next?' Eva asked.

'Freya kept looking for an answer every day, searching high and low for something, anything that could save her town and free her from the eternal loneliness she now felt. One day she stumbled across an ornate mirror, a wash of technicolour swirling around blocking her reflection until suddenly she was staring at a reflection ... but it wasn't her own. It was a man ... your great-great-great grandfather to be precise.'

That story stuck with Eva long after her father passed away. It followed her wherever she went, the mirror practically gazing into her soul. Her dreams were filled with swirling colours, little girls crying and ornate mirrors. The last one wasn't just confined to her dreams; Eva would see the blasted thing every time she walked past the library.

She was 17 now, a woman in her own right. Her mother had held on for as long as she could, until one day she dropped to the floor like a marionette who'd had her strings cut. Her heart had given out, the doctors had said. The stresses of life catching up to her, Eva guessed.

Eva had been studying the mirror ever since her mother passed away. Before, the mirror had been covered up with a blanket, her Mama refusing to look at the object that stole most of her husband's last days. Eva would sneak in at night, just to get a glimpse at the object of her father's fascination ... until her mother found her curled up asleep at the foot of the mirror, her face stained with tears shed over a man she didn't really know at the end. Her mother had locked the library that day, effectively shutting down any hope Eva had of discovering whether her father had been telling the truth about Freya.

Until now.

The mirror had come to life.

Eva had been sitting in the library, a common occurrence these days now that she was the only one in the castle. After her Mama's funeral, Eva locked herself away, claiming that the grieving process was too much to handle alongside her extended family and friends' well wishes. The truth was that she wanted, no, needed to unearth the mystery of the mirror once and for all. If even a small fragment of the story her father told her was true, she needed to see for herself. See the girl who had been haunting her dreams from the moment she heard the story.

Freya had become Eva's best friend, in a way. Of course, it was all in her head, but Freya had frequented her dreams every night for eight years and so she became her best and only friend. Eva had always imagined what the girl would look like; she'd turn up in Eva's dreams every night looking like someone different, a carousel of nine-year-olds repeating the same phrase.

'Find me, Eva. Find me ... and save me,' the girl would say each night in a different voice but with the same five words.

'You cannot stay holed up in this room, it isn't what your parents would have wanted.' Of course, there was Marj. Marj was an old lady who lived in the mansion with her. Eva sometimes forgot she was there, having grown accustomed to Marj's presence in the background of her life. She had been the maid for her mother since before Eva was born and looked after her since she was just a baby.

Usually, Marj kept to herself, having been on the receiving end of Eva's anger and frustration over the mirror for far too long. Occasionally, the woman would come down to the library in a misguided attempt at pulling her away from the object. 'When was the last time you slept?' she'd say, placing a hot, home cooked meal in front of her. 'You need to start looking after yourself, you'll be no good to the girl if you waste away like your father did.'

'I see her, every night when I close my eyes, she's there Marj, staring into my soul. Looking at me like I've wronged her, someone who I have never met before. I know the story could be fake, a fairytale told by an old decrepit man desperate to be something ... but she's in my dreams. Every. Single. Night,' Eva said, forlornly looking at the mirror that had taken all of her time. 'I would want someone to find me, I wouldn't wish for her to be alone, either. So, that's what I'll do. Save her, even if we can't save the town. She needs to not be alone anymore.' Eva was frantic, eyes skittering around the room, somehow focusing on everything yet nothing. She was determined to get to the bottom of it, even if it was just so she could finally get a full night's sleep, instead of the fractured rest she'd had.

Eva had had issues discerning dreams from reality for far too long due to this blasted mirror, so although she was doing this to save Freya ... she had selfish reasons too.

Marj was right, of course she was. Sleep, however fruitless it may seem, was very much needed if Eva wanted to crack the case ... or just function like a human rather than a depressed and cranky shell of herself, haunting the library like a benevolent ghost. She'd retired to her bedroom not long after Marj left; she didn't need the maid to know she'd been correct, Eva would never hear the end of it. After her nightly ritual, Eva slipped into bed, her auburn hair splayed against her white pillow.

It took a while for Eva to fall asleep, her brain rattling around in her head like a bird stuck in a cage; she didn't know what would greet her when she closed her eyes— darkness, or Freya. Eventually, she succumbed to sleep, her body aching with tiredness and eyes stinging.

This was different.

Eva woke up to light. Bright sunlight shining on her, chasing away the sleepiness that shrouded her. Her dreams usually consisted of the young girl standing alone in the middle of the forest, screaming at her to find her and save her. This was a lovely break from the torment that frequented her sleep, and Eva was worried about what was to come; she knew that peace came with a cost, always.

Freya was nowhere to be seen, another deviation from the usual narrative that controlled basically every aspect of her life for the past years. She was all alone, and for the first time in weeks, months, years even ... she felt okay. Eva knew this was a dream, knew she'd have to wake up at some stage, but that was the last thing Eva wanted to think about.

'Who are you?' A voice echoed throughout the forest, trees swaying in time with the melodic tone. Eva shot up, coming face to face with a young woman. She would have been the same age as Eva, maybe a year or two older (Eva was terrible at guessing people's age), shocking blonde hair cut jaggedly around her shoulders. Her clothes were torn, mud and leaves speckled her outfit.

This was Eva's dream, yet she didn't feel in control.

'I'm Eva Kingler. Who are you?'

'Kingler? As in Jax Kingler?' The woman said, grasping onto Eva's arms, slightly shaking her.

'He was my father. But you already knew that, you're in my head,' Eva said, pulling away from the woman.

'Was?' the woman said, sadness flitting across her face for a second before her previous air of indifference came back. Eva decided to play along; it was her dream after all.

'He passed away ten years ago, looking at that godforsaken mirror.'

The woman broke down then, tears leaving tracks through the dirt caked upon her face. It was then that Eva realised something. Something massive.

'You're Freya ... but it can't be. You were nine years old when my great-great-great grandfather discovered the mirror, and he said you couldn't age until the spell was broken,' Eva said, shock evident in her face. Here was the woman that had haunted her dreams for years, no longer a little girl but a woman.

'He was wrong. I still age, but at a rate slower than a snail it seems,' Freya said. 'Wait, you know me? You know who I am?'

Eva sat with Freya and told her the whole story from the beginning; her great-great-great grandfather's story, which was told to generations of Kinglers, her father's descent into madness and Eva's constant nightmares.

'That wasn't me, that was the mirror. It sucks you in, poisons your brain until you succumb to its madness. It's part of the curse. The mirror used to be a thing of beauty, a connection between my world and yours. Back when our ancestors ran the world, they discovered the mirror in a cave. Well, caves, as they were from different worlds. The mirror allowed for the two clans to traverse through to my world and vice versa. Our families formed a bond, growing and evolving with each other as the years went on. Until one day there was a fight, and the leaders of each clan didn't see eye to eye ... It got so bad that they decided then and there they'd never use the mirrors ever again, erasing centuries of friendship and comradery just like that. The mirrors were placed at the bottom of Lake Saman, until they washed up one day out of the blue. My grandmother found ours, and Nico found yours,' Freya said. 'Now that mirror is my only hope. It's the only thing that can get me away from here and into your world, the only object that can save me has been cursed to trap me forever.'

'What can I do to help?' Eva said. This is what she had wanted to do since she'd first heard about the mirror and the mystery girl trapped within. Eva knew that this was real, even if it had taken place in her sleep.

'Go to the mirror and you'll see a bump in the bottom left corner of the frame. Press it twice, and then hold it until the colours disappear. You'll see the forest, and hopefully me if this all goes to plan. It's hard to see, but it's there.'

The women hugged, a bond solidifying what was already there; these two were connected by history, by love, and by their dreams.

Eva woke up the next morning, stretching her arms and forcing a yawn out. She hadn't felt this relaxed in forever ... and then she remembered why.

'Freya,' Eva said, jumping up and racing to the library, not worrying to put her dressing gown on let alone proper clothes. Freya had been trapped in that mirror for far too long, Eva couldn't let her wait anymore.

She flung the doors open, and there it was. The mirror, the one connected to Freya, unassuming and beautiful all in one.

Remembering the instructions Freya had told her in their shared dream, Eva got to work. She would free Freya, and they would work together to save her world, just like her people had once done. They would bridge the gap between the families and bring life back to her town, with the hopes of reconnecting the clans and reinforcing their past connection. Her dreams had become a reality, and Eva couldn't wait to start her journey with Freya.

GRIEF OF THE MIND

Ronan Clarke

Revan made his way through the trees, looking around for any sign of how he had gotten here. The road ran through the dense clutter of centuries-untouched oaks, stretching out to infinity in either direction. Despite the impossibility, these woods were still familiar to him in their twilight rustlings and creeping fog, though he wasn't sure from where.

He had woken up amongst the old trees a few hours ago, just as the sun reached its zenith, its soft orange light filtering through the canopy. But the sun was setting now, the earlier beauty fading quickly as panic set in. Had he been in an accident? Was he dreaming? It certainly didn't feel like it.

A branch cracked to his left, alerting him to a presence. He didn't let his body language show that he'd noticed anything, instead he continued looking ahead, walking at the same pace. He let his mind out into the woods, seeking out any life around him. Trying to touch the edges of their thoughts and learn their plans, he could plan how to avoid them.

There.

Suddenly, memories of this place flooded into his head as he touched a familiar mind. He held his head in his hands and resisted the urge to collapse to his knees as tears starting to flow down his face. 'No. This isn't possible.'

A giggle belonging to a young girl came from the bushes and he shook his head, refusing to believe this was reality. He tried to reach out with his mind once more, to prove to himself that he had imagined it, but he couldn't focus on his power, couldn't feel even the ants beneath his palms. His mind was too clouded with thoughts of the past, of Emily.

'What's the matter, Revan?' the little girl's voice asked. 'You look scared.'

'You're not real. I don't know if you ever were. Get out of my head!' Revan screamed.

He began hurrying forward once more, then, leaving behind the voice that had once belonged to his sister, crying out for him to wait. The trees seemed to grow closer around him as the sun fell completely behind the horizon, lengthening the shadows until they clawed at the edges of his vision.

A fallen log barred his path, propped up on a moss-encrusted boulder. He vaulted over it, landing in a run. He continued down the impossibly long path, the trees growing closer, taller, older, thicker, as if he was travelling back in time. To a place where nature lived in harmony with people, providing for them, hiding them. To a place where a small family lived amongst the ancient trees, sheltered and safe.

The giggling chased him, swarmed him, crowded his mind. The path stretched on unending, time seeming to slow down to enthral his mad dash in perpetuity. Voices crept into his thoughts; voices he'd not heard in many years. He tried to shut them out, focus on running, but to no avail.

Murderer! A snippet of a half-familiar accusation rushed forward through his mind as he vaulted another fallen log, almost causing him to slip on the moss-covered stone that propped it up.

Freak! Monster! A familiar voice surged through briefly.

Your sister deserved better. The old woman from the town. She'd always hated him.

Every time the voices grew discernible, he tried reaching out with his mind, trying to detect the source. He found nothing, but each time he brushed against the girl's mind, however briefly, he felt like screaming. He blocked it out and kept probing, the pounding of his heart and the beating of his feet against the leaf litter drowned out, muted as he reached out further.

You always were a sadistic little bastard, weren't you?

'Leave me be ...' Revan breathed.

'Killing bugs again? Revan?' came the clearest voice yet, a woman's, marred by tears, 'What is wrong with you?'

He tried vainly to block the voices out, tried to focus on the sound of his feet pounding against the leaf litter, on his heartbeat, on anything other than the voices.

'Revan! What have you done?' the crying woman's voice came again, even louder.

He knew that memory; he'd heard that question a thousand times before. He winced and reached his mind out, trying to find the source, tracking the words back to their progenitor. There. Just as he'd thought. Wiping tears from his eyes he kept running, shutting off his mind to all but that one voice, trying to ignore the others, ignore that incessant giggling.

Then, the voice he'd latched onto grew clear once more. He shook his head, closing his eyes as he kept running, trying to isolate it to permanently remove it from his thoughts, thinking he'd accidentally touched her mind again. But the voice remained clear, raising in volume and pitch, becoming a scream. An oh-so-familiar tea-kettle scream.

His eyes snapped open, and a middle-aged woman of medium height was sprinting towards him, tears streaming down her face, blood trickling down a bitten lip. Mascara stained her cheeks and the flour on her apron. Her shoes were pristine, ill-suited to running through the forest. As her scream pierced the stagnant air, she raised a kitchen knife above her head.

Revan swore and braced himself for what he knew was about to come. His mother plunged the knife into his left shoulder and twisted the blade. 'I know this is your fault!' she screamed, spittle flying onto his face. 'What did you do to Emily?'

Revan screamed and tried to pull the knife free, futilely trying to push the woman back with his hands. 'Not again,' he breathed, 'not again.'

As his mother pressed him back, twisting the knife more as she pushed it further in, Revan roared, and pushed her back with all his force. Her physical body staggered back, the knife coming free. But her mind, her soul, her memory, it kept moving, taking the body with it.

Even though he knew he could control it this time, he couldn't stop his mother from slipping on the tiles in her uncontrolled staggering. Though there were no tiles this time, no ancient pottery to break her fall – It all played out the same. Dead leaves whipped out from under her foot and she fell back, landing face first on the path. Revan staggered back, knowing full well what was coming next.

He began to walk away, though he was unable to take his eyes off the body. His breathing ragged, he reached up to feel the wound on his arm, only to find his sleeve still intact, and the same grizzly scar where it had always been.

Slowly, what was once his mother lifted herself up on her forearms, blood dripping from her face. She turned slowly to face him, and he winced as he saw a face that had been burned into his dreams every night. What was once a pretty face was now sliding off of the skull, lacerated and opened up, as if you were to peel off a beauty mask.

As a piece of skin the size of his hand fell to the path, Revan turned to keep running. A log loomed a few metres in front of him, propped up on a lichen-eaten stone. That same log, that same boulder. Every time. He slowed to a stop and sank to his knees, leaning his head against the rotten wood as his vision blurred from his fear and tears, his hands covered in the blood only he could see. 'Please,' he begged the ether, 'let me bring them back. Take me back, I can do something to stop it this time. I promise.'

He sat there for a few minutes, awaiting another memory to assault him, but it never came. He stood and turned to see his mother had disappeared, replaced with silence. The wind blew through the tunnel of trees, urging him towards the place he had once called home.

Body shaking, he climbed over the log and began walking briskly down the path once more, looking warily from side to side. He tried to get his emotions back in check, so he could use his power, but he found himself completely unable to. He hadn't been so useless for years. Not since—

He closed his eyes for a moment, breathing deeply. But as he opened them, the figure of a young girl stood before him, her features shrouded in shadow, arms outstretched as if to catch him. He slipped as he lurched backwards, almost losing his balance on the autumnal leaves.

'Get away from me!' Revan yelled, shaking his head and backing away, 'you're not real.'

'That's so mean,' the girl said, 'you act like you haven't seen me in years.'

'I haven't!' Revan snapped, 'Emily is dead, you're just a memory. A nightmare. So is she.' The wind stopped, then, leaving him perfectly alone, with only this grisly apparition for company.

The figure stepped out into a ray of moonlight, and Revan turned away as his little sister's face smiled over at him. She was still wearing that pretty floral dress she had that day, though the once pale blue was mostly red, now. He tried to reach out once more with his mind, and finally pierced through as though a veil had suddenly lifted. He found her mind, that familiar mind he hadn't sensed for twelve years.

Emily stepped towards him and wrapped him up in the biggest hug her little arms could muster, her long brown hair filling his vision as she buried her head into his shoulder. 'It wasn't your fault, Revan.'

She released him and he sank to the floor, tears filling his eyes and beginning to trickle down his face as he lay back against the side of the log. He lifted a hand and placed it against her cheek. She smiled and leaned against it, no sign of anger or regret in her eyes.

Revan watched as her face started to pale, her left eye darkening. Even in the dim moonlight he could see the blood running down her cheek, down her neck, the branch from the ancient birch piercing through her skull where her eye should have been.

He started sobbing, slumping back to sit on the grass and leaves. 'I never should have scared you like that. If only ... if only I could have controlled these worthless mind powers. You could have ... you'd still be ...'

He trailed off, breaking down into heaving sobs. Emily stepped away from him, that smile still on her face. 'I'm just a memory, remember. None of this was your fault.'

A cool wind swirled through the woods, and by the time Revan looked up, Emily was gone. He opened his eyes, saw the lights of his worn-down Land Rover illuminating what was once his childhood home, now a long-since forgotten relic in the woods.

He got out of the car, wiping tears from his eyes. The house had always seemed bigger when he was younger. The old birch tree, too. He grabbed the box from the back seat and walked over to the house.

He cracked open the box and grabbed the bottle stored within. With one last sigh he threw it onto the porch, hearing the glass shatter open and the petrol within soak into the wood, his eyes already turned back to the contents of the box.

He grabbed the matches and the second bottle and closed the box, kicking it to the side. He lit the match and threw it to the porch, not even waiting for it to catch before walking towards the old birch.

He placed a hand against the knotted bark, closing his eyes a moment. He took a deep breath and brought his hand back, swinging the bottle at the trunk. He had to hit it a couple of times before it shattered, cutting his hands, but he didn't care. Alcohol this time soaked the wood, and he struck a match to hold against the bark. As the tree caught, he stepped back, throwing the matchbox down at his feet as he walked back to his car.

Once he was a safe distance away, he turned to watch the old house burn, and that awful tree along with it. No more dreams. No more memories. It was time to move forward, take a step outside of those infinite trees.

As he drove away, past that old boulder with the log on top of it he reached out with his mind one last time. And there, for nothing but the briefest of moments, he felt his sister's thoughts. Felt her smile.

RESIDENTS OF A BATHROOM

Jack Carter

The human drags his sorry-to-be-alive body out of bed and into the bathroom. The residents of the bathroom shudder as the human starts to strip off his clothes.

'Not again, I can't do this, I don't want these eyes and mouth anymore!' the soap screams.

'We don't get a choice, Pilchard, hold yourself together man,' the shampoo commands from the top ledge.

'Easy for you to say, Larry, you only squirt into his hands and watch your lavender flavoured piss get massaged through his hair. Here he comes!' says the toothbrush.

The human opens the shower door, turns on a hot waterfall, steps under the hot running water and grabs the soap. The soap, crying, loses his top surface as he is rubbed over the entirety of the human's pitted skin.

The shampoo is left only having to spectate once more. 'Be stoic, Pilchard, this is what you were born to do.'

The towel watches on, hoping that Pilchard slips into every gap and crack. 'Wait, wait, you're not done yet, go back. Pilchard, what about his crack?' the towel screams.

The human places the violated soap back on the rack. Pilchard's body lies dead still in shock, murmuring, 'Mummy, please.' The human's hands wrap around the toothbrush and the toothpaste.

'Remember, Colgate, keep your bristles stiff, relax your breathing and, as we trained, reach for those hard-to-reach places,' the toothpaste coaches the toothbrush as a part of his insides vomit on to Colgate's face.

'Yeah, I'll try, ya slimy lump of fluoride; even though I'm completely paralysed like everyone else in this torture chamber. Oh, how pleasant—pizza.' Colgate grates back and forth over the human's decay, picking out decomposing lumps with his face, while the giant hums 'American Pie'.

'Straighten up, Colgate, you're leaving too much behind—breathe—focus—relax,' says the toothpaste.

A voice bellows from near the human's tonsils. 'Have you ever dragged your face across a coral reef and eaten dog shit at the same time?'

The toothpaste replies, 'No.'

'Then shut unghdkf.'

The shampoo looks down and says to the soap, 'Pilchard, it's ok now, it's over.'

'Oh yeah? How do you know he doesn't have to shave?' Pilchard manages to squeeze out through his running tears.

'I didn't think of that. Fingers crossed, my son,' answers the shampoo.

Colgate gets his five-second rinse under the showerhead and is placed back on the rack next to the toothpaste. The toothpaste doesn't make a sound and the toothbrush watches on as the human has his final rinse.

'I'm not doing this, no way. It's one thing using dog poo as a metaphor, but I'm in line for a real choc dip,' says the towel.

'You have nothing to complain about,' says the toilet. 'Have a look at the pieces of toilet paper, all lined up and ready for execution by being smeared with shit and then drowned with no burial or relations to say goodbye, whilst their cousins become books, wallpaper or aeroplanes. Both you and I get washed, not regularly, but we do. Now take that shit and own it, do it for the paper!'

The human turns off the shower's valves and opens the glass door. The towel doesn't move an inch. 'Maybe I'll get lucky, he doesn't always go in there,' says the towel.

'That's it, positive thinking,' says the toilet.

The human squashes the bathmat.

'Oh yeah, there's some soiled foulage in there,' the bathmat reports.

The towel is taken off the rack and closes his eyes and mouth. The human starts drying his hair, moving down to the face. The human uses the towel as a two-man saw across his back. On to a quick rubbing of the tackle. The human then moves down to his ankles. The towel's mouth relaxes with a smile, and he opens his eyes. The human works up to his knees, to the thighs and follows with a light drying of the outside of his cheeks.

The towel returns to the rack. 'I thought I was in for it.'

The human moves to view his reflection in the mirror and doubles back to the towel. He grabs a fist full of the towel's face and scours deep into his hidden soiled foulage. The human releases the freshly painted towel and walks out of the bathroom.

'Are you okay ...?' asks the toilet.

The room falls silent, as they hear the screams coming from the undies' drawer.

TRAINS OF THOUGHT

Reordan James Carey

STATION

There was an old station that sat in my head ...
Its derelict platforms a dark, lingered stain.
Though dark tiles untrodden lined walkways all dead,
The rails still bustled with thousands of trains.

There were old ticket stubs turned to dust on the benches,
A book full of sketches that mould made unfair.
The drip of *Decay* as it ran through the trenches
Where nobody else breathed the wet, stagnant air.

There I tip-toed the scuffed yellow line on the floor
And stared blankly, through steam, at trains as they stopped.
I watched one called *Desire* that opened its doors
But it was no Passion, so my faint smile dropped.

There were trains I rode often, and more if I counted
The brief trips on *Whimsy* I took every day.
They looped back to the platform, the voyage surmounted
By that old train called *Memory*, that slipped all away.

There were trains that took aeons to return to the station
And ones, despite effort, turned to rust in the dark.
The first, trains like *Innocence* and *Inspiration*,
The other, *Cold Dread*, that would never embark.

Their engines unmanned, though their carriages, beckoned
By *Frenzied* timetables, old *Rumour* let rot.
Like *Lust*, which was said arrived each seven seconds
Though the platform sat empty more often than not.

There a screech as I swayed by the departure board.
A passenger poised as *Purpose* passed by.
A train called *Apathy*, that I just ignored.
A solo conductor with no boarding cry.

There is one train I'll wait for, its bright cloud of steam
Will sing the old station to sound, sleeping *Sorrow*.
I'll step over yellow, to the train that's called *Dream*,
And trundle away down the tracks to *Tomorrow*.

MAINLINE

Thunder, old rolling stock, brake with your cries.
Scream out exertions and rattle the ties.
Tracks that have bled
Through the white gravel bed,
Tinged pagan purple by hedonist skies.

Twist now, old loco, tear into the dark.
Shovel old memories into the sparks.
Hollow shell filled

By the pressure you build
That whistles your worries away to the larks.
Follow, old tender, black soot a' blowing,
Paint night the tunnels and hide where you're going.
Loosing the wheels
As the firebox squeals
And dusts everything, like a seed meant for sowing.

Hold me, old wagon, as I break away
Through the cargo entrusted the previous day.
Sleep, calm and hale
Amidst the night mail
Riding the dream train and hoping to stay.

Siding

There's a young man, that stands in a cornfield
With a smoke figured hand 'bove his eyes
And he glares through the unlight of all three new moons,
For tonight is the night he will die
And he wonders if he should be watching,
The train whose engine passes by.

There's a cow that can speak in the barnyard
And a tree clothed with only one leaf
And the young man, that steps through the barred iron fence
For tonight he is playing the thief
And the tree he'll be leaving is leafless
And the cow he'll be leaving as beef.

There's a drip from the flesh as he scurries
A dark stain that runs slick cross his hands
And he lays it to rest in incoherent streams
For tonight it ignores his demands
And the cow sings from under the water
And the young man just listens and stands.

There's a snap from the bones of the forest
And a crack as his body capsizes
And the rifle that's pushed 'gainst the hole in his chest
For tonight he runs out of disguises
And the rifleman leaves him a' rotting
And the young man on dying ...
arises.

DEAD-END RAIL

See a door in a tree that is woven of wood,
But not from the wood of the tree as it should,
And a door knocker made of a metal that shouldn't be found in
the forest at all.
Go on, enter space that's far bigger inside
Than the bark of one oak tree could ever abide
And a corridor crafted of shifting stone that's unstable and yet
never falls.

Pitch headfirst down a slide that is shaped from the stone,
Feel it batter your flesh and yet shatter no bones,
And careen through a bustling necropolis, watching the undead
that lived there of yore.
Feel the cool wind rush past in the dark, stale air

And return the old cavern's bright, yellow-eyed stare
As you hurtle through bedrock, till tunnels run out, at the end
on a dusty wood floor.

All clocks stopped and silent, thirteenth of July
The year of destruction, a quarter past five,
The third, final visit, the date still the same, if you are to believe
what you've read.
Buy a ticket with money you do not possess,
Follow friends from the past in all manner of dress
And sit in a lawn chair, eyes on the compere who is someone you
know to be dead.

A creak from the stage, then you're one with the fray
As the red curtains open upon *Cabaret*
And a performance erupts that's so brilliant it leaves you the
moment it enters your brain.
Then break down in tears when it comes to its end,
And the hall falls apart 'round your departed friend,
Feel the space coalesce in a flurry of form, till you're sitting once
more on a train.

TERMINUS

Dense steam unfurling.
Watered light through concrete clouds.
Hot coffee, cold sweat.

WHAT KEEPS ME UP AT NIGHT

Sofia Abbey

CHARACTERS
ASH
ASH AS LADY MACBETH
ASH ON LAPTOP
ASH GRAFFITIING
ASH DANCING
ASH THROWING TANTRUM

The stage is a bed. Strewn on the bed are three pillows, delicate and pretty. Nailed in the middle of the wall, a meter from the floor is a bedside table. There are six lights positioned around the space, all switched off. Peeping from above is a giant spotlight. Fairy lights frost the cornices of the room. A disco ball dangles from the ceiling's centre. A cloud-shaped night light is plugged into the wall. Swinging low in the corner is a dingy light. The sixth light is a lamp perched on the bedside table. Soothing music plays in the background. A soft glow filters from nowhere illuminating six duvets. They are strewn across the bed, concealing six figures beneath. The duvet closest to the bedside table is draped over 18-year-old ASH. She tosses and turns. After a moment, she bolts upright, revealing her mismatched pyjamas. The music dies but the soft glow remains. She turns on the bedside lamp and faces the audience.

ASH (*to audience*)
You know that moment when you're finally drifting off to sleep and then you think of the most humiliating moment of your life?

> (ASH *turns off the lamp. She fumbles around in search of comfort.* ASH *groans. She switches the lamp back on and shuffles towards the audience, duvet wrapped around her.*)

I suppose you want to know what it is. People always want to know. It's a question that pops up quite a lot. *What's your most embarrassing story? What's the most mortifying thing that's ever happened to you? What's the most shameful thing you've ever done?*

> (*The spotlight turns on, shining on a duvet.* ASH AS LADY MACBETH *rises like the undead. She is dressed in a white gown. The spotlight locks onto her. She behaves eerily.*)

Well, last year, I was in a production of *The Scottish Play*. I was Lady Macbeth.

> (ASH *watches as* ASH AS LADY MACBETH *steps forward, drilling her manic eyes into the audience.* ASH AS LADY MACBETH *recites Lady Macbeth's*

second soliloquy of Act I Scene 5 quietly. ASH speaks over her.)

It was opening night, and my entire family was front and centre. Mum, Dad, my older brother and sister. My stepmum and stepsister. Nan and Pop. Aunt Camille and Uncle Patrick, who I hadn't seen since I was seven. Even pervy cousin Edgar, who was studying at NIDA, made an appearance. Everyone. In the same room. It was unheard of. Anyway, so there I was, nailing every fucking line ...

(ASH gestures towards ASH AS LADY MACBETH. With an air of cockiness, ASH mouths along.)

ASH AS LADY MACBETH
The raven himself is hoarse
That croaks the fatal entrance of Duncan
Under my battlements. Come, you spirits

ASH (*to audience*)
The audience was mesmerized. Four hundred people sitting in utter stillness. I can't explain it. It was like, even the smallest movement would shatter the fantasy.

ASH AS LADY MACBETH
That tend on mortal thoughts, unsex me here,
And fill me from the crown to the toe top-full

ASH (*to audience*)
And then...

(ASH *pulls her duvet over herself.*)

I can't even say it.

ASH AS LADY MACBETH

Of direst cruelty! make thick—

(ASH AS LADY MACBETH *pauses. She appears alarmed.*)

Make thick my ...

(ASH AS LADY MACBETH *opens and closes her mouth. She sucks in a breath and freezes. With haste, she crawls back underneath her duvet. The spotlight switches off. ASH uncovers herself from her duvet.*)

ASH (*to audience*)

Yeah.

(*The figures, still veiled beneath the blankets, sit behind ASH in a line and drag a finger up and down each other's spines. ASH shivers.*)

I remember at that moment I wanted to crawl inside a hole and die. Dramatic, I know. But the feeling ... Embarrassment is powerful. It consumes your mind until there is nothing left.

Silence.

Yet, at the same time, so many thoughts—*too many thoughts*—race inside your head.

> (ASH *stands. The veiled figures, giggling and whispering, chase her.*)

They're laughing at me. They're recording me. They're talking about me. I will never hear the end of it. This will haunt me forever. It will never go away. They saw everything. Every mistake, all the hesitation and second-guessing. They watched me fall. I am a failure. I am a joke. I am an embarrassment.

> (*The veiled figures suffocate* ASH.)

Then the shame consumes your body. There is a sensory overload.

> (ASH *escapes. The figures smother one another. The sound of flames, the sound of nipping, the sound of sandpaper, the sound of slamming, the sound of plummeting and pleading marinate and play in the background.*)

Your cheeks are lit aflame. The air nips the nape of your neck. Inside your mouth is like sandpaper. Your throat is choking itself. Something slams into your chest. Your stomach plummets and the entire time you are begging, pleading your feet to move. But you're consumed. And you think nothing could possibly end it except, perhaps, sudden death.

(*The veiled figures stop. They separate and lie on the floor, resting.*)

Beat.

(ASH *smirks.*)

There is something so arousing about shame. When someone offers to share their shameful little secret or story, you morph into the Cheshire Cat.

(ASH *imitates the Cheshire Cat's smile. Her eyes sparkle. She leans in, sinisterly.*)

And there are different types of shame too. Not everyone thinks the same thing is scandalous, that's why nudists exist. So, depending on what you're into, your reaction will vary from ...

(ASH *takes on a nihilistic persona.*)

... Wow. No way. Wow ... to ...

(ASH *takes on a passionate, giddy persona.*)

Stop! No. Stop. You did not. You did not! How? I could never. I would have died.

(ASH *resumes usual demeanour.*)

Humiliation comes in various forms. There's the taboo. Which nobody loves. But it is the most fascinating. It's like seeing—

> (*The cloud-shaped night light switches on. ASH ON LAPTOP peeks from beneath a blanket. She is young, a laptop settled in her lap. She is completely engrossed with what is on screen. ASH notices and approaches. She slithers under ASH ON LAPTOP's blanket and peers over her shoulder at the screen. ASH winces and eyes the audience.*)

Everyone my age loves second-hand embarrassment. You can tell because Netflix is so successful.

> *Beat.*

Once, when I was little, I watched this terrible film. It was about a schoolgirl who was obsessed with this guy in the grade above. And throughout the film she does all these dumb things to impress him. But of course, he's completely oblivious. So, eventually she devises this plan to walk past him at lunch time, fill up her water bottle and *accidentally* spill it down her shirt. All with the sex appeal of Megan Fox. On her first attempt, he doesn't even look at her.

> (*ASH ON LAPTOP's eyes dart between the screen, the floor and the roof.*)

So, she does it again, in the same lunch break. Still doesn't work. So, she does it again. She performs her little show six times. And on the seventh lap around, she slips over and whacks her jaw on the metal seat he's sitting on.

(ASH ON LAPTOP *slams the computer shut and pulls the blanket so it swallows her. The night light switches off.* ASH *withdraws, cringing.*)

I always need to shower or something when I watch or read stuff like that. I coil up. Showering is like my way of unwinding. So many people find second-hand embarrassment funny though. I don't get it.

(*Dance music plays. The disco ball spins, flashing fluorescent lights.* ASH DANCING *shimmies from beneath a blanket. She's in a party dress.* ASH DANCING *spins* ASH *around. They dance together.*)

I also don't get when my friends show me videos of themselves being *quirky* or *cool.* I think that's so embarrassing. But they act almost proud. When old videos of me trying to be cool pop up, I delete them straight away. Most of them I don't watch. Don't need to. It's always me doing the splits. Or attempting to.

(ASH DANCING *blows a kiss at* ASH. ASH *pauses, suddenly uncomfortable. She avoids eye contact with* ASH DANCING *and tries to walk away.* ASH DANCING *follows her.*)

ASH DANCING

I used to do gymnastics when I was five. Watch this, watch this!

(ASH DANCING *does the splits.*)

Are you filming? You should. Film it and send it to me.

ASH

Only if you go away.

ASH DANCING

Alrighty.

> (ASH, *flashing the audience an apologetic look, guides* ASH DANCING *back under the blanket. The music and disco ball stop.*)

ASH (*to audience*)

In 40 years it'll be retro, and my grandkids will think I was hilarious. But right now, it's cringey.

(ASH *ponders.*)

Hmmm ... what are other kinds of embarrassment? Oh! There's the kind you feel when you stoop to a low point. When you forget who you are for a hot second and become an imposter. When you mutate into someone else's version of you to please or impress or sabotage.

(*The dingy light flickers on.* ASH GRAFFITIING *creeps out from beneath a duvet. She is dressed in a school uniform.* ASH GRAFFITIING *cautiously stands and approaches a wall, checking over her shoulder.* ASH *looks the other way.*)

It's difficult to admit you're weak. But the initial denial allows time for the humiliation to fester and eventually grows so monstrous that you can no longer look at yourself through rose-coloured glasses.

(ASH GRAFFITIING *whips out her pen and begins to scribble on the wall.* ASH *claps once.* ASH GRAFFITIING *jumps. She races back and hides under the blanket. The dingy light flickers off.*)

Losing control of your emotions is a big one for me. When I was little, kids would laugh at you if you cried or screamed or simply reacted. *It's not a big deal. You're a sook.* Now, expressing any sort of emotion is encouraged. *You owe it to yourself to be honest. There's a reason you're feeling this way.* And that's cool. We love progression.

(*The fairy lights come to life.* ASH THROWING TANTRUM *rips off the blanket she is hidden beneath. She's dressed in daywear. She marches around the room, muttering to herself.*)

But there's something about anger, about being angry that's ...

(ASH THROWING TANTRUM *screams and throws a pillow across the room. ASH cringes then bursts out laughing.*)

And seeing someone angry; comedy gold.

(ASH THROWING TANTRUM *dives onto the ground beside her duvet. She pulls it over herself. The fairy lights go out. The soothing music plays. ASH drags her own duvet back to the bedside table and wriggles underneath. She takes a pillow and fluffs it.*)

I believed once that society manipulated people into talking about their shame. So, they had a weakness to exploit. But if you think about it ... people unprompted and willingly share their embarrassing story. There are BuzzFeed articles and Reddit threads. Magazine columns. TV shows. Movies. Even t-shirts. All devoted to someone's embarrassing story. Why do people like to talk about their shame?

Beat.

At this rate I'll never fall asleep. Alright, goodnight.

(ASH *turns off the lamp. The soft glow vanishes. There is complete darkness. The soothing music plays for a moment before it is disrupted by the sound of a door slamming. The fairy lights turn on. One of the figures is missing. ASH curses.*)

ASH (*to audience*)

What now?

ANONYMOUS (*offstage*)
Can you just shut up and leave me alone?

(ASH *stills.*)

No! Just fuck off.

(ANONYMOUS *is revealed to be* ASH THROWING
TANTRUM. *She storms onstage glaring at someone
offstage.* ASH *tosses the duvet and stands up.*)

I hate you!

(ASH, *frightened, speaks to* ASH THROWING
TANTRUM. ASH THROWING TANTRUM
is oblivious.)

ASH

Shhh. Don't say that.

ASH THROWING TANTRUM
I wish you would just fucking die!

ASH

Shut up! I don't wish that.

(ASH THROWING TANTRUM *thunders across the bed, muttering to herself. ASH follows her, tugging at her arm.*)

ASH THROWING TANTRUM

Fuckwit.

ASH

Stop!

(ASH THROWING TANTRUM *shakes ASH off and hurls the pillows around the room. The dingy light flickers on. ASH GRAFFITIING tiptoes out from her duvet. She sneaks back to the wall she was scribbling on. She looks around before pulling out her marker. She writes 'BELLA HAS CHLAMYDIA'. ASH sees and races over, snatching the marker off her and throwing it away.*)

Stop writing that.

(ASH GRAFFITIING *pulls out another marker and continues writing vulgar things. ASH glances between the audience and ASH GRAFFITIING.*)

I would never write that.

(*The disco ball spins, flashing fluorescent lights. Party music plays. ASH DANCING shimmies out from beneath her duvet. Her make-up is messy. Her dress is slipping off her shoulder. She dances drunkenly. She approaches* ASH.)

ASH DANCING

Hey!

(ASH *tries to avoid her.* ASH DANCING *swings her round.*)

ASH

No!

ASH DANCING

Hey! Watch this!

(ASH DANCING *staggers, almost pulling* ASH *down with her.* ASH DANCING *laughs it off.*)

I used to do gymnastics when I was five. Can you film me? Please film me! I want to show you something.

(ASH DANCING *sways dangerously. Her breast peeps out.* ASH *fixes* ASH DANCING's *dress.* ASH *refuses to look at the audience. She is beyond mortified.*)

ASH DANCING

Don't stop recording! I haven't even done the best part.

(ASH DANCING *vomits all over* ASH. ASH *screams, drowning out the music.* ASH DANCING *drops to the floor and continues vomiting.* ASH *uses* ASH DANCING's *discarded duvet to clean herself off. The cloud-shaped night light switches on.* ASH ON LAPTOP *peers from beneath a blanket. She is engrossed with the screen. Moaning noises play.* ASH *hears and whips towards* ASH ON LAPTOP. *She sprints over to her.* ASH ON LAPTOP *unzips her pants.* ASH *slams the laptop shut and throws the blanket over* ASH ON LAPTOP. *The moaning can still be heard.*)

ASH

Stop it! Stop it!

(ASH *tries to unplug the night light. It does not budge.*)

Come on. Come on.

(*She runs over to the lamp and switches it on. She turns to see* ASH THROWING A TANTRUM, ASH GRAFFITIING, ASH DANCING *and* ASH ON LAPTOP *have not disappeared.* ASH *flicks it on and off in frustration.*)

No! Please. Stop. Fucking stop!

(ASH *grabs a pillow and swings it at the lamp. It breaks. All the lights shatter. The moaning and the music die. There is a tense minute of silence and darkness. Suddenly, the spotlight pierces through, a pale red. It illuminates the stage. There is only ASH, a pillow and a single duvet on the bed. She plucks the duvet off the floor, unveiling ASH AS LADY MACBETH. She walks towards the audience, reciting Lady Macbeth's second soliloquy of Act I Scene 5.)*

ASH AS LADY MACBETH

The raven himself is hoarse
That croaks the fatal entrance of Duncan
Under my battlements. Come, you spirits

ASH (*to audience*)

I was a pillar of power. The audience was under my command.

ASH AS LADY MACBETH

That tend on mortal thoughts, unsex me here,

ASH (*to audience*)

I was not bound to my body, but suspended above, hearing myself articulate every word with precision. Feeling the tension as I teased and enticed with the right amount of pause. Seeing as I glided across the stage. Then ...

ASH AS LADY MACBETH

And fill me from the crown to the toe top-full
Of direst cruelty! make thick—

ASH (*to audience*)
... back inside my body I went. And I could feel ... warmth. Something slithered down my leg.

ASH AS LADY MACBETH
Make thick my ...

ASH (*to audience*)
My period. And just like that, I was no longer Lady Macbeth. I was no longer on stage. I was no longer in control. I was consumed.

> (ASH AS LADY MACBETH *sucks in a breath. She opens and closes her mouth. After an awkward pause, she darts off stage. The spotlight fades to white. It shines solely on* ASH.)

My family said nothing. Did nothing. No mockery or coddling. No ice cream. I bawled the whole way home and they talked about the weather. I went to the shops with Mum, and we bumped into a family friend who asked how the play went. Mum acted confused. *What play?* I try to pretend it didn't happen too. But it did.

> (ASH *sits on the ground and fluffs the pillow. She yawns and she drags the abandoned duvet over herself.*)

It's funny how when you're little, you're afraid to fall asleep. What if you have a nightmare? But as I've grown up, I don't need to be asleep.

(ASH *puts her head on the pillow and closes her eyes. The spotlight fades.*)

My thoughts are what terrorise me now.

RECURRENCE

Drake Esparon

Noah awoke to the smell of coffee, the strong scent wafting in through the open tent flap. He breathed deeply, slowly got up from his bedroll and exited the tent. He'd slept in his guard uniform, straightening it as he walked towards the fire in the centre of the circle of tents. One of his fellow guards was crouched over the pot of coffee. Without saying anything, Noah sat beside the fire and poured himself a mug, enjoying the aroma as he drank the coffee. *Hopefully I can find the herb today, I'm sure boneset is found in this region,* he thought. *The sooner the mayor's fever subsides, the better. Last I saw him he was on death's door.*

'I am going to resume the search today,' he said to the guardsman.

'I wish you good hunting,' came the monotone reply.

Noah tipped the dregs of his coffee into the fire, stood, and made his way to the edge of the encampment.

Looking at the two trails before him, Noah opted for the right path, where he knew there were mushrooms whose stems were as tall as the pines, the glowing gills of which mingled their light with the dappled sun filtering through the pine needles, and small endemic life darting through the colourful foliage to create a breathtaking spectacle.

Without hesitation, his steps confident and steady, he walked the dirt path, searching the forest floor for the herb that matched the description he'd been given. He searched for a short time, wandering from the path to find amaranth and ghoul's bane, but not the purple boneset required to break the mayor's fever.

Returning to the path now, he was not alone. He came to a halt, looking at the thin silhouette of a man that stood ten feet away. As the silhouette stepped from shadow, Noah realised this wasn't a man at all—at least, not anymore. The skeleton started walking towards him, its feet clacking against the stony forest floor. Noah's experience herding drunkards had left him woefully unprepared for a battle with the undead... Steeling himself, Noah drew his sword from his sheath and swung it at the skeleton's neck, feeling the bone cleave beneath the blade as it collided. His aim was true, as with a thunk the skeleton's head fell to the ground and its body crumbled onto the mossy forest floor. Noah panted in relief, looking triumphantly at the pile of bones, then sheathed his sword proudly. *Now, if only I can find that blasted boneset for the mayor, I might finally make Captain one day.* Grinning widely at the thought, Noah got going again.

He continued his search, coming upon a flash of purple through the dense foliage up ahead. Delighted, he moved towards it at pace, before scrambling back as he realised it was not at all what he was looking for, but a purple crest adorning the helmet of an enormous skeleton as it bounded towards him, its armour clattering and clanking, metal on bone.

'By the gods!' Noah exclaimed as he turned and ran towards the campsite, his grin long gone. Glancing back he realised the armoured skeleton was gaining ground. Gritting his teeth, Noah put all thoughts of conserving stamina out of his mind as he strained to run even faster. Not paying any attention to the terrain, he felt his foot catch on a root and collided face first with the leafy dirt. Dazed, he stood up to see the skeleton approaching, brandishing its sword over its head. Before he could unsheathe his sword, the skeleton brought its weapon down and there was a brief flash of anxiety before a heavy fog descended, and his vision faded to black.

Having trouble killing skeletons? Remember they are weak to blunt force damage.

With a start, Noah woke, his hands going straight to his neck to check it was still intact. *Was that a nightmare?* He tried to calm his breathing, then smelt the familiar aroma of coffee drawing his attention to his surroundings. *Wasn't I in a tent?* He looked around the log cabin, not recognising it. He raised himself from his bedroll and walked out of the cabin to see his fellow guardsman crouched over a pot of coffee boiling above a campfire. Unsure, he sat beside the fire, drew a mug of coffee and focused on the strong taste. *Well, I'm definitely awake,* he thought, as the heat from the bitter coffee welled in his stomach. Shoving the disturbing dream out of his mind, he got up and prepared to search for the boneset again.

'I'm going to see if I can find that herb now,' Noah said to the guardsman, feeling strange as he did.

'I wish you good hunting,' came the monotone reply.

The first thing Noah noticed as he left camp was that the path was a lot more defined than he remembered, and the mushrooms which he could have sworn were tall and thin were large and blocky. From some angles, they could even be mistaken for buildings. Instead of taking the path he took in his dream he decided to take the left route, even though his gut told him otherwise.

He scanned the underbrush for the purple herb, the occasional flash of lavender giving him a sense of false hope. After a while he couldn't shrug off the feeling of familiarity and, recognising a distinct green mushroom with red dots, he realised he was on the original path, halting as he reached the position where he had encountered the first skeleton. He scanned the area, however nothing was there—just the dirt path winding into the distance. But then came a long, drawn-out groan, somewhere close to his right. Turning pale with fear, he saw the horrifying figure of a zombie shambling towards him, bent over, its arms dragging across the floor. He wanted to flee, but felt his feet stick to the ground with a compulsion beyond his control. With trembling hands, he drew his sword against his will—*Why can't I stop?*—and manoeuvred out of the way as the zombie lunged, jaw snapping, teeth gnashing. As the zombie reeled away, Noah brought his blade down on its grisly neck, striking it to the ground. Noah watched it convulse to its death, Noah himself shaken. *I can't feel the compulsion anymore, but by the gods, what came over me?*

Noah headed back to camp. He would return to his search for the boneset later. He needed to consult a map to re-orientate himself. Yet as he walked, the vibrant forest foliage darkened and branches snapped behind him. *What ridiculous game is this?* he wondered, as a larger and more muscular zombie lurched towards him in battered armour, the clanks of its worn-out sword against the mossy rocks causing something within him to stir, compelling him to stay and fight. This time he refused the urge, battling it and the terrain as he ran. But what he had taken to calling *the compulsion* bore down on him with greater force the further he ran, as though a higher entity controlled him, forcing him to stop and face the armoured zombie. An out-of-body experience, Noah's hand drew his sword and his feet posed in a fighting stance. As the zombie approached, Noah launched himself toward it, his sword gliding through the air as he swung at its exposed neck. With a clang the zombie parried his strike. Unwilling to give ground, Noah went on the offensive, the clash of metal against metal resounding throughout the forest.

Attempting a fatal blow, he lunged his sword at the zombie's heart, yet the monstrosity sidestepped the manoeuvre and, using the opening, thrust its sword through Noah's heart. Sharp pain coiled throughout his body, as a thick fog rolled in, subsuming his senses, so that he could barely make out what seemed to be words appearing before his darkening vision.

While zombies are slow, their teeth and claws are poisonous so always carry an antidote.

'Argh...' Noah woke, yelling, his clammy bedsheets clinging to his sweaty torso. He lay there trying to recall the words he saw before he awoke, but all he had was a vague recollection of the word 'zombie'. *I know I died, so how come I'm not dead?* Looking around, he realised he was inside one of the rooms in the barracks. *I'm back at the city?* Out the window he could clearly see the sturdy stone buildings stretching towards the horizon. *Did any of the events in my memory even happen? I have to go find the mayor and see if he is still fever struck, and try to figure out what's going on.*

Getting up from the bed, he smelt the aroma of coffee and noticed he had woken up a guard in an adjacent bed. The guard looked at him bemused before rolling over and going back to sleep. Walking out of the room, Noah saw a guardsman crouched over a pot of coffee in the mess hall. Opting to ignore the coffee, he walked out of the barracks.

'I wish you good hunting,' called the guard in a monotone voice.

Noah proceeded to the mayor's residence at the other side of the city, looking for the tell-tale gargoyles adorning the mansion. Turning a street corner, he did a double take as he saw a flash of giant mushrooms taking the momentary form of buildings. On edge, Noah quickened his pace, now alert to anything out of place. It was early morning—the sun had barely risen, so the streets were near empty, except for a farmer carrying his shovel towards him. Noah prepared to greet the man, however he once again felt the compulsion to draw his sword, his hand moving against his will.

Stop!

His hand clenched the hilt and unsheathed his sword. The farmer stood in disbelief. Noah raised the blade above his head, but just as he was about to strike, he opened his hand for an instant and the sword clattered to the cobblestones. Noah quickly kicked it away. No more! The farmer whacked Noah over the head with his shovel, then bolted around the street corner, shouting, 'Help! This guard tried to kill me!'

A moment later, the current captain of the Guard emerged, the farmer close behind.

'What is the meaning of this? Is it true that you attacked that farmer?' the captain asked, commandingly.

'I didn't, but something else...' Noah stuttered.

'Yes or no, soldier. Did you move to kill that man?'

'I was not myself, Captain. While it is true I raised my sword against him, I was compelled. When I realised what I was doing, I managed to drop my weapon.'

'Realise this—you are suspended. Be thankful that I do not have you arrested.' The captain then turned to assuage the farmer.

Noah retrieved his sword from the ground, briefly catching sight of a black cloak ducking behind a building. It would be a lot harder to find work without his sword. But as he stood, he felt pain in his back, followed by the tip of a dagger protruding from his chest. *At least he'll get some use out of it,* he thought as he fell to the ground, indifferent about his death. *Figures,* Noah thought. As he lay there in a pool of blood and the fog descended to envelope everything, the cityscape distorted, and all that he could see was made up of glowing white lines that moved and pulsated. Noah admired this view for mere seconds before his vision once again faded to black. He was determined to change his fate, resolved to overcome the compulsion. He may have lost his life to it, but it could be resisted, it could be beaten.

I will take control.

Backstabs deal critical damage. Avoid showing your back to the enemy.

EPHEMERA

Adam Brannigan

Toward their own butchery vulture's hiss dreams uncoiling
their last meanings coiling again

half awake,

sliding on our belly the awakened world shatters while
yesterday's winds snore on

we were,

asleep on bones tossing and turning uncomfortable
underneath a witch's pelvic des/ire

awakening,

stretch follows yawn catches the light of our closed eyes
behind scar/red vistas

wondering if,

last night's dreams will become forgotten sounds of
fingernails lactic scars of your belly

wondering if,

blood is enough if blood is enough if *blood* is /ever enough

PEEKING THROUGH THE CURTAIN

Nerina Brassey

It seems bleak looking at the
sheer curtain
Of conditioned commonality.
Peeking in
Like an invader from another
world, searching
For freedom, finding
conformity.

But as I look closer,

men are the ones
conforming, women are the
ones controlling.

Through the sheer curtain

boundaries are strengthened,
patriarchy is strong.

The unwavering gaze from
the unwanted eye,
Is seemingly protected by the
veil.

But still, women are
conditioned to the
perpetuated promise of
freedom.

Through the sheer curtain

it seems like women cease
control.

But as the curtain thickens,

the women remove the veil
of conformity to resume with
the normalcy of everyday life.

The male takes a break, and
the women take the power.
Is it an act of subjugation
or submission that enables
women to take charge of
their dwellings?

As the men mingle outside
their homes, women are
in full control of their own
home.

But what women can freely
do must be done in private.
Always in private.

As I look, I see stylish shoes,
trendy bags, elegant clothes.
I see women having fun,
socialising, dressing up.
I see these women feeling
free, unbound and
playing with one another
These women are enabling,
empowering,
encouraging each other to
take control
within this conventional life.

Step by step.
Freedom is naturally
achieved.
Through the independent
dependence
on men to support and
satisfy the
ruler of the dwelling. To
ensure that
happiness reigns throughout
the public
perception as it does behind
closed doors.

As it is a precise balance of
conformity and

Freedom.

This sheer curtain comes and
goes,

but as it thickens, life never
wanes.

Whether it is from tradition
or respect.

Step by step ...

Women empowering women will continue to remain.

CRAZY SHIT

Natalie Richy

We say we're losing our rights and freedoms,

I remember giving so many away.

Are we dreaming or lost in sleep?

Counting sheep, in sweet ignorance of our fortune.

The Nuevo Mass Awakening

fuels our refusal to be subordinated.

'Next thing they'll knock on the door,' we say,

'Take our rights, our voices away.'

Am I entitled to my choices or have the luck to choose?

Does this make me special, more special than you?

Am I entitled? Not. Thinking on humanity's cost?

A confusing path where our unity be lost.

Just asking, is this where apartheid starts-to-rise-up?

I didn't earn this, born on the right side of luck.

I eat organic food, won't be subjected to lies. No more

Fake News Fake News—Looney Tunes, rather surf the wave dunes.

Calm like a goddess. We cling to our paths,

Sudden flood of choice 'round fear let's do the maths.

Phil's scared of losing control.

Jake's afraid of catching the plague.

Trisha's role to save the soul and

Stace is spaced by being traced.

Nobody wants to put toxins in their body.

Rob thinks it's ALL made up!

I remember at school when we went to the game and a kid

wandered off—

The rest of us were locked down,

no longer allowed to move around.

That was so fucked up.

What do we know 'bout the right way to go? If this is about control,

then dividing us, the oldest trick in the scroll. Dare we look

for teaming, for scheming and for who is deeming what?

Look from whose book comes-forth-the dreaming lot.

Cacophony of voices demand some more, claiming their right

to scratch and gnaw, peek through the window, burst through the door.

Try to claim us, 'till we, its message can't ignore ... the draw of

sirens: luring, streaming, blaming, shaming ... thriving call.

Crazy shit!

and It H-U-R-T-S my ears.

PROGRESSION

Aari Rondo

In torment I stood on the dunes looking to the horizon.

'Is it worth it?

There's a lot of people on one bank.

There's a lot of people getting slammed.

There's a lot of people making it too.

There's still no way it's good enough for this kind of crowd.

The waves have been like this all week.

There's been a crew like this all week too.

What else will they all do?

There is nothing else to do, there's nothing we can do.

This is the new normal, now everyone loves it too.

We started off like this, now it's their turn.

Get out there, it's still worth it.'

THE TOWN

Gia Doe

My mother said it takes a village to raise a child.
Whether that village was big or small, she failed to tell.
The village that raised me was one of discrepancy,
A place disguised as paradise but burdened by circularity.

We grew up safe,
As safe as it could ever be.
Each blinded by the sun and deafened by the water.

Naïve and privileged, rebellious in turn
Our forthcoming was aligned with those who stepped before.

The boys moved in synchronicity with their fathers,
Working in the sun until they were too frail to endure.
While temperate girls wished for small-town lives
With minute careers and mouths to feed.

The lesser ones found a place in hardship and their own upheaval.

The minimal nightlife appearing exhilarating to those
As the moments of exhilaration screamed louder than the mundanity of the day-to-day.

Every so often a calamity shifted perceptions,
Where a friend was stolen from us
Or a contact erased.

The stagnant ones saw a moment of uprising.
A glimpse of what could be
And a hint to what they could become.
But these attitudes only ever lasted the time of the aftershock.
In seconds it seemed we were business as usual,
Numb and amassing the moments that shaped us.

Few saw this village as a ground level,
A place which one could be grown from
But more significantly a place that should be grown out of.

The cycle is embedded in us
As we follow the footsteps of those perceived above
Becoming trapped within our own time warp
A small-town syndrome that endeavoured to vortex us all.

And so some of them went,

But most of them stayed

A struggle on either end

In which the world is within one's grasp but so far from reach

Where the town will most definitely shape you,

But could your being shape the town?

THROUGH THE CRACKS

Roshai Yarrow

I am strong. I am strong? Am I strong?
I stare at her, *at me—those hazel eyes.* I challenge her—
that brown hair... I care for her?—*my freckled nose.*
I can get through this. I've been through worse.
Haven't I?

I am a statistic; I am a survivor of a broken family. I read once, in an article by Parker or someone, that one-in-four children are from a broken family—*check*—and one-in-three of those do not see their other parent often—*check.* But I am not weak; it has built me, made me stronger, made me more resilient, made me more empathetic. *Did it, though?* The article spoke of how it can be damaging for the children—*check*—how it makes them less ambitious—*wrong*. It breaks us first. It confuses us. *But does it?*

I remember the hurt in the faces of my siblings, reflecting my own. My brother and sister would snot-cry when dad drove off.

'See you soon,' he'd say.

We all knew that meant in a few months. We were all children, but I felt responsible for them; the burden of being older. I had to live the aftermath. My mum checked out. She had a lot going on. She was young. She was alone. She was a single mother of four. Verging on poverty. Taking all the handouts we could. Mum would drop my younger sister and me down the street so we could walk the rest of the way to the food bank. We would wait, hand in hand, for our mother and brother to go in ahead. This allowed us to get double the food. I remember the smell, the aroma of all the different breads. The wall along the back would have sesame rolls, sweet icing rolls and freshly baked loaves. In front was the fruits: the bags of oranges and the quartered watermelons, the halved rockmelons and pineapples. The table when you walked in had cereals and rows of stacked tinned foods. They never asked questions, never turned us away. I'm sure they knew. They would just give you a basket and instructions—

'Only one box of cereal, sweetie,' the lady would say, 'one type of bread, two pieces of fruit and up to five tins.'

I collected the food. My sister always begged for sweet rolls, but the last time we got them, instead of the bread, we ended up not having enough bread for lunches—*man, I was hungry.* The lady would nod as we left. She knew. I have no doubt that she knew, but she never stopped us. *Did she know that we were embarrassed?* After all, isn't it expected that your families are fed and clothed, that they have shoes and showers and brushed hair? But what happens when there is no money for food? Or new clothes that fit? Or if your shoes were so small they hurt your feet? Society does not accept or forgive this. It's not tolerated and it's not normal. So yes, she knew and still she didn't stop us. She pitied us. *She saved us.*

Not from everything though. Or everyone.

As I got older, I stopped looking.
If you know, then you know.
But not my brother. My small, sweet baby brother. I would see his little eyes searching, every soccer game, after every goal. He would look back into the crowd looking for him...
'He didn't come?' my brother would say. I'd shake my head, not strong enough to say the word.
I grew older and stopped looking. But my baby brother didn't.
He got older, he remained hopeful. I grew, and so did my resentment towards our father. I watched my brother's innocent eyes in the rearview mirror as I drove him to his formal and still, after all the years, he searched the crowd.
'He didn't come again,' my brother said that day, and I shook my head, frowning into the mirror.

Even then he looked. Hoping for the surprise. *He still hoped.*

We were older and my—*not so little*—brother, dedicated as he was, achieved his biggest dream. *Wrong again, Mr Parker.* There he was with his platoon, marching the oval, in his green uniform. Behind him, the band marched: trumpets blowing, drums banging, feet stomping. My little brother, after weeks of torturous training, was graduating as a member of the Australian Army. The platoon stopped in the middle of the grandstand, filled with the cheering and crying families. There he was, my not so little brother, second to the front, near the left, almost right in front of us. He tried to hide it, but I saw it. *Because I recognise it. Because I always look for it.* He looked directly at me, and I shook my head. In that moment I saw the emotion: hope, devastation, confirmation, and finally, acceptance.

I watched it.

I saw him grow.

He stood taller.

He wasn't letting the absence of his father take his moment.

I was so proud.

My two sisters, my mother and I screamed and cheered louder.

It made us stronger.

It made him stronger.

It made me stronger.

I am strong. I won't be grouped into a statistic. I won't fall through the cracks of society. I won't be damaged. I will be successful. I will be inspirational. I will be a role model.

I stare at myself—*those hazel eyes.* I challenge myself—*that brown hair.* I care for myself—I powder my freckled nose.

I can do this.

'I am strong.'

THE WHITE JACKET EFFECT

Emma Holmes

Hospitality. An industry designed to serve.
You see the shiny tables, the mild glow of the mood
lighting. You see the fancy meal, wear the fancy clothes to
match. You see the server, always smiling, ready at your
beck and call. You see the room of contented diners—
chatting, laughing, drinking, high on life. You pay for the
service; you pay for the food; you expect perfection: 'How
hard is it to get an order right,' right?

Chef, how far on table 45?' asks the new waitress. I don't know her name. Until she's survived a month, I won't bother to learn it.

Chef looks at the dockets lining the pass. I check the dockets over his shoulder.

'I don't have a 45!'

I reach past him and point to a docket about halfway down the rail, 'There it is, boss.' The waitress sighs and gives me a quick, tight-lipped smile. *Disaster averted.* I go back to the eight frypans I'm juggling across the stovetop. *Tea towel in one hand, tongs in the other.* I swap the front pans to the back burners, adding pasta into the pan I'm holding, giving it a final toss before spinning and placing it on the heatproof pad behind me for Chef to plate.

'Hot handle, Chef, she's been in the fire,' I say as I spin back to the stove.

New pan. Garlic. Oil. Chilli. Fire. Go. Tongs in one hand, tea towel in the other.

'Four minutes to the pass on table 18, 52, and 45,' calls Chef across the kitchen.

'Yes, Chef!' choruses the room.

We are an orchestra, Chef our conductor. Each of us has our role: entrees, mains, pastas, pizzas, desserts; even the dishies play their part. Eleven of us in total. We work in synchronisation; not always playing at the same time, but always reading from the same sheet of music; always in time.

Pan. Pasta. Toss. Spin.

'Hot handle, Chef.'

Tongs and tea towel.

Accompanying our orchestral production is the background music of a busy kitchen: the clang of tongs onto metal trays; the thunk of plates hitting the metal benches; the slide of the plates being taken from the other side of the pass; the shuffling of feet, always accompanied by the boisterous 'BEHIND' calls; the crackle of the fire from the stove; the whir of the gas of the fryer; the obnoxious creak of the under-stove-oven door; the soft bubbling from the pot of boiling water; and through it all, the communication from chef to chef, section to section.

Pasta. Sauce. Herbs. Check for seasoning. Toss. Spin.

'Hot! *Fuck!* Yep, Chef, that one's real hot.' I watch the red line form up my arm, parallel to two very similar burns from *yesterday? Day before? Last week? Oh well.*

'You good, Embo?' calls Sam from the pizza section.

I raise my burned arm in response, grinning.

'Tongs and tea towel, dude, shoulda known better.'

He raises his arm to show his scars for the night. It's apparent the pizza oven is biting back tonight as well; his palm is red and already starting to blister.

'Tongs and tea towel,' he says. He knows the story.

Early in my apprenticeship, when I was 17, one of my first chefs would get furious with me if I forgot to have both a tea towel and a pair of tongs with me at any given time.

'TONGS AND TEA TOWEL!' he would yell.

To really drive the point home he started turning the pan handles into the open fire when I wasn't looking, only to turn them back just before I grabbed them with bare hands.

That's how his chef taught him.
It's one way to learn, I suppose.
Pity I'm still burning myself 14 years later.

New pan. Oil. Garlic. Prawns. Fire. Go.
'Um, Chef, table 45 said...' *Oh no.* The new girl is back,
'...they ordered the prawn entrée, not the prawn pasta.'
'You're all fucking IDIOTS!'
I try not to flinch as the plate hits the wall. I knew it was going to be one of these nights when Chef came in carrying the Mt Franklin 'water' bottle. The kitchen is silent for a second. The poor girl is frozen in shock, or maybe fear. Chef grabs his bottle and stalks out of the kitchen. He won't be back tonight. Tomorrow, we will all pretend nothing has happened. *At least he didn't shout much tonight.* I hate the shouting.

Last week he took one of the guys into the coldroom and screamed at him so hard we could hear it from the carpark.
Four hours later when I went down to the entrée section to check on him, poor Aiden was still on edge.
'C'mon, Aido, you made a mistake; he reacted like an arsehole. Don't let him get to you like this.' I nudged his shoulder, trying to cheer him up. His posture had slumped a full foot from his actual height.
'I know, Em, I just feel like such a worthless piece of crap when he yells like that. And I can't do anything; it takes me right back to before my mum left my dad.'
'Fuck him, mate. He's just angry because his wife threatened to leave him if he doesn't stop drinking.'

He looked at me, a resolve in his eyes, pulling himself back to his full height, 'She fucking should,' he declared.

There's my boy.

My mind flashed back a few years to Aiden's first days in the kitchen. He was my first apprentice. Having just turned 15, he carried with him a tough guy bravado that had probably gotten him through his schooling—*would get him through his apprenticeship.* It was only when he spoke about his sisters and his mother, *single mother*, that his face would soften. The kid had been thrust into a 'man of the house' position far too young, yet he was kind and soft. He had a hunger to prove himself and was easily motivated by competition, *same as me.*

I had always been the same. Fuelled by my desire to be better than the next guy, determined to succeed.

Growing up in a house with three brothers, I watched my single mother—married too young and then remarried to a second Mr Wrong not long after—struggle with her independence, struggle with her identity. I swore to myself at a very young age that I would never be dependent on any man. Ever. I WOULD be a strong, independent woman, even if it killed me.

'You need a real man to help you with that, Sis?' my older brother would mock. Too bad if I did need help, now asking was impossible. *Still is.*

It doesn't matter now. Now, I can do anything.

The new girl looks about to cry. I sigh. *Maybe I should have learned her name.*

'Don't stress, hun, let's fix it. What do you need?' I ask.

'Just a prawn entrée please, Chef.'

'Alright, boys, I need one prawn ASAP. If you have one for somewhere else, use that and get another one straight in, ok? How long?' I call. *Shit. Pans. Turn. Lower heat.*

The oven door down in entrée section slams. 'Two minutes to the pass, Chef!'

'Nice one, guys.' I turn back to the waitress. 'Let them know it'll be three minutes, ok?'

'Thanks, Chef.'

'Well, that could have been worse,' says Chris, blowing cigarette smoke past my face.

I angle myself away from the smoke before replying.

'True. It's getting really bad though, he's drinking most nights now, still driving home too.'

'Yeah, I thought he was going to throw the plate at the new girl's head for a second there, poor chick,' says Sam, joining us in our makeshift break area—scattered milk crates for chairs, old tins emptied of their contents for ashtrays.

I yawn, 'Fuck me it's been a long week.'

I haven't had more than four hour's sleep in weeks and it's starting to take a toll.

Sam lights a smoke beside me.

'I thought you quit,' I say, raising an eyebrow.

He shrugs his reply with a nod back towards the kitchen. *Fair call.* I'm once again thankful I never took up smoking.

'What day you up to?' asks Chris. He takes the cigarette out of his mouth long enough to drink from his Redbull.

'Eight. You? Also dude, that shit is poison and it's 11pm.'

'Yes, *Mum*,' he responds with an eye roll, 'But. It's day 12 and we still gotta clean the kitchen, so I need my go-go juice.'

I don't say anything else. Redbull and cigarettes aren't so bad compared to what some of the other boys get into.

A few weeks ago, I walked in on the new grill chef doing cocaine off the shelf in the storeroom. He paused, face halfway to the shelf when I entered the room.

'You want?' he asked, offering me the straw in his hand.

'Nah, man, you know I'm the no drugs kid,' I replied.

'Give it a few more years, you'll cave.'

'Probably not, dude,' I replied, turning to leave the room. *Definitely not.*

'Wait, no drugs? At all? Not even weed? I mean, that's pretty standard, isn't it?'

Is it?

Hospitality. An industry designed to serve.
Just not the people who work in it.
While you treat your families to a Saturday night meal,
our families slowly forget what we look like.

Why do we choose this life?

I have a theory. Formed from 15 years working alongside many different people from many different backgrounds.

—We are all broken.

We are the children of abusive homes, broken homes; we are the introverted, creative types; we are the mentally unsound, the adverse, the oppressed. It's a fate we come to accept, lacking the self-worth to believe we deserve better. Holding our arrogance in front of us, like a shield of honour, while our personal lives fall apart around us.

I'm one of the lucky ones.

While my cuts, my burns, heal to scar tissue—stronger for the pain; for others, all that remains is a gaping wound, left festering.

The green light on my phone flashes with a new notification.

<Missed call>

Scott: WTF Aiden died?

<Missed call>

Scott: U suck

Me: I'm at work... I didn't know... I cant believe it... I thought he was doing good

Scott: Things can change quickly

Me: What happened?

Scott: He committed suicide by the looks of it.

I drop my tongs and tea towel to the bench and make my way out of the kitchen in stunned silence. *Air. I need air.*

The reality of the situation hits me. *Sometimes you make it, sometimes you don't.* While this environment has worked to make me stronger—to set walls so hard around my heart that I am impervious—for some, it's too much. For some, it works only to break them down, leaving them isolated and damaged with no way out. Trapped in their heads.

Where do you go when you can't stand to be with yourself? *You get out.*

Some choose drugs for their escape, only to find themselves waking the same, no better for their high. Still stuck.

Some check out for good; I've seen it too many times.

So get out. Get a different job, right?

For some of us, it's too late. We know the monstrous nature of our captor, yet we stay. It's Stockholm syndrome. We build ourselves into the environment of the kitchen to the point where we are unable to comfortably function outside of it. We are the pair of tongs, without a tea towel, grabbing for the hot handle of the frypan of life, trying not to get burned.

There is a reason chefs and mental asylum patients alike are characterised by their white jackets.
Hospitality: an industry designed to serve.
Order up.

UTOPIA

Hannah Sticklen

From the moment I started that petition in sixth grade, I knew I had a passion for Mother Nature. A hopeful eleven-year-old me started the petition to try and stop the deforestation of the Amazon. I can pinpoint the exact moment when my little world turned upside down. It was on a Wednesday during geography class. While I intently watched a David Attenborough series on the small boxed TV, my heart sank into my stomach. I remember seeing thousands of trees being chopped down. Animals fleeing with fear, eventually stranded with nowhere to go. Mama orangutans struggling to keep themselves alive, let alone their babies. I recall scanning my peers' faces halfway through the documentary and seeing their expressions, similar to mine, shocked. When it ended, there was silence. You could cut the tension with a knife. This was my first experience realising something that makes me feel deeply passionate. It allowed me to use my voice and stand up to create change. My petition had only about thirty scribbled signatures on it. Those thirty signatures may not have made a huge impact in that moment, but they had a huge impact on me. It was the start of a lifelong journey. A journey to self-discovery. A journey to veganism.

In my utopia, there would be no suffering. No suffering to animals, people or the planet. Everything would live in harmony, coexisting with each other. Imagine the world finally being at peace. No hunger, poverty, devastating flooding or heat waves. The list goes on. This may seem like I'm 'dreaming big' for now, but I believe there is hope for a better future as more people turn to a plant-based diet. The earth and human survival will reap the benefits. This concept is also evident in the David Attenborough documentary *A Life on Our Planet*. He has firsthand experience in seeing how much the earth has declined over his sixty years of life.

Sit and imagine this: your entire world stripped away from you in the blink of an eye. Devastation caused by big metal machines driven by humans. The reality is that the livestock sector alone is one of the leading contributors to significant environmental problems happening right now. Since 2011, when I created my petition, 80% of the Brazilian Amazon rainforest has been cut down for cattle ranching and grazing. Soy farming has also been a massive contributor—70 to 75% of soy farming is used for feeding livestock, whereas only 6% is used for direct human consumption. The other 20% or so is converted to soybean oil and used for frying foods, creating biodiesel, and even producing plastic and paint. The deforestation of natural habitats for these farming practices have caused a massive reduction of biodiversity and 'dead zones' of species. This means species that were already on the brink of extinction are now completely gone. Also, the emissions released into the air from agricultural farming are alarming. It is estimated that even if fossil fuels were eliminated immediately, these emissions would still make it impossible to reduce warming to 1.5°C. This extreme heat is causing corals to die, droughts, water shortages, flooding due to rising sea levels, and islands in the South Pacific to disappear completely. In fact, natural disasters have tripled in the last thirty years. This is a concerning statistic, and most of these events are never seen or heard in the media. Especially in recent times, with Covid-19 overruling all. I know it can be hard to stay connected and aware of what is happening around the world, but it is imperative to try, for Earth's sake. This is a very real problem, and it is impacting so many lives! More than 20 million people a year are forced from their homes because of climate change. It will not stop until there is a universal shift.

The quickest and easiest way for these disasters to be eradicated is on a personal and individual level. Looking at what you buy and put on your plate will decrease the demand for livestock. With less land being used for agriculture, it can then be reconfigured to entirely human-edible crops, such as fruits and vegetables. This will allow for an additional 350 million people to be fed. Other parts of this land can also be restored with a rich biodiversity of plants and animals. Restoring natural habitats will help to remove up to 8.1 billion metric tons of carbon dioxide from the atmosphere each year. This change will benefit the planet in more ways than one. It will uplift humanity and bring my visions of an ideal world to life.

However, there is so much uncertainty for our future if the food system doesn't change and the demand for animal-based products increases. By 2050, the demand will be 70% higher than it is now. In turn, this will require an extra 593 million hectares of land. This, in comparison, is the size of two Indias. These statistics terrify me. I think about what the future may look like for my children and my grandchildren. Will they get to see and experience the wonders of the natural world like I did growing up? Will they be able to live without the constant threat of flooding and fires? Will they have the opportunity to encounter an abundance of animals if they become extinct? These are all thoughts that I keep inside because I fear that if I verbalise them, they may come true. It scares me to think that I am even having these thoughts in the first place, but I want to continue to have hope. Hope that through creating awareness, people will become educated and make conscious choices.

The reality of the livestock industry, which leads to the brutality of slaughterhouses, is one of my main reasons for choosing to be vegan. I know that the majority of

people could not step foot inside a dirty abattoir. No one
wants to see or hear the things that go on in there: faeces
on the floor, blood and guts covering the walls, screams
of pain. Just thinking about the smell makes my stomach
turn. However, it is important to get a perspective of what
it is like to work in such a place. I came across a news
article on BBC called 'Confessions of a slaughterhouse
worker'. It explained, through personal experience, the
raw, *harsh* reality of what it was like working in an abattoir.
To survive there, it was necessary to dissociate—learn to
be numb to death and suffering. It's tough emotionally
and physically for the workers when it comes to killing
animals. They must detach from the fear lurking in the
animal's eyes; otherwise, they would be haunted by
nightmares. Even those considered to be 'tough' men.
I believe that as human beings we all have qualities of
empathy and kindness ingrained in us. I could hear the
echoes of sadness and regret as I read their story. It is not
human instinct to kill. Not only do slaughterhouses hurt
animals, they hurt humans too.

When people ask me 'why are you vegan?', I struggle
to put everything into a simple explanation. My response
is normally 'many reasons'. I feel people won't understand
me if I open up and that it will be an invitation for them to
judge me because of the 'vegan' label. People automatically
think you are a rabid vegan, who protests and goes to
extremes. I had an experience recently that brought this
insecurity to life. I was having a friendly conversation with
a guy at a friend's birthday dinner. He was a country boy
and a meat eater. We had been chatting for most of the

night. When it came time to order our meal and I asked for the vegan menu, I saw his perception of me instantly change. His face dropped, he put his guard up and he never spoke to me again. I did not judge him because he was non-vegan, yet he judged me. This man taught me a great lesson. Preconceived ideas can lead to quick judgements. I prefer to live my life a different way: be loud, be bold, but be kind.

To create a movement, it's up to the cumulative effort of all individuals to create change—a concept that has stuck with me, inspired by one of the most influential vegan activists, Earthling Ed. I wholeheartedly believe that if masses of people become open to incorporating plant-based alternatives in their diet, even just a few times a week, we can create change. It is not about being 100% perfect but about being aware. We do not have another decade to spare. The planet and humanity need this shift now. Through my childhood, my personal experiences and education thus far, it is possible to see the light at the end of the tunnel. To see glimpses of my utopia, where harmony flows through all living beings: plants, animals and humans.

Sources

One Green Planet, *Soy consumption and deforestation*, Nadia Schwingle, 2021.

BBC News, *Confessions of a slaughterhouse worker*, 2020.

YouTube, Earthling Ed, *Veganism could save the planet Here's why*, 2021.

Oxfam International, *5 natural disasters that beg for climate action*, 2020.

HOW DARE I CALL MYSELF A WRITER

Dakota Brown

'Every child is an artist. The problem is to
remain an artist once they grow up.'
—Pablo Picasso

My mum thinks I'll become a writer.
She still brings up a short story I wrote in grade
four, where my classmates and myself were
pirates, and the teacher our captain. In those pages we
lived every child's illusion of escapism. We sailed towards

the horizon and reached it. We glowed amidst the sun as she swooped us up in her golden palms and showed us the world waking up. We raced dolphins around Atlantis and danced like nine-year-olds do when they don't have a care in the world. I enabled us to escape; to be happier, freer versions of ourselves that didn't exist within the four walls of the classroom.

I don't even think that short story was an assignment. I guess I wrote because I wanted to, because something in me needed to.

I blush when my mum brings up my pirate fiasco chronicles now, in front of other people or not. Eleven years later and the idea of that story—any mention of it—makes me cringe. My mum doesn't understand why I shut her down when she brings that piece up and I don't think she ever will.

Because, of course, how dare I call myself a writer.

Even though I can't remember grade four that clearly, I know that I didn't blush or cringe, or push away from receiving praise as an author, when I was nine. I ate it up. I stood proudly in front of my classmates, their inquisitive eyes looking up at me, hanging onto every sentence I read from my precious story. I smiled, maybe even smugly, as they applauded my work and asked to hold my tiny publication in their hands. I found delight and contentment in answering their questions, knowing that I had produced something that moved people—even if it was into escapism.

Oh, if I knew. Knew that only six percent of adults end up in the careers they dreamt about as kids. Maybe then I could have better prepared myself for the letdown.

I let people call me a writer. A kid with talent that means something. A creative.

I believed it; I wanted it—until reality hit.

Since then, no one has looked at my work and given feedback that made me want to rip out the identity I had carved for myself, slash it, burn it, and start from scratch. Apart from constructive criticism that I've come to accept every writer must swallow, feedback on my work has otherwise been positive.

So why do I feel like I'm lying by calling myself a writer?

The common notion of being a writer is that we struggle. We don't have a solidified source of income. We work on one manuscript, one screenplay, one idea for months, years, even decades. We pour our entire soul into it, leaving nothing behind in our desire to produce something that someone important believes in and runs with. We lose so much of ourselves in our work, of who we are and who we could have been in another career, only to receive rejections heartbreakingly more often than interest.

And what capacity of the human heart, its willpower and hope, is left standing after that?

This perception of writers isn't one I've made up; it's definitely not one that even crossed my mind at nine. But it's one I've been subconsciously influenced to believe as I've grown up, and, as reality has irked its way into my head.

It's a perception that has evolved from high school teachers cocking their heads and asking what my 'backup plan is' after I stated I was going to be a writer.

It's a perception that has evolved from family friends tentatively avoiding conversation that would trap them into listening to my intangible career plan, and instead waffling on about their own child's dreams of studying medicine.

It's a perception that has evolved from my friends calling my degree a 'marketing' one instead of the 'creative writing' undergraduate that it rightfully is. Whether they forget, or think my degree is less than proper or practical or applicable to real life, I don't know. All I know is how to let their passive judgments slide, and to stop confiding in them my dreams of being a writer.

It's a perception that has evolved from being taught creative writing at university for years, only for those same tutors to hint at how hard it is to become successful in this industry.

It's a perception that has evolved from the government incentivising 'pragmatic' jobs by offering students almost zero debt, whilst doubling the degree price tag for future creatives and art lovers alike.

It's a perception that has evolved from the government ignoring the importance of The Arts and its work in delivering comfort and optimism to millions throughout a worldwide pandemic, and instead utilising this moment to push people into studying careers that the Australian economy *needs*, and not what the individual is passionate about.

The Education Minister, Dan Tehan, put this bluntly when he said: 'It's common sense. If Australia needs more educators, more health professionals and more engineers then we should incentivise students to pursue those careers.'

And so I ask myself, more often each week now:

Why am I studying? What am I even aiming for, as I approach graduation?

'Follow your dreams,' they say.

'But make sure to uphold society's expectations of your contribution to the economy,' they whisper.

So where does that leave me?

Huddled in my room, too scared to ever release my words, reassuring myself that I wasn't meant to write in *this* lifetime. Trying to convince my inner child that although this reality leaves me with a gnawing sense of unfulfillment, I will someday cram this hole with another form of satisfaction, and all will be OK.

So why do I feel like I'm lying by calling myself a writer?

Because, after everything that creatives take on, as the invincibility of being a child—openhearted and unapologetically proud of your work—begins to fade, and realism sets in, shouldn't I still want this?

If I loved writing and knew without a second thought that being a writer was my fate, wouldn't all these obstacles just crumble under my self-assurance?

Perhaps.

And so, how dare I call myself a writer.

What an insult that is to those who have had the power to block out the judgements, the pity, and the ignorance, and make a name for themselves. How can I justify calling myself a writer—even just in my head—when I've spent years spitting on my own dream, morphing myself into someone who is too ashamed to confront all the judgemental comments, and instead back the dreams of her inner child.

'You don't want to live in stress about money, do you?' said an aunty.

'I hope you're not naïve enough to depend on your creative works for a long-term income,' said a hospitality employer.

'You have so much more potential. You're smart—study medicine,' said a family friend.

'You're the first in your family to go to university. Don't you want to make them proud?' said an unwanted opinion from someone close.

It's ironic, really, that this piece is published in a book devoted to recognising new writers, and yet I still feel as though I am the furthest of ever being one. Some would say it's imposter syndrome, that I'm being humble to the point where I can't appreciate my own abilities anymore.

That's not the case.

It's shame.

As much as someone telling me how impressed they were with my work propels me back into the dreamtime state I occupied at nine, this brief euphoria is always overshadowed by reality, and shame. Instead of running with these compliments and encouragements, I dwarf them with disgrace in myself.

Disgrace that *this* is the best I can produce for the world—little words—not scientific developments, medicine or even a steadfast political viewpoint. Disgrace that *this* is the footprint, not a legacy, that I'll leave; a woman who could string a strong sentence together, like that matters.

Disgrace that there's still some desperate part of me, too tiny to even have a voice, clinging to that childhood dream, when in reality I need to let go of it and grow up like my adult peers.

The idea of never returning to my own *Neverland*, where I was a proud, unashamed kid writer, bold in my abilities and star-struck by what the world had to offer, plagues my heart whenever someone asks of my dream career today.

It's hard to describe what it's like dreaming for something so hard as a child, only to grow up and be conditioned into ignoring that inner child's yearning for something more. Despite my cynical view on being a writer today, I've pulled out that little girl—her hope and confidence—as much as I could for this piece, in order to tell my truth.

And to put that truth simply:

You know that weird longing you get once you wake up, that unfulfilled craving to jump right back into a sensational dream despite remembering nothing about it apart from the feeling it gave you?

Same.

I MUST ASK...

Jordan Brennan

What is knowing?

How can we know?

How do we remember?

Where do memories go?

    Is the mind a machine? The ears blow steam as the brain turns over.

Where was your first kiss?

When will be your last?

How comes the future?

Where goes the past?

                         Who can access these archives?

Are we alone in the universe

or is there company?

Could we live in unison?

Would we live in harmony?

             Interstellar neighbours we could grow fond of ...

Who are our creators?

What do we come from?

Evolution is a theory,

not witnessed phenomenon.

How do we know that fossils once breathed the same air as we do?

Where goes our conscience

When we're set in the ground?

What really happens

When eyes aren't around?

Does the world only contain what happens in our current moment?

What's the purpose of endings

if time can't stop?

What exists?

What does not?

Does the simulator become reality if that is the world we've grown in?

Will I find answers

To these questions asked?

Maybe the progression of life

Will see these unmasked.

AWAKEN

Giorgio Alzetta

I'm here because of someone else's dream

No one follows the path of Love directly

Not anymore

The situation of the world (Kali Yuga) won't allow Love easily

You really want Love?

Dig deep so the dirt we came from gets under your nails

And Love will find you

And become your friend

It found me to let me know

The path I follow was anyone's but my higher owns

It revealed the truth through an untruthful image

A family who resembles progress

But disregards all others that aren't kindred

Ignoring the world family!

The Vasudhaiva Kutumbakam!

I don't agree with it

I agree with It!

With Love!

It's all we've got

It's all we've ever had

It's all we will ever have

Awaken from your slumber!

THE LIGHT
OF GRIEF

Ornella Riggio

MONDAY 3 MAY 2021 – LOSS & DENIAL

G et up, get up, get up,' you always told me, in a tone so jovial it would make the Grim Reaper smile. But I died when you did. There's no soul occupying this body, nor do I believe there ever will be.

I got up today because you told me to. I opened the windows in this stale, insipid apartment and the wind barrelled in to fill my lungs with fresh, cold air, as if I had just taken my first breaths in this world. I sat on the unmade bed and glanced at the picture of us on the bedside table in that hideous seashell frame you made me buy. I cracked my first smile in weeks. You loved the ocean, frolicking in the shallows and chasing me through the sand dunes. Your sun-kissed glow overshadowed my pale, awkward self. I love the ocean, not because of the atmosphere, but because it reminds me of you.

I kept my eyes closed for a little longer to escape the unforgiving reality. *Get up, get up, get up.* I had to work today. I had to escape the memories of you that consumed me. I tried to catch my breath. I felt like I had to relearn how to live. I said to myself, 'Ok, let's take it slow.'

Step 1: Brush your teeth.

Step 2: Put on your bra and undies.

Step 3: Put your pants on, one leg at a time.

Step 4: Put your shirt on, one arm at a time.

Step 5: Find your shoes.

Step 6: Walk out the door. Come on, Rose. Walk out the door.

Apprehension crept up my spine when I walked into the chaos at work. I heard nothing but the echo of my breath and anarchy in my heart. Eyes pierced through my phony exterior and I felt naked. Each step was harder to take; I was balancing on a beam, destined to fall. It happened a few weeks ago and though they all knew, no one said anything. They just stared at me like I was a foreign reptile at the zoo.

By some miracle, I made it to my desk. I gazed at the only ray of light that warmed this cold, relentless office and I saw you. I knew you would always be around. I knew you weren't gone. You noticed me and began to walk over;

I felt my heart in my throat. I fixated on you like you were a work of art. You were coming, but you weren't coming fast enough.

'Come here, Helena, come faster, please!' I called, but no matter how fast you walked, you never got to me. I was desperate. I needed to hold you, needed to touch your sun-kissed skin, needed to breathe in your jasmine-scented hair. You were saying something I couldn't comprehend; all I could hear were other voices dulling your sweet tones. I closed my eyes and covered my ears. The sounds were consuming me. When I opened my eyes, I was confronted by panic-riddled reality. Teresa from HR hovered over me.

'Rose, are you ok?'

'She was just there, Teresa. She was there, standing by the light,' I responded.

'Come to my office, dear.'

I followed Teresa to her office. The stale room smelt of three-day-old ham and old coffee.

Coffee. I remembered when we were on a road trip to Sydney, it was probably 5am and the wrinkles between your brows told me you needed caffeine. We stopped in this small town and I ran inside an old, rundown café to buy you possibly the worst coffee in history. You took one sip and spat it out the window. You glared at first, then began to laugh like I'd told a perfect joke. Only you could find the joy in this situation. In any situation, really. That's what I loved most about you.

An echo overwhelmed my thoughts.

'Rose. Rose! Are you listening?'

I snapped back from whatever realm I fell into and focused on Teresa. 'Yes, sorry. I was listening.'

'Why don't you take the rest of the week off? I don't think you're ready to be here just yet.'

'Yeah, sure. Whatever you think is best.'

I don't know if I was ready, Helena. I didn't know if I would ever be ready for real life. Living in the dream of you is more comforting. I glanced at the ray of light on my way out of Teresa's office. You weren't there anymore. But the fact I saw you there made me realise you weren't gone. I knew you wouldn't leave me. I smiled for the second time today as I walked home. I have nothing to worry about, you haven't left me.

FRIDAY 7 MAY 2021 – ANGER

Sweaty palms. I wake up shaking. You haven't called me; you haven't walked into my apartment. You are gone. You are not here, and I don't understand.

I walked around the city today, passing all the stores we used to go to and trying to walk off this unwelcome feeling consuming my soul. Tonight, I'm making your favourite: carbonara. So, I went to the deli you love on Market Street, even though I can't stand the smell of those stinky cheeses. I could tell you hated it, too, by the way your nose would scrunch up as you walked in. I stood in line at the deli waiting for my turn. The old Italian man was working today, and his hair net barely covered his receding, greasy greys combed back into a pathetic version of a rat's tail. His teeth were stained from years of smoking his pipe and cigars. I was so fascinated by the tattoos trickling down his arms to his knuckles I almost missed my number being called.

He snapped at me in his thick Italian accent, 'Lady, what do you want?'

'100g of spicy pancetta, please,' I said.

'Not today, no pancetta.'

'You don't understand, sir. I *need* this specific pancetta. I cannot make my carbonara without it.'

'Not my problem. *Next.*'

The entire world stopped. I felt the rage unbuttoning. I couldn't stop it. I blacked out and caused an unwarranted scene in that homely little deli that would scare the poor Italian man's ancestors. I don't remember exactly what I said, but the rage took over my body and released itself all over the broody man.

When I woke from what felt like an exorcism, I walked out of the deli, horrified with what had transpired. I made my way home, exhausted and embarrassed.

I'm angry, Helena, but not at him. I'm angry at you. I'm angry at God. I'm angry at that disease. You don't understand, I can't do this without you.

FRIDAY 28 MAY 2021 – BARGAINING & DEPRESSION

The rain washes away the little joy hanging onto my heart. I spent the last few weeks living in your wonder, pretending you're here, creating 'what if' scenarios. But as the days of 'what if' pass by, there is only one that painfully sticks ... What if a year ago I'd made you go to the doctors the moment you first felt the pain?

You would still be here today. I could have saved you, but I didn't. It is all my fault. I deserve to feel agonising pain, the same pain I let you feel. I'm not worthy of joy, of love, of the comfort of this bed. My phone rings all day, every day; I refuse to answer unless it's you calling me, you telling me you are here, telling me to breathe, telling me everything is ok. My heart calls for you and receives no answer.

In your last moments on this earth, you told me everything would be ok. But it will never be ok; this pain will never escape my body. You were too valuable to me, Helena. There are so many things I regret not telling you, like how I love the way your chubby cheeks squished your eyes when you smiled. Oh, that smile, full of soul and kindness; full of an abundance of love. That magnetic mystery, people were drawn to you.

It's hard for me to keep writing, I'm weak. Maybe tomorrow will be easier. Maybe not.

SATURDAY 4 SEPTEMBER 2021 – ACCEPTANCE

It's been a long time since I have written about you, Helena. I'm coming to terms with my new reality. I'm stumbling through this new life. Despite missing huge chunks of my heart, the love you left behind has kept me going. Once again, you have been there, pulling me out of the darkness.

You may be gone, Helena, but your soul isn't and I don't think it ever will be. Speaking and writing about you helps. You wouldn't believe the beautiful stories I've heard from your friends and family; I'm in awe of how your life has affected others. Your story isn't finished and I'll make sure it never is.

I wrote you a letter. I hope you like it.

My soulmate, Helena,

Sometimes I think about the nights we would stay up laughing and drinking wine on the roof. You would look me dead in the eyes and tell me how proud you were of me and how people must be jealous of the love we share. I was always under the impression a man was supposed to be my soulmate, but I found you instead. I'm not mad about it, but I'm mad you left me. The bad news is that I'll never get over you, yet this is also the good news. You will live forever in the broken pieces of my heart. Grief is something you never get over. I won't wake up tomorrow thinking I'm ready to move on. It's something that will walk beside me every day. I'll learn to manage it and honour you at the same time. In this pathetic sadness, I'll find comfort in knowing you wouldn't want me to suffer. The only way I can rationalise this loss is knowing you were too good for this world. You were a true angel on Earth who has now returned home. This is not goodbye, Helena. I will see you again.

Until then.
All my love,
Rose.

LYRICS OF LIFE

Shona Marie

Tragedy transpired in a twinkling. Thereafter a flicker of light. At times I wondered, if granted a virtuous wish, might that fateful day have been constructed another way. Most often, I realised not. Because Wilson and I were lovers. We aligned like stars.

Our introduction had been awkward. We sat opposite one another riding our mundane morning train into the city. Wil worked at the city fish markets, driving a forklift. I pushed a steel trolley

around one of the tallest buildings ever constructed—
Riverside, high on level 35. Our offices called for a two-
hour daily train commute. I'd done it because my job had
been important—I was solely responsible for transporting
all communications between the mail room, and a team
of wealthy divorce lawyers. Not that those pompous arses
ever used public transport. More like valet parking. But
hey, I wasn't begrudging. I was indebted to the suburbs—
open roads, clean air, wide spaces, no hype. In fact, I'd
welcomed the peaceful dawn transit with complementary
air conditioning since our summers had begun to boil. Each
season felt warmer than the previous years, so I scoured
special seating arrangements for myself. Stranger's odours
offended me, empty chit chat, unwelcome. Over time,
I'd begun to guard the smooth palms of my hands from
humanity's germs. At times, my feelings were frightful. I
believed my life forever burdened, by recurring thoughts,
melded with an overpowering sense of touch, and smell. I'd
chosen never to share my secret. Because it made me weird,
but I overcame this hardship by wandering the jolting
corridors wearing black, tattered, fish netted, fingerless
gloves. That way, I could clutch the train's rubber hand
grips without exposing my foibles. 'Just finished ladies'
night shift,' a pimpled prick once asked me. 'Dude, don't
go there!' I'd hissed. As luck had it, he gave me the bird
and disappeared. After that, my mitts became my faith.
Hidden hands divided me from the dorks, and the dirt,
and were particularly helpful when sidestepping others,
during frequent and unexpected track nudges. Eventually,

I'd stumble upon an empty seat, beneath one of the few, functioning, cooling vents, to retreat and read.

One morning, I plonked my stuff on the floor, looked up and our eyes linked. But only briefly. We were sheepish and both glanced sideways, out the window. I remember being shell-shocked by the sight. I gulped, endeavouring to look past the giant golly plastered on the glass, full of fizz, gifted to us by the previous occupant.

'Gross,' we said in unison. I'm amazed I wasn't sick at that point. Then we started laughing. I stamped my feet, repulsed.

Wil shook his head in disgust, thrust one fist into the cushioned seat, coughed, and said, 'That's a shocker and a half.'

I chuckled. I thought Wil's voice sounded like a green frog stuck in a downpipe. One year on, his voice became a song to remember.

It was no accident. I found myself pinned beneath the wheel, bewildered, my body throbbed—lyrics blared— ... *in time I was falling*—lights blinked, red, yellow, and blue. We were surrounded by shards of glass. I turned. Screamed. Wil's crippled body faced me, lifeless. If only the flash of a falling star hadn't have passed.

We'd stuck by each other like saliva, post meeting on the train. Wil constantly made me laugh. He'd said his Poppa wanted to shake the hand of the lady who'd turned towards, what he'd said, sounded like the grandest golly in time, someday. I don't know about that, but I don't think his Poppa realised just how soon that day would come. Because one month later, Wil and I unshackled ourselves from our parents, and moved in together. That too, happened like a flash.

'Cha-Ching!' Wil's arm skimmed past my face; finger pointed.

'Ouch, do you mind,' I protested, reaching out and caressing his powerful bicep.

I felt so tall, settled high, in the big crimson rig Wil drove. I liked my newfound, unencumbered, panoramic view of the wide-angled world we lived in. Wilson was my man. Around him, I wasn't afraid. I wasn't afraid of heights; I wasn't afraid of anything. And whenever I was in his company, I was flying high. I knew everything in life was fine when Wil was mine.

I suppose that Sunday morning drive, returning to my parents' house, had demonstrated we were destined to be together. Wil went wild when he spotted a bright red Smeg fridge, beside a solid Sealy queen mattress.

'Oh, snap!' he'd said, braking suddenly. Then, 'Sorry, sweet. Whatdya say, wanna pick em up, make a home, make em ours?'

Wil's query stunned me. Both items stood strong, curb side. Taped to the fridge door was a handwritten cardboard sign. It read 'FREE—still works! No stains!' I too thought the furniture looked grand, unsure why someone would just throw things out. *Perhaps our stars have begun to shift in agreement*, I pondered.

'Is that a proposal, Wil Roberts?' I blushed and covered my mouth, embarrassed. Then, excited by the notion, I said, 'Sure, I'm with ... this oil burning beast of yours ain't no slushbox, but it sure gives me reason. What's up back anyway?'

'As if! I've got myself a buff pickup, thank you very much,' he gushed, 'and the tray's near empty, bar the chute. Who knows? One day, you and I might share this top-gear beast. Grease, grubs, and a backyard of shrubs.' He grinned and stroked my stomach. 'Whatdya reckon?' It was then that I knew, Wil Roberts touched me in a way I'd never let anyone touch me before.

Within days we'd found an affordable unit, and by the end of the week we'd moved in. Life together ran swell for months. But the onset of an early winter caused the fish to spawn prematurely. Soon after, Wil found himself redundant. So, he started studying and working from home—tinkering with oiled car parts and offering minor car services to our friends, to help with expenses. Car parts were strewn across the coffee table. I loathed the littered living area, but I spun away. I was happiest when Wil was happy.

'I have to bounce, babe. Big day today. Let's dance tonight?' I jested.

Wil stood, wandered over and drew me into him. I sensed his enthusiasm.

'Giddy up!' He grinded my hip like a horse on heat and tipped my chin to make eye contact. 'The scorching samba ... a little wet waltz—a sneaky skinny dip, then we got a deal. Whatdya say?' His jaw was soft and his dimples performed when he smiled.

'Oh, snap,' I whispered, brushing my lips against his cheek, then raced to the bedroom to grab my camera, unable to resist the sudden urge to snatch a pic. Returning, I said, 'Sure thing, but only if you smile again for me, baby.'

I lie in wait, in wonderment, between silk sheets, staring at our humble pictures, turned portraits. Sometimes our photographs cry out like poisoned toads. Screaming, shouting, stifling my life with the same deafening lyric ... *in time I was falling*— Still, Wil's olive-green eyes shine back, dimples dancing. And I can't reply. I can only crumble ... like a castle ruin. My house is mute. I am culpable. I don't dance; I won't sing.

Every day is a doldrum, every thought a chore. I know I won't harm myself. But I'm living under the mindful eyes of my parents, among others. Mum says continuing with work is essential. Dad says happy company will create happiness.

It's a short stroll from the carpark to the platform. Spring justles the eucalyptus leaves. I whistle with the lorikeet chatter; a wagtail dances in circles, battling for a branch. In, out, zipping here, bobbing there, without a care, like the fine tip of an artist's brush. I power up my Walkman, ... *in time I was falling*—there it is again. Again and again, and again. I can't escape it. I press stop, to skip the undesirable beats. And then, a fractious flutter. BANG! Right there, in front of me, a wee wagtail slams into the windscreen of a parked car. I begin to shake, stunned by this brittle bird, lying motionless. Black eyes open, body contorted, feathers scattering across the scathing metal bonnet. A small soul begone. The lyrics continue playing *... in time I was falling*— They're in my head, they're raucous. I rip off the headset, throw it to the ground, and begin stamping the shit out of it.

'Are you ok, love?' a female voice asks, startling me.

'No! What? Where ... where are the shards of glass?' I scream.

'We think it's time, Dana.'

'Time for what?' I ask.

'Time to polish your past.'

'What do you mean?'

'There comes a time to let go. A time to drive your own journey. And a time to steer your own dreams.'

'I can't let go,' I cry, tossing, entangled in the bed sheets.

'We understand ... It's been a trying time ... Three long months of your life.'

'It's been a hole!'

'At one time, flying high was top of your list. Yours and Wil's.'

'It doesn't matter anymore, he'll never know! What would you know, anyway?' I gasp for air, nodding erratically—left, right, left again—my throat constricting like a corset.

'You're not imprisoned, Dana.' The tone was doting. A faceless shape. Disturbing, yet peaceful.

'What if I can't come back? Where will I go?'

'What if you can?'

'Will I find Wil? You must know Wil and I forged a dream ... A joint venture in the sky ... A future as one ... Bonded by our parachute strings. His proposal to me was stellar. Sweetened, with his smile. His commitment to marriage ... it had hit me like a supernova.'

'We felt it too, we were the choir.'

'Then you know that I demanded to drive. Go ahead and prove what's yours is mine, I'd exclaimed. It was a pathetic joke, yeah ... excuses, I know. But Wil agreed ... Why? He was kind ... willing, like his name. And I killed him. I killed him! I'm an absolute soul killer.'

'Why blame yourself, Dana?'

'That beastly car! I said it at the start. Wil managed it. He'd tamed his beast. But not me, I lost control. I couldn't see. I was blinded. I lost every—every piece of—'

'Grab on, Dana. Nothing is absolute. You can grab hold of a soul. Grab onto Wil's.'

'How?'

'It grows inside you. But you must be willing. Willing to wake up and wipe your blame. Wake up ... wake up ... wake up, Dana.'

'But I haven't heard the kookaburras calling.' I was thinking out loud, blinking my eyes open, and hearing engines whirring; power tools drilling; birds twittering. All these intermittent noises telling me it was later than my usual waking time. I feel different, disorientated, confused, yet content. What is happening to me? I wonder, lying twisted and restricted in the softness of the sheets, while streams of sunlight enchant my bedroom like a fairy-tale. I begin inching towards the side of the bed, my long cotton

pyjamas edged up around my knees. After smoothing
the lengths of my pyjamas down my legs, I wander into
the bathroom, knowing a cold splash of water will aid
my awakening.

Leaning against the ceramic basin, I stare at my jaded
reflection. The tiles are chilling against my bare feet, but I
remain, willing myself to remember. BOOM! My memory
moves me like an explosion. I turn my eyes towards the
ceiling, seeing, and remembering every spoken word—
the wisdom of my dream, as clear to me as the song
of whipbird.

I stir naturally today, not woken by dreams, but by a flock
of laughing kookaburras. Reaching for a shawl, oblivious
to time, I step outside, straight into a cool breeze blowing
through the eucalyptus trees. A chill lingers but I'm full
of warmth, captivated by the swaying leaves shaping
shadows like strange ghosts. Their silhouettes linger until
the shaded night's sky begins to shimmer, and on the
horizon, I see the glitter of day peeping through.

After spending so many days concentrating on the
lyrics, which plague and curse my life, I find solace gazing
upon the morning's waning crescent moon.

'Be with me, or begone,' I whisper with confidence,
wanting nobody to realise my deepening doubt.

Later, I'm grateful when Dad offers to drive me to the
privately owned airfield. We leave around midday and
when we arrive, the asphalt is dotted with small planes.
It's turning into a clear day, not a cloud around. A small
sign signals us to check-in at reception. We weave our way

through more parked cars. Goose bumps cover my arms. I'm hoping the airplane is superior to the discoloured tin shed, operating as an office, but I feel calm when we meet the instructors. All three (one woman and two men) are encouraging and lead me into a small room to watch a short instructional video. When the video ends, I've got the pasties, dry mouth and my nerves are trembling. But that passes when they hand me my kit. I change, donning a pink and white Nomex suit—the tag says it's lightweight and fire-resistant. Finally, my heebie-jeebies are jolted when I'm given a pair of fitted, leather gloves and a space-age, death-defying piece of armor (otherwise known as a helmet). My feet are jolly too, dressed in my own comfortable toe-covered sneakers—an instruction upon booking. And in the full-length mirror things are beginning to look and feel real.

Dad smiles when I exit the changerooms and I hand him my personal belongings.

'I'll make a wish when I'm up there, ok. Don't worry, Dad.' I grimace, thinking nobody notices me, stuffing my Walkman into the suit's deep pocket.

'We'll take the shots. That'll need to stay behind,' says the middle-aged instructor, thinking it's a camera.

'No way! My music comes with,' I plead.

'Rules are rules. It's way too dangerous, Dana.'

'Nuh! If I'm doing it, so's this song.'

'Huh!' he says, raising his hands in disdain.

'Dana!' Dad interrupts, 'what are you talking about?'

'Life don't matter to me anymore. There's always going to be a maybe ... maybe we live ... maybe we die.'

My instructor nods in agreement, clutches my shoulder, and I shudder with surprise.

'Aiight, Dana. It seems you've been through a lot. I've an idea.' He smiles. 'Put your helmet on, the plane is fuelled and ready. I'm coming with, and you can carry the song in your soul, ok. Do you know what I'm saying?'

I only hear one word. Soul. I do understand. So, I pass the Walkman to dad and inhale a few deep breaths. Gasoline and oil ignite my senses. I almost can't breathe.

'Is it going to be windy up there?' I ask, rubbing my hands to distract me from my gloved and sweating palms, while evaluating the idea, that I needn't grip anything—as it's all just thin air, anyways.

'The wind speed is 21 knots, perfect skydiving weather. But we ought a move. Things can change quickly. C'mon, Dana, speed it up.'

I quicken my step and catch up. 'Is that ours? It's so small. It's—'

'Larger than life, really. I call her Liv.' He chuckles beneath his breath and I begin preparing for a rickety ride. A couple of groups climb in before us. We enter last. The cabin is tight with six adults. Two long benches run either side of the craft and a pile of chutes pack the centre floor area. Everyone begins belting up as the three instructors complete their fourth and final safety checks.

'Aiight! All set then?' the pilot twists and asks, then fiddles with a few switches and the engine rumbles; the propeller spins alive. He signals two thumbs up and we begin to roll. The air circulating the cabin cools and what feels like twenty minutes has us hovering at 12,000 feet. We witness the first two tandems, tumble out like a couple of haybales swept up by the wind, and I know my turn's coming.

'Are you guys ready? The wind's changing. I'm going to do a loop. Then I'll come back around,' the pilot calls. We move closer to the exit. I see an abundance of blue, white, and yellow. I'm tethering on the edge like a loose tooth—I don't look down.

'Ready?' he shouts, squeezing my shoulders from behind. I readjust, bracing myself with my fingers, which only pinch the thin rim of the aircraft's opening.

I can't turn. I'm strapped to the front of his body, battling with the lyric in my mind. I hear it, repeat it ... *in time I was falling*— ... *in time I was falling*— ... *in time I was— falling*. Without warning, we lean left, as the aircraft takes a turn, and I squeeze my eyes. But the sun's rays beam like a sovereign's sword and its affection forces me to watch the perfect outline of his face forming.

'Wil?' I whisper.

... *in time I was falling*— I know the lyrics like I know my mother. They're getting louder, and louder, and louder. Tears warm my cheeks. His eyes twinkle like glitter.

'I love you, Wil. I'll hold you soon.' I sob, squinting, and he's gone, lost in the sun's glare.

'Aiight, Dana. This is it! On one, we go! Arms wide, ok. And we don't fall—we fly. Two—one.' Forward we roll.

'Yeeeew—' he raves.

Shona Marie

My name is Dana. I dance with feet bare; I praise the glorious lights of life, satisfied our souls stay like stars ... mailing lyrical echoes, to and fro ... eternal arcs in motion—

UNTETHERED

Amelia Connell

The flower was the palest cream, its edges gilded in deep gold.

Elysia cocked her head, watching a bee land on it.

The flower had been blue yesterday. She was sure.

She blinked and the bee flew away. Elysia tracked it with her gaze until it disappeared among the trees.

The gardens were different. Everything was slightly wrong, as though the plants had all moved an inch overnight.

Her mind was blessedly empty as she wandered among the pale flowers. Her dress brushed against her ankles, the soft slide of silk silent in the midmorning air. She cupped a rose in her hand, the white petals glaringly bright beneath the sun.

She'd have to go in, soon. Her mother would be wondering where she'd disappeared to. Elysia's eyes slipped closed.

Maybe she should take the flower with her. Present it as though it could quell her mother's endless rage and save Elysia from her violent outbursts—

She pressed the back of her hand against her mouth as searing pain cut across her thigh.

Her eyes shot open. The room was dark, save for a single lit candle beside the tub. The scent of mildew hung heavy in the air. The knife in her hand was slippery, the handle wet. Something dripped against the concrete floor.

Drip. Drip. Drip.

She looked down. Her skin was burnished in the candlelight, glistening and covered in suds. Shaving ... she'd been shaving and must have slipped.

Blood ran down her thigh and dripped to the ground.

Elysia dropped the knife and pressed her hand against the wound. She reached for the towel hanging over the tub, pulling it down to press against her thigh. The candle flickered as the pale terrycloth darkened.

The wound throbbed and she looked up, meeting her own gaze in the mirror.

No. No, no—

Dark eyes stared back at her, lanky black hair pulled into a haphazard bun. Her face was wrong, her nose too small, her brows too arched.

Her mouth moved and she spoke. It wasn't her voice. 'You're not supposed to be here.'

Elysia slumped to the ground with a gasp, the rose crushed in her fist. Shivering, she rolled to her back before lifting her head and staring down at her thigh. Her dress fell to her hips when she bent her knee, and her pale skin was smooth, unblemished.

Elysia dropped her head back against the grass and stared at the sky. Threading her fingers through her hair, she pressed her palm against her forehead. Her hand was sticky and she pulled it away, blinking.

At first, her hand was merely a silhouette, outlined by the sunlight beating down on her. Her eyes focused and she sucked in a wheezing breath.

Blood, almost dry, caked her hand. A few strands of her blonde hair were caught and she tugged them free. She dropped her shaking hand and let the sun blind her.

The psychologist her mother had hired said she hallucinated, said there was something wired wrong in her brain, and she slipped away when her thoughts drifted. He said her consciousness simply vacated the premises and returned at its own leisure.

When she came back to herself, hours—or once, days— later, something was always different. Sometimes it was a sense in the air, a taste in the back of her throat.

Once, at breakfast with her mother, she'd left with an orange in her hand only to return and find a strawberry. When she gasped, her mother slapped her and said, 'Shut up and eat your breakfast.'

Nobody else noticed when things changed. To them, the world was constant, a flat sheet of paper. To Elysia, the world was like dry pasta dropped in boiling water and every day it was left to cook into something unrecognisable.

She groaned and sat up. The sun had passed the apex of the sky. She'd been gone for hours.

The crushed rose in her hand slipped free. Deep crimson petals fell to the grass, vibrant against the green, like drops of freshly spilled blood.

Elysia stood and stalked through the gardens, ignoring the hues of burgundy and eggplant speckled throughout. Every flower had changed, as though someone dipped them in paint.

It was like the setting of a gothic daydream had replaced her mother's formal gardens. Trailing arms of English ivy climbed the stone statues and willow trees stood where wisterias once swayed.

Elysia trailed her fingers through the dangling leaves of a willow. Her mother would be outraged to see her finely manicured gardens thrust into disarray. It was a pity she'd never know the difference. With a sigh, Elysia pulled away and started the trek up the hill to her mother's estate.

The door to the kitchen was thrown wide. Elysia toed off her boots and slipped inside in only her socks. Maia, their cook and so much more, stirred something on the stove and the heady aroma of mixed spices filled the room.

Elysia smiled at the sound of Maia humming a jaunty little tune she used to sing Elysia to sleep with. Crossing the kitchen, Elysia looped her arms over Maia's shoulders and propped her chin on her own bicep. 'Tell me that's my favourite stew and I'll love you forever.'

Maia snorted and petted her hand. 'Child, as if I'd make anything else on your birthday.' Elysia laughed, squeezing her shoulders and kissing her cheek. Pulling back, she walked to the kitchen island and hefted herself onto it, letting her feet dangle.

'So,' Elysia drew the word out. 'How angry is she?'

Maia turned and folded her arms. Her lips pinched. 'It doesn't look like you'll be eating your stew tonight, sweets.'

Elysia's shoulders slumped. 'Or any time this week, I suppose.' She looked at her hands and tugged on a hangnail until the skin burned. They were clean, at least. She'd washed them beneath the tap outside.

'Likely not.' Hands landed on her shoulders, and Elysia looked up.

'Deep breath, sweetheart. We can't have you floating away just yet.' Maia smiled softly, arching a brow.

Elysia rolled her eyes.

'Hey. Just three more years and the money is yours. You can go anywhere.'

Elysia shook her head. 'You know she's trying to prove I'm unstable. I won't get a cent of my inheritance if the next psych proves her right.'

'So, prove them wrong.' Maia's warm hands cupped her cheeks, and Elysia's fingers grasped her wrists. The gesture was familiar. Comforting. Maia was more of a mother to Elysia than her own had ever been. 'You like to daydream.

So, what? You can be flighty or distracted without being insane.'

'It's more than that.'

'Stop telling them that. Lie, Elsie, and take yourself away from here as soon as you can.'

Elysia's mouth opened, but a ringing bell interrupted her. They both looked at the closed door to the rest of the house, as though her mother would burst in at any moment.

'I have to go,' Elysia murmured, tugging Maia's hands away from her face. 'It'll only be worse if I make her wait.'

Maia stepped back to watch her slide from the bench. Elysia turned and left without meeting her gaze. She felt it drilling into the back of her head until she closed the kitchen door between them.

Her mother was in the formal receiving room. It was empty of staff and sparsely furnished. Fire crackled in the fireplace, spewing sparks into the chimney when a log snapped.

As always, it was slightly too warm. The windows were sealed, condensation beading on the glass like the sweat dripping down Elysia's spine.

She stopped in the centre of the room, staring at the side of her mother's face as she watched the fire. After several minutes, her mother inhaled and stood.

Their eyes met and Elysia shuddered, dropping her gaze to the floor as her mother crossed the room. Her eyes were a void, darkness devouring her pupils and leaving only empty, aching black.

The sound of her mother's heels clicking against the floor stopped. A cold hand cupped her chin, long nails digging into her jaw as her face was tilted up. 'Messy hair and grass stains.' Her mother clicked her tongue. 'Should I expect a bastard heir in nine months, girl?'

Elysia sputtered, her eyes darting to her mother's. 'No.'

The grip tightened. 'Then you have another explanation for your absence this morning?'

'I—I was gardening.'

Her mother yanked her face to the side. Her mother's disappointment always tasted like old coins: iron and bitter. Volatile. She huffed and dropped her hand. Elysia stiffened. 'You were not.'

The blow was hard, a backhand across the face. Her mother's ring dug in, the pain sending Elysia to her knees. She cried out and clutched her cheek as blood oozed from the wound.

'You are pathetic.' The other cheek this time. Elysia fell to the floor, curling her arms above her head. She knew her mother only stopped when she surrendered.

Her face throbbed and Elysia closed her eyes, shutting out her mother's voice. Thoughts drifting, she slipped away into the dark.

Elysia's hands cupped someone's jaw, stubble itching her fingers. A man was kissing her, pressing her tight against an icy brick wall. Panicking, she shoved.

The man stumbled back, his grip tightening on the backs of her thighs. Her eyes widened as she went with him, hands falling to his shoulders for balance. Her legs squeezed his waist and he staggered, his foot catching on a bottle.

'Lena, what the fu—'

They toppled, and Elysia pulled herself free of his grip, her feet finding the ground before she slipped and landed on her butt. The bitumen was cold and sticky through her leggings.

She stared at the man on the ground, half shrouded in darkness by the light of a streetlight. He'd landed beside a dumpster, his eyes open.

They were in an alley, the sounds of a city echoing through the surrounding streets. The scent of rotting food hung heavy in the air and Elysia gagged, pressing a gloved hand to her mouth.

He wasn't moving.

Elysia dropped her hand and reached out to shake his foot.

A dark puddle spread beneath his head.

Elysia sucked in a breath, her eyes falling to the bottle. It was cracked, not shattered. Several versions of herself stared back, brown hair pulled back in a bun on either side of her head.

Oh—

'What have you done?'

And she was gone, sucked back into the black.

Elysia returned with a sob, her face throbbing as she launched upright. The fire still crackled in the fireplace, but her mother had left. The sun was setting, a haze of blue settling beyond the windows.

She stumbled to her feet. Her mother would be in the dining room by now, and Elysia would rather be anywhere else.

Elysia kept her fingers on the wall as she walked down the hallway. Her breaths were loud, though she'd subdued her sobs to sniffles.

She trembled when she reached the door to the kitchen, her sweaty hand sliding on the doorknob. Maia would be inside, finishing dinner. Maia would know what to do. Maia always knew.

Elysia pushed the door open. 'Maia, I need—'

She froze in the doorway.

The kitchen was dark, the stove cold. 'Maia?'

The door to outside swung in the breeze, the creaking hinges the only sound in the empty room. Elysia crossed the kitchen, yanking open the door to Maia's private quarters.

If she was in the bath, she could have bloody well answered—

The room was empty.

None of Maia's clutter lined the shelves, no towers of books leaned against the walls. The bed was stripped; the barren mattress and a folded pile of sheets were all that remained.

A thin layer of dust coated everything, as though Maia had never been there at all.

'No,' Elysia's voice was a whisper, cracking the silence. 'No. Maia!' Elysia spun, running to the back door. Her hand slammed against the wood, flinging the door wide.

Never had she returned and found someone missing. Not once in twenty-three years.

But she'd never killed anyone before, either.

'Maia!'

Silence answered her. Tears traced down her cheeks, the salt stinging her cuts.

Maia was gone, and soon, so was she.

Elysia opened her eyes to an unfamiliar ceiling. It was a buttery yellow. She sat up, aching down to her bones.

Blinking, she tried to force her eyes to focus. With a sigh, she reached for the glasses on the bedside table and slipped them on. She looked up and stiffened.

Painted on the wall in large, jagged letters were the words:

Do not speak. Do not look in a mirror. Write.

Beneath the words was an arrow pointing at the desk below, a journal and a pen were the only things on the surface.

Elysia hesitated a moment before crossing the room and tugging out the chair. She sat and flipped the journal open.

Hello? she wrote.

'Hello,' her mouth said, the voice raspy, hitching. Elysia hadn't spoken. 'Don't panic. I've been waiting for you.'

I don't understand.

'I'm not surprised. Your scientists haven't discovered this yet.'

Elysia blinked. *Discovered what?*

'The ability to travel between past and future selves. Like reincarnation, kind of.'

What?

'It's like interdimensional travel, but easier.'

Elysia looked up, squinting at the wall. *Who are you?*

'I'm you. A version of you, anyway. We're the same soul passed through different bodies, different lifelines. We're different people, but the essence remains the same.'

I don't— The voice interrupted before she finished writing.

'I know. You don't understand. But you're making mistakes and affecting other lifelines, so you need to learn. Quickly.' A pause. 'You have a tether. Something that changes before you travel, every time, yes?'

My mind wanders.

'And when you're focused, like now, you remain where you are?'

Yes.

'Good.' The voice was softer, almost affectionate. 'You already know the basics. What's your name?'

Elysia.

'Elysia, you *cannot* travel without intention. If you do so by accident, you *cannot* react the way you did with Lena.'

Elysia stiffened, the pen hovering over the page. She rolled her lips between her teeth. *How do you know about that?*

'We know almost everything our lifelines do, Elysia. You've seen the consequences, so I hope you know better now. When you do things like that, *everything* changes—

for you and for your host. You need to stay focused and stay in control.'

How?

'Work it out. You and I are at our limit. We shouldn't interact with our past and future selves for any longer than this. Any questions?'

A thousand raced through her head, but only one made it to the page. *I'm not crazy?*

'No, sweetheart. You have a gift. Use it wisely.'

Her hand moved on its own, scrawling a single word: *Goodbye.*

The darkness took her back.

The thought circled her mind for days. Her single point of focus, her tether to reality.

She'd been practising.

Elysia sat on her bedroom floor, her eyes closed and her legs folded beneath her. Books lay open across the floor, nonfiction tomes filled with placeholders.

Her mother locked her in her room days ago, and food arrived with a maid at sunrise and sunset.

This wasn't a life.

Not one she wanted, anyway.

She was calm, her breathing even.

Inhale. Her mind was empty.

Exhale. Her thoughts began to wander.

Inhale. Elysia was gone, swept away by the current of her memories.

Once, she woke in a flower garden, her gloved hands buried in dirt and a large hat flopping over her face.

She'd frozen, blinking at the petals stuck to her sweaty, mud-streaked forearms. Fingers curled over the brim of her hat, lifting it to reveal a smiling man.

He gestured with his hands then paused, staring. She blinked at him and disappeared.

Elysia now knew he'd been signing words to her. Knew he'd said, *Come inside, darling. It's too hot out here.*

Maia had fed her insatiable hunger for knowledge with books for years, and it took less than a day to find what she needed. A week to learn the language.

Now, she was here. Back in the picturesque little garden, with her floppy hat and flourishing flowers. The sun was setting, turning the afternoon golden.

Rule one: *travel with intention.* Check.

The man waved in her periphery and Elysia turned. *Come inside,* he signed. *Dinner's ready.*

Elysia smiled and stood. *Coming.*

Rule two: *do not speak.* Check.

She paused just inside the back door. She took off her gloves and dropped them on the side table. Her hat followed.

Flicking on the light in the bathroom, she stepped inside and rinsed her hands.

Rule three: *focus.*

Elysia sucked in a breath and looked up.

She met her eyes in the mirror. She smiled.

Check.

THE GATEKEEPER

Elizabeth Brown

He stood facing the ocean, his hands clasped behind his back. 'I think it's going to be a hot day today, Theia.' He extended a weathered hand and a hummingbird landed on it with a flurry of brown feathers. Two beady eyes stared up at him.

'What?' he asked, amused. A string of sweet symphonies flittered into his ears. 'You don't say? Well, let's have a look then, shall we?'

Turning his back to the rumbling ocean, they began strolling up the sandy pathway. Tropical flora tunnelled around them. As his bare feet felt the familiar stone steps, he ducked his head and stepped through the cascading vines.

A shiver shook his frail frame. Theia chittered.

'I know. But it's hard to remember how cool it gets in here when the sun is an endless warm bath.'

Theia ruffled their brown feathers in agreement.

'Let's see what we have here.' He crouched down to kneel on the wet stones and slipped a hand into the cavern's pool. As he withdrew his hand, it dripped with spools of white, unravelling like yarn. Clasped gently in his palm was a golden seashell. He tenderly tilted the seashell until a pulsing, milky orb rolled out.

'This one is still warm, Theia,' he said, voice thick with excitement. Theia's eager chirps ignited a twinkle in his opaque eyes. 'Indeed, little one. A new dream is a precious gift.'

Gentle energy throbbed from his weathered hands, melting the protective glaze of the orb. Apparitions exhaled out like steam. The billowing dreams mushroomed up to the cavern's ceiling before cascading down against the cave's black walls. A bitter shadow shifted within him, an all too familiar chill lurking around the outskirts of his existence.

Turning to peer down at the hummingbird, the little man gave her a weary stroke. 'It's getting stronger, Theia. We are running out of time.'

The little bird chirped.

'I know she's not ready, but what are we to do?'

She nuzzled his palm, a silent encouragement.

'It's time to wake her.' He sighed. Together, the old man and hummingbird stepped into the flowing fountain, disappearing into the stream of dreams.

Black. Suffocating. Fear lurches up from my stomach, punching a fist through my chest. I try to scream but my mouth won't open. I can't move my hands or my feet. I'm sure they're there but I can't feel them. My heart hammers in its cage. My eyes frantically zigzag the black abyss, scanning for something. Anything. My airways close. Body surrenders. Eyes shut. Two milky orbs float behind my eyelids. A bird chirps.

Grey. I think it's fog. Although I know it's cold, I don't shiver. I look down. A golden dress drapes from my shoulders, and the hem plays peek-a-boo with red-tipped toenails. They're mine but I can't feel them, can't feel the rocky ground they stand on. A grassy runway rolls away to a belvedere, where a little brown bird perches. A hummingbird? As I'm carried towards it, propelled by a gravel conveyor belt, I see something tied to its neck. A shell? The edge grows nearer. I try to step off, but I can't move. The rocky ground rumbles, reverberating avalanches of panic through my body. I stare desperately at the little bird, silently screaming for help. It vanishes. An invisible drawstring tightens around my windpipe, a tourniquet turning into a guillotine.

Mauve. It's her favourite colour. Used to be a beautiful colour too, before she wore it so much it became nauseating. A sick reminder. The room is doused in it. The flowers. The gaudy get-well gifts. The visitors. Her outfit. My outfit. I feel like I've been dipped in an acid vat. A nauseating fragrance of antiseptic and mashed potatoes wafts into the room. Well-meaning hands touch my arms, my back. Faceless strangers with clipboards and white coats come and go. The ventilator plays like a broken record—click, chhss, click, chhss, click—making my blood boil. 'Wind Beneath My Wings' plays quietly from the speaker beside her bed. The track stops only to start again, Midler's voice droning on. I'm standing at the foot of her bed. She looks childlike, a skeletal shadow of a mother half dead. Someone taps my shoulder. It's an old man in a beige linen suit.

'It's time.'

Brown. I'm alone. Dust. Drying ink. I'm lying on a bed of papers that rustle and rip as I sit up. My papers. Lives, stories, journeys, feats, sacrifices, entire worlds lay beneath me. A colossal reminder—etched in ink—a taunting memoir shoved into the escritoire. I, the scribe, to my failure. I grab a handful of the papers and rifle through them. The golden calligraphy swirls off the pages, plucked free and unravelling in the air. The letters pivot and pirouette, twisting into coiled seashells. They bob, suspended on invisible threads, like puppets, before vaporising. As I grasp the faded sheets, flames flicker to life and lick the edges, a blackened kiss receding with an amber hunger. The pages furl in a silent howl, keeling over. They combust, floating away like ashen snow.

Blue. I know that smell. Wildflowers. Grassy meadows. The salty tang of sea breeze. Home. Why did I stay away for so long? I know why. Dad, Ja—the sound of flowing water slices through my memories. Water? That can't be right. My ears lead the way, guided by the unmistakable hush of cascading water. My feet, bare and dirty, fleetingly kiss the dewy carpet as I move across the meadow. A ring of giant oaks protects the clearing. I step beyond the cloaked ring—

'Hello, Ruby.' A tanned old man in a beige linen suit smiles at me. A little brown hummingbird perches on his shoulder, their black eyes inspecting me.

'Uh, hello? Who are you?' I ask.

'Apologies. I've forgotten myself. I must admit, it's been a time or two since I last spoke with a Realing. It's rather exciting!'

'A what?'

'A Realing. It's what we call you here.'

'Here? Where's here?'

'Depends on who you ask, my dear. Come along now. There's so much to do and no time to lose!' With that, the little old man swivelled on his heels and strode off.

'Wait a minute. Excuse me!' I shout.

The stranger pivots. 'Bless you, dear. Do you need a tissue?' Before I can respond, a white fluffy cloth is dangling in my face.

'Wha—no. Thank you. Sorry, but what is your name?'

'Gatekeeper. Did I not mention that?' His frown creases like ripples in the sand.

I shake my head.

'Right. Deary me. Well then. Here.' He thrusts the cloth into my hand.

'I don't—what is this?'

'A sliver of cloud. Also fantastic for cleaning. Hard to come by, though. Best to hold on to it. Come along now.'

'Gatekeeper. Who are you?'

'My dear, please try to keep up.'

'Where am I?'

'Where do you think you are?'

I look around. It's the first time I've noticed my surroundings, or lack thereof. There's nothing and everything. Images ripple like puddles, contorting in a matrix of colour. 'I ... I ...'

'I know. That happened to me the first time too. Quite the rush, isn't it?' His childlike giggle rattles around my desolate mind.

'I've lost it. It's finally happened,' I whisper, hugging myself. Breathe.

'Oh, my dear Ruby. Calm yourself. The only thing you've lost is, well, your father, Jack, and sweet Guppy the Goldfish—my condolences for the entirety, by the way. An awful run of luck, really.' He rests a hand on my shoulder and liquid calmness melts over me.

'Better?' he asks.

'Better.' My lungs inflate with air. 'But, Gatekeeper, I still don't understand. Why am I here? And where is here?'

His eyes never focus on me—two opaque mirrors sit where blue eyes should be. His face, though tanned and weathered, has a translucent quality like sheer curtains. Beyond, a mesmerising nebula.

'You, my dear, have weathered many storms during your life but now your time has come. It is my duty to help you on your way.'

The hummingbird chirps abruptly and nips Gatekeeper's collar.

'You're right, little one. A very audacious duty indeed.'
An affectionate stroke settles the bird.

'What do you mean by duty?' I ask.

Gatekeeper's gaze lifts from the bird and stares through
me. 'I am The Gatekeeper of Dream Island, Keeper
of Dreams.'

I gawk at him, my mind blank. *How on earth did I dream
this up?*

'Ahh, it's not a dream, my dear. You're very much awake
right now.'

'So, you're saying this is real? You're real?' I ask.

'As real as the day you were born.' A smile lights up his
face. He turns his body, a silent encouragement to walk
with him. As we move, the whirlpool of images and colours
shifts and contorts, cocooning us in an infinite tunnel. We
walk together; I, trying to make out the complex collage,
and Gatekeeper, muttering to the little bird.

'Does it understand you?' I ask.

At first, he doesn't look up or acknowledge my
question, continuing to mutter and stroke the bird. But
after a string of nonsensical sounds, he says softly, 'They
do. Theia understands me more than I understand myself.'
He looks up at me. 'It is imperative that you form a bond
with them—Theia is the key to controlling this place.'

'Controlling? Why—wha—what do you mean? Why
would I need to know how to control this place? And what
is this place? Where are we?'

He meets my questions with an endearing smile. 'Always
the inquisitive child. Come. We must first walk the path.'

We stand in a dark cavern, the only source of light coming from the pool of water in the centre. It's unlike any body of water I've ever seen before. The surface glimmers a brilliant white but occasionally indiscernible things disrupt the surface layer, and a velvet abyss lurks below.

'What is this place?' My voice is barely a whisper.

Gatekeeper stands beside me, Theia still perching on his shoulder. 'This is where we collect lost dreams.' He smiles at me before bending forward and dipping his hand into the pool. When he straightens, he's grasping a blackened seashell in his palm. 'Humans have an innate way of losing things in life. Moments, time, love, dreams ... the list, unfortunately, is endless. And for every lost thing, there is a place it goes and dreams, my dear, come here. It is our duty to return them to their rightful owner.'

I stare at him, trying to absorb his words and their meanings. It's like I'm learning a foreign language; nothing makes sense right now. *This would make a great novel.*

'It would make an excellent story, my dear, but it would have to be a non-fiction piece, for this is no work of fiction.'

I look at him, aware of his eerie ability to answer my thoughts. He just smiles back at me while mindlessly stroking Theia's head. I let it go. *Absurd.* 'Okay. Let's say I believe you. What do I have to do with this?' I ask, waving my arms at the cavern.

Theia chitters, and he sighs. 'I will admit, I am to blame. There were signs but I thought I had more time. It seems I am no better than Realings. In my selfishness, I have threatened everything, and I am no longer fit to fulfil my duty. That is why you must replace me.'

'Why me?' I ask.

'Because, my dear, there is no bigger dreamer than you.' He opens his hand, offering me the seashell.

I gingerly take it; its exterior is smooth and cool but there's an inner warmth trying to reach out, calling to me.

'You were born a dreamer, but you became a carer. You're innately good. I see you with your mother, how you were with your father and Jack. How you treat strangers. You see the best in everyone, even when they present their worst. Do you know how rare that is, my dear? Only those of the purest disposition can place the dreams of others before their own.'

'So, the inability to follow my own dreams in real life scores me a job doing exactly that? How ironic,' I mutter.

'Well, yes. They chose you, before you were born.'

'What?' The question flies sharply out of my mouth.

He shrugs nonchalantly. 'We are dealt the dreams we're destined to find.'

'No,' I say.

He looks at me with raised eyebrows. 'What do you mean, no? This has been written.'

'I don't care. I don't want this.' I cross my arms defiantly.

He sighs. 'Dear Ruby, before you decide, there is something that may change your mind. In becoming the Gatekeeper, you are granted one fulfilment: your greatest dream. But it is my duty to inform you—there are consequences. Consequences that are heavy to bear.'

'What kind of consequences?'

'Beyond returning lost dreams to their owner, it is the Gatekeeper's duty to protect the sanctity of dreams. To do this, we must absorb the darkness that invades these cavern waters.'

'What do you mean?'

'I will show you.' His hand glides into the water. He withdraws his arm, and there, grasped in his palm, is a replica of the shell in my hand, only it's black.

'These,' he says, holding the shell out, 'are nightmares. They trickle into the Stream of Consciousness and attach themselves, like leeches, to the shells as they wash up. If we do not remove them, they fester—darkness secretes into the dreams and erodes them. A dream becomes defective once exposed to this putrid energy and cannot return to its owner.'

'So why not just dispose of them elsewhere?'

'Darkness like this has a way of eating away at whatever it touches. If we do not absorb the energy, the island will, and that risks the entirety of our existence.' Cupping the black seashell, Gatekeeper leans over it and whispers in a tongue foreign to my ears. The shell quivers, the energy peels itself off and snakes into his hands, up his arms. It spreads, black blood bleeding into water, staining his mesmerising translucency. He shivers, becoming more sheer.

'Are you okay?' I ask, watching him sway on the spot.

He closes his eyes, and a blackened hand presses into his chest. 'Quite alright, thank you, dear.' He smiles wearily. With his blackened hand, he caresses the shell once, its coat golden again. The golden shell rolls off his fingers, soundlessly sinking into the pool. We stand, side by side, and watch as the shell disappears.

'Where does the shell go now?' I ask, looking up at him.

His eyes are still on the water. His voice comes out distant, like his mind is down in the depths where the shell sinks. 'Somewhere between here and there.'

His vague response frustrates me. 'I'm sorry, Gatekeeper, but I can't help you. I have a life. Responsibilities. My mother. I can't—won't—leave her.'

His eyes leave the water to focus on me. 'What if I told you there was a way to save her?'

My heart follows the sinking shell. Flashes of her skeletal body fill my mind, bringing with it a waft of antiseptic that burns my nose. The ventilator clicks, the sounds of her hospital room haunting me.

'It's too late,' I whisper.

'My dear, if you become Gatekeeper, your greatest dream will be fulfilled.'

'But I don't know what that is!' I shout, exasperated.

His eyes reflect sympathy, only making me angrier. *I don't need your pity.*

'I do,' he says casually. It takes me a moment to comprehend what he's saying.

'And how do you know?'

He chuckles, mindlessly reaching to stroke Theia.

Theia chirps, fluttering inches away from Gatekeeper's outstretched hand. Their incessant twittering makes no sense to me, but Gatekeeper seems to wither below their wings.

'What are they saying?' I ask, watching the exchange with unease. There's something in the way Theia's fluttering that makes my stomach quiver.

Gatekeeper's tone comes out quick and breathy, like it's an effort to speak.

Theia's fluttering grows larger and sharper.

'Gatekeeper?'

His head swivels toward me, two black eyes finding me.

A gasp escapes my mouth.

He tries to speak, but no sound comes out; his mouth opening and closing like a voiceless ventriloquist.

Theia's shriek is ear-splitting as they fly backwards, putting more air between them and Gatekeeper.

The blackness in his hand is spilling like ink, oozing into his arm. It's spreading quickly now, seeping into the corners of his core. His mouth is shaped in a silent 'oh' and he takes a step towards me, but his legs give out and he stumbles, falling hard against the cavern's walls.

Theia streaks through the air and lands on my shoulder, their chirps bursting out short and sharp.

'I don't know what you're saying!' I shout, unable to control my panic.

Beady black eyes stare back at me.

A hauntingly familiar voice echoes in my mind. 'My dear Ruby. It is time.'

Mum? A tear whispers down my cheek.

I look around. Gatekeeper is dragging himself up the wall. Theia hovers close to my face, gazing at me. *It can't be.*

'I need time,' I plead, desperation clawing at my insides.

Theia chitters, hopping on the spot.

Gatekeeper stands. His once mesmerising nebula now reflects a starless, midnight sky. He raises his arm, a blackened finger reaching out.

The sweet voice urges, 'Ruby, now!'

White.

THE ROUNDABOUT MAN

Kate Sanderson

His hand extended towards me, grasping a bouquet of lobelia. Freckles dotted his sun-tanned hand. I always bought flowers from him after my grocery run. The market stall was made of a foldable camping table, with a single plastic chair that looked as if it had been stolen from the community hall, or even the local primary school.

I didn't know his name, and I assumed he never learnt mine. Every Saturday he sat on the outside edge of the town centre roundabout and sold bouquets of lobelia. He smelled of fertilizer and cigarettes and sunscreen and grease. A thin scratch reached from the base of his thumb to the middle of his wrinkled hand.

I took the flowers and placed my money in his laid-out palm. A polite smile, a wave of thanks, and I turned my back on him.

He was the Roundabout Man. The nameless who waved at cars and sold flowers from his garden on the weekends. I've never met someone that had not seen him sitting on that roundabout. His house was behind the trees that lined the road, and sometimes at night, lights glowed between the tree branches. The driveway forged its way through a thin opening into the trees, directly onto the edge of the roundabout. If I listened closely, past the birds, I could hear the humming of the diesel generator that powered his house.

'Does that old man ever do anything other than sit and sell flowers?' I overheard the shop keeper question one morning.

'He is older than that roundabout, surely someone will send him to the nursing home soon,' the chicken farmer gossiped every pub trivia night.

He was fragile; his skin sagged over his bones, and his muscles barely held up his hand to take my money. He was also always covered in scratches and bruises. I never knew what to believe. The Roundabout Man had never said anything about himself before, and it felt disrespectful to ask. He sold flowers and waved at cars. I bought the flowers and waved back.

I put the shopping bags on the kitchen floor and monitored a rip in the bag that threatened to widen and dump milk everywhere. I turned on the tv, so there was chatter while I put the food away.

The local news reporter—fixated on the teleprompter—recited the main headlines of the day: 'Mr Owen Miller has won the Sheep and Livestock Fair with his merino sheep. Congratulations. In more concerning news, a man who was last seen at the local butcher has been missing for seven days.'

I peered at the screen, which showed security footage. The blond man carried a shopping bag, which had something strange poking out the top.

'Fourteen hours after the man was reported missing, his grocery bag, which contained one point five kilograms of minced chicken, four pork and veal rissoles, and a dozen purple petals, was found in the old cider mill's orchard. If anyone has any information on his whereabouts, please contact authorities immediately.'

Flower petals?

The framed photo of my childhood friend, Christie, watched me from beside the landline phone. I had given her purple lobelia the day she went missing, and those same flowers were found scattered around her sallow corpse. I had watched Christie step onto the bus, she was on her way home, only she never made it and I never saw her again.

I watched the man on the security footage, the ice cream tub in my hand slowly defrosting, water dripped down my wrist. Did his disappearance have any relation to Christie? In this town, people frequently went missing. Surely the purple petals are just a coincidence? They must be a grocery store bouquet for his house, or his partner, or his sick grandmother.

Christie had held onto those flowers I'd gifted her. She had looked out the window and given me a soft smile before the bus drove away.

I blinked, the image of the man left the screen, and the news reporter changed the subject.

The biting wind pinched my exposed skin. The grass tickled my thigh as I kneeled over Aunt Dana's grave. Her tombstone was cracked and moss grew in the engraved letters. I placed the bouquet beside a half-burned candle. The shadows of trees loomed over while the leaves created a dance that projected over me and her grave.

I stood up. The flowers were placed, and a windy hill was no place to mourn. She was my aunt, but basically a sister. One last wave goodbye, or a hug would have meant so much before she was found rotting in the old cider mill. She would have laughed at me for being so sentimental and thrown me into the grass.

I walked towards the edge of the cemetery, in this direction you could look over the town and see the mill's orchard stretch across the valley. Farmhouses twinkled over the hill side.

I turned and saw a hazy figure in the distance with their back facing me. I got closer, my footsteps crunching twigs and leaves. They stood beside the gate and bent down, their knees supporting their weight as they got lower to the neglected grass, squatting in front of someone's grave. They reached towards the tombstone, their hand brushing the dirt from the name.

Another twig snapped under my foot.

The figure—a man—grabbed the flowers left on the grave, his jacket sleeve falling down his arm, his weak leg wobbling under his weight.

An overgrown patch of grass shuddered as I stepped through it.

The man took a pair of scissors from his pocket and began to sever the heads of the flowers from their stems. He stashed them in his pocket, grabbing the fallen petals from the dirt. When he finished, he stood and turned to leave. As I walked closer, his figure spun and saw me. The Roundabout Man—hat covering his weathered face— stared at me.

I looked at the grave he was beside. It was Christie's. I squinted at him, and at the cuttings in his hand. The wind sung through the trees. Christie's grave cowered under his shadow. I went to say something, anything that could crack the solidifying silence, but he nodded politely and left before I could speak.

Why was he visiting her grave? She never liked the Roundabout Man, found him unnerving. Unlike everyone else in the town, she refused to wave at him as she drove by each morning. I guess he didn't like that.

Christie's grave glared at me, as if it felt abandoned. I put flowers there only a few days ago, it knew that. I knelt and adjusted the framed photo, so the sun couldn't bleach her. Its stare softened.

It was blurry, the colours bleached together.

The Roundabout Man. He stood on the other side of the road. His stall was over-run with lobelia. He was waving at me, waving me over to buy the flowers. Waving me closer to him.

I stepped closer. The grass beneath my feet felt like a carpet made of dead mice; lumpy and squishy and putrid and rotting.

I looked at the Roundabout Man. His leathered hands reached towards the bouquets, reached towards me. I stepped back. The scratch on his thumb was bleeding. It became longer, and deeper, stretching down his forearm. The blood licked his skin.

I stumbled, falling onto the dead mice grass.

He sprinkled me with a dozen flower stems. A polite smile, a wave of thanks, and he turned his back on me.

I sat up in bed. The night air seeped into my lungs. I tore the blanket from my body. Why did he have that cut there? The scratch looked like nails had raked down his arm. Did he hurt himself after hurting other people? It looked about a week old. That blonde man had been missing for a week. I went to the bathroom. I washed my face. Why did he take Christie's flowers? Why did he take each petal? I stared at the mirror. The moon was the only light. It made me look ghostly. Ghastly. I needed to know why Christie died. The Roundabout Man had to know something otherwise he would never have gone to her grave. What did he know? I gave her his flowers once. Now she was covered in worms and damp dirt. I shoved my feet into my shoes and headed towards the roundabout.

I wobbled the door handle. I looked back towards the driveway, and double checked there was no car. The garage was filled with bags of fertiliser and fuel for the generator. The moonlight reflected off the rusting kitchen surface and danced as I tried to twist open the door handle. Nothing. I cupped my face and looked through the glass panel. The kitchen stood silent, just soft light caressing the edge of the countertops, highlighting the jars of flour and sugar. The kitchen window was open, allowing for the bitter night wind to wash across the tiled walls. I pulled it out further, creating a gap for me to squeeze through.

I needed to get in.

I needed to know.

I needed closure to ease my unrest.

The window creaked. I ducked under the windowsill, pressed my skin against the prickled brick wall and listened. My legs became sore. The only sound that caught my attention was the breeze. I peeked through the window again.

The white countertops softly glowed in the dark. I lifted myself onto the windowsill and crawled in. Pots filled with water and soap and the residue of multicoloured sauces cluttered the sink while jams sat on the shelf. Fatty butter and a used knife were left next to the bread bin. Newspapers and bills sat on the dining table. I flicked through them, ensuring that I placed each sheet where it was before.

In the cabinet dividing the dining room and lounge sat a box. Perhaps it was a collection of medals, or coins, or whatever things that old men collect. I pulled it out and carried it to the kitchen so the moon could illuminate the contents.

I carefully removed the dust-covered lid and dug to the bottom. An envelope, thick and crisp and white, hidden underneath family photos. I took it out an ran my finger along the edge. It had weight to it. I opened the unsealed flap and peered inside. A stack of small photographs stared back at me. I pulled out the first few and flicked through.

A photograph of the chicken farmer's ex-wife. I held another up to the window, allowing the moon to show me the image; a man, grinning, holding a trophy and a bouquet of lobelias. A photograph of a woman who I had never seen, her black hair chopped at her shoulders, dressed in a wedding gown.

I fiddled with the envelope, seeing what else was inside. I pulled out purple petals. So many petals. They rained to the floor, covering my feet and covering the tiles. Purple petals. Like the ones found with Christie's body. At Aunt Dana's grave. In the missing man's grocery bag. Always purple petals. I dropped to the floor and scooped them back into the envelope. Photographs fell to the ground as I put the petals back. A photograph of Aunt Dana. Her brown hair, glowing underneath the summer sun, her skin, tanned and warm. She stood in the orchard; the photo taken from behind a tree. The moisture from the petals bled onto my fingers. The photos began to stick. I shook them, which made them fall to the ground, adding to the mess on the floor. The bleeding purple petals stained the photographs. The moonlight felt like a spotlight. I placed the envelope in the box, burying it deep under the photos. But the petals still stuck to my fingers. I opened the envelope again, removing the petals from my skin.

A photo caught my attention. A photo of Christie, sitting next to me. The bouquet of flowers I gifted her after her father died resting on her lap. Her head on my shoulder, waiting for the bus. I had never seen a photo of our last moments together. She was found dead a month later. A petal floated from the back of the paper down to the kitchen counter. I shoved the photo in my pocket and continued scooping petals.

Then, the sound of the diesel generator interrupted the still night. He was home. I shoved everything back in the box, careless about its placement, and scrambled across the tiles back to the dining room, back to the cabinet where the box had been. I had to get out through the kitchen window again, it was the only way. My footsteps were quiet through the dark, buzzing house. Suddenly, I was blinded by a torch shining in my face, the light creating spots in my vision as I climbed onto the counter. He grabbed my ankle, grabbed at my clothing as I crammed myself through the window opening and fell on the ground, the bricks scraping my elbow. The scent of rich dirt invaded my nose, then I heard the kitchen door unlock and unnatural light washed over me. The spots in my vision danced around me, mocking me and pushing me back to the ground. I pushed myself up and staggered through the flower beds, dirt clinging to the soles of my shoes and flowers tickling my knees. I reached the edge of the tree line and glanced back, his silhouette standing in the door frame, torch light continuing to watch me.

The houses on this street were small; match boxes lined up on the bitumen like dominos. The morning sun devoured my eyes. The trees grew thicker the closer I drove to the town centre roundabout. He only opened his stall on Saturdays. He wouldn't be out today. He would be gardening.

The roundabout grew closer.

My shoes were caked with dirt, I had tried to hose them off when I got home but the dirt clung on.

The roundabout.

He stood in the narrow opening of the trees that allowed his driveway to exist. He held a single flower. His glower impaled my throat, my heart. I didn't wave. My breath was a bubble of air caught in my lungs. A pair of scissors severed the head of the flower from its stem.

THE WHISPER CHRONICLES

Blaine Yarrow

I've been having unusual dreams. I'm finding it hard to tell what's real and what's not. I find myself lying awake at night, listening to the sounds of the town outside, too scared to fall asleep. I hear noises which are not really there—noises which make the hairs on the back of my neck stand up. I think I am going insane, but both my dogs keep staring at the place the noises are coming from. I remember my baby sister looking at that exact same spot.

I need to start writing this down. Either I am going insane, or there is something much more sinister going on. I watch the alarm clock and wait for morning to come. When the sun comes up and light fills the room, I rush towards my desk, pull out my favourite pen and a blank journal. I begin writing the title of the journal, 'The Whisper Chronicles'. It is in this journal that I would write my account of the happenings at 13 Crimson Court.

JANUARY 16
Just as I started to fall asleep last night, I heard the whispers once again. Faint, foreboding, far away, but also very close. The dark whispers were not coming from anywhere in particular this time, they were just there, all around me. I tried to listen; I concentrated as hard as I could. Worried if I clenched my teeth any harder they might crack under the pressure. Still, as hard as I listened, I was only able to hear one coherent word: die. Die? Was my brain telling me that I wanted to die? I didn't feel like I wanted to die, or was something else telling me to die?

JANUARY 22
It has been six days since my last journal entry. The voices were quiet for so long that I'd let my guard down, which I should not have done. Last night, the voices pulled me from my sleep, physically, mentally or both—I am not sure. I know I woke up on the floor. I heard the familiar, but foreign voice of a young person on the radio talking to someone about buying a heavy-duty rope. When I approached the radio to listen more closely, the voice stopped and I realised the radio was not turned on. I became frustrated; unable to identify the owner of the

voice. No matter how hard I thought, I could not recognise the voice or who it belonged to.

JANUARY 28

Today was the most unbearable day at work. It was so bad; I was genuinely eager to leave and get home. When I walked in through the front door, I could smell something odd—burning almost. The smoke alarm was not sounding, which I found to be quite unsettling. What happened next was so fast. I heard voices, but this time I saw a familiar shadowed figure floating above the ground in the kitchen. I saw the figure. Everything went blank; I fainted ... It was like I held my breath underwater for too long, then rushed to the surface to get air, but instead of breaking the surface of the water, I blacked out. So, not only have I been hearing voices, but I have also now started to see things that are not there.

FEBRUARY 3

I could hear the voices again last night. They taunted and teased me. Relentless in their endeavour to de-hinge my mind. I could only hear bits and pieces—whispering— only could see small shadows shimmering around the room. My only line of defence was to pretend I did not hear what I heard; to pretend I did not see what I saw. The voices and shadows plagued my room for the rest of the evening until dawn came and hurried them all away. I cannot help but think that my life would be easier if I had no life at all. It is not that I want to die, I want to live, but it is the fear that I am being driven insane which weighs heavy upon my mind and soul. I really need to try and find a shrink to talk to. I need to figure out if I am going crazy or not. Maybe if I take my journal with me, they will be able to help me get better. All I know is that I cannot go on living this way.

I finished my journal entry and placed the book on the desk, exhausted by my life. I leant forward and rested my head in my hands. Some time passed before I peeled myself from the chair and made my way to the shower to get ready for bed. As I headed towards my bedroom, my sister rushed past me and into my room. I turned to grab her, to get her out, but I got caught up by what she said.

'Who are you?'

I immediately looked to the place where she projected her voice and I could see it. The haunting figure of a familiar individual. They appeared to be floating ... I could not stop staring. I knew this person. The more I looked, the more I saw; they were not floating, they were hanging by a rope as if they had been hanged in times past. It was like pins and needles in my veins, they started at the top of my head and made their way to my toes. I know who this person is and so I should—I have stared at this person in the mirror for the last eighteen years. As I gazed into my own eyes, I heard the voices again, but this time, they came from the other me. Voices muffled, almost as if it— as if I was trying to speak, while being strangled. I stepped forward, and as I did, I heard the same word very clearly.

'Die!'

JUDE

Kira Whyte

Jude Miller led an unfortunate life. She wouldn't tell you that, though. If you asked her how she was, she'd laugh and say something dismissive or cliché.

Completely fine. Nothing interesting to tell, really!

Everyone lies about their underlying troubles sometimes. Jude was an extraordinarily ordinary civilian. Every so often, she wondered if her fairytale ending was still waiting for her.

Her home was adequate, though barely liveable. She had been in Melbourne for a large portion of her life. The house sat tucked in the comfort of a cul-de-sac, surrounded by dead grass and a collection of broken cars. Her neighbour insisted on fixing each of the cars, but

Jude had never held him to the expectation. She'd often thought about renovating her home, for its withering age had crept up over the years.

One day, I tell ya. I'll fix this old thing up, good as new.

It was within the confines of those decaying walls that demons etched at her mind and body. Like many, her vulnerability seeped out behind closed doors.

Jude took her keys out of her bag and unlocked the front door with ease, as she had done for the last nine years. There was a tinge of rat poison wafting in the air, blending with the dust she hadn't found time to clean. She'd become accustomed to the smell, it lived with her.

I'll clean it soon; I just haven't had the time. But soon, I will.

Jude walked down the hallway, silently inspecting the unkept bedrooms. She was pleased to find that nobody was home this afternoon.

She moved toward her bedroom, locating the source of her fabricated relief. It was an embarrassing habit she wouldn't disclose to anybody outside of that community, especially given she'd helped others overcome the detriments of this drug within her job. The darkness of its hues enticed Jude's sensibilities, creating an enveloping satisfaction merely from the act of holding. *This substance will help me to forget,* she told herself. She knew things were, in fact, not as they should be.

Jude hadn't known the effects of heroin until she met her lover, Josef. Her childhood had been stock standard, heavily religious, rejecting the dark corners of humankind. She often mulled over whether it would have benefited her to know the culture of the drug war. Her father's fault for sheltering her, she thought. It'd been ten years since his death. While she had originally rebelled against his confining religious regulations, she yearned for them now. Josef had introduced her to the seductive world of substance abuse, though she would rather not dwell on such terminology for the drug.

'Get your filthy hands off that, I just got it.' Josef's low voice interrupted Jude's moment with the small bag.

Jude froze, putting the bag down and turning around to face her soon-to-be husband. Instantly, she recognised evidence of frustration in Josef's expression. Jude subtly swallowed, knowing the typical outcome of a tough day at work. She still had shades of purple, blue and orange scattered strategically across her thighs and stomach from his last bad day. As if her body was a canvas for Josef's emotions. He never hurt her above the neck; it would be too obvious. Too reportable.

He grunted, and walked toward the cabinet to collect his poison, and left Jude in the bedroom to be alone with her relief. She followed him, failing to resist the voice in her brain telling her to indulge in the contents of Josef's plastic bag. He went to the kitchen, a ritual followed every afternoon, to cook an egg or two before submitting to a needle.

'Where's the pepper?' he demanded, rummaging through the spice cabinet. Jude had found dried oregano from three years ago sitting in their pantry not many days earlier. She stepped back as Josef began throwing the spices on the floor, spilling a rainbow of green basil and red chilli flakes. For a short moment, Jude admired the herbed art.

'Why don't you ever clean this shit up?' he cursed. 'Can't find anything in this place.'

'The pepper is in its usual spot,' Jude responded, instantly regretting having said anything.

It wasn't long before he launched himself toward Jude, inflicting his frustrations onto his fiancée. His violence was a staple occurrence in their household, and Jude had learned it was better to resist fighting him off. Disturbingly, Jude experienced a dissociative feeling when he hit her similar to when she was using. An explicit escape that she couldn't replicate in any other way. Because as he was hitting her, she didn't have to worry or wonder when it would happen. Living in a state of fearing violence, and her withdrawals from the drug were what scared her the most.

Eventually, she returned to her unfortunate reality. Her eyes slowly opened; regaining consciousness, she was face down on the aging carpet of her bedroom floor. She wasn't sure if Josef had dragged her there or if the fight had ended in this room. The blood cascading through her nose formed a small pool on the surface beneath her head. Her eyebrows scrunched. He had hit her above the neck. These were cosmetic issues she would have to deal with in the morning before work.

'Makeup will cover that. God, I hope Leah doesn't see it,' Jude stammered.

Dabbing her nose with her uniform, she made her way down the haunting darkness of the hallway. Voices were coming from the living room.

'There you are, darling,' Josef smiled, surrounded by a group of their friends.

Tuesday nights, just as any other, were an opportunity to gather. Mary rose quickly and walked towards her bruised friend. She glanced at Jude's uniform and inspected the red stains for a split second before meeting her sore eyes again.

'Jude, join us. You look like you need a hit.'

They never spoke of relationship troubles. Mary dealt with her own dark household secrets. It was easier not to ask. Better left unsaid.

Josef wrapped a tender arm around her, gifting her a needle with the other. Jude gazed down at the tar-like fluid. She didn't hesitate to take it from him and suppressed a sigh of relief. There were no words to be said, her face hurt. She needed the escape.

'There's a little too much in there, don't ya think, Seffy?' Mary's partner, Nathan warned.

'Thought I'd spoil her a bit,' Josef replied, squeezing Jude. She ignored the pain of his grasp.

There was a lot in the needle. Jude dismissed it, perhaps it would be the best escape. Mary helped tighten the tourniquet Jude had stolen from work around her frail arm. Jude watched as the liquid invaded her body and she fell into euphoric bliss. At first, the high was familiar. Every cell in Jude's body lit up, sending her into wondrous illusions of hope and reverie. There was a change in pace. Her euphoria rapidly twisted, she felt her body temperature rise. She was aware of very little, but conscious of her heart rate. The irregular rhythm was thumping in the chest of her petite frame. She felt that her heart would blast through her fragile, bruised skin. The feeling devouring her was not a regular high.

Jude had faded away from her living room. Her heart rate dropped, and her vision welcomed absolute darkness. Slowly, a light peeked through her eyelids.

Have I been asleep all night?

Her hands stretched across a soft duvet. Her back melted into a mattress she knew couldn't be from her home. On the walls around her were posters of various musical artists. A mid-sized guitar sat in the corner of the room. A floral design splayed on the face of the guitar; it was one of Jude's favourite art projects. Her small, bright yellow radio was playing a soft tune from atop her dresser. A cool breeze swept through the room.

Jude was in her childhood bedroom.

Her feet carried her off the bed. She was confused, but she asked no questions. Her body took her out of the room in an autonomous motion. A comforting voice called for her in the kitchen. Jude's father stood in their pleasant house. He stirred a cup of tea in the mug Jude had gifted him 16 Father's Days ago.

'Blossom. How are you?' He spoke calmly. It was as if he were there, like he was still alive.

A tear fell down Jude's cheek. She hadn't cried in a long time. The barriers Jude built for herself crumbled. Her tears signified the vulnerability spilling over the surface of her unconscious mind.

'You are dying, blossom,' her father said, passing the cup of tea to his daughter.

Jude looked at the tea and then back to him. She couldn't speak, only listen.

'Drink your tea, blossom. Save yourself.' He smiled. Every wrinkle, every spot and hair follicle were precise in Jude's memory. The commanding tone in his voice was unfalteringly how it would have been ten years ago.

Jude picked up the tea, feeling its warmth as she brought it to her lips. Her hands weren't shaky in this reality, her face didn't feel wincing shoots of pain at every expression, her feet stood firm. She felt strong. Her body embraced the tea with grace, as slowly her father dissolved from view. Empowerment echoed alluringly through her body. She didn't feel sorry bidding her father goodbye, she knew he was always with her. Feeling the power of his love again cradled her, sending her into a cascade of hopefulness. But darkness met her once more before she reconciled with the truth. Her new reality pulsed a pattern of electronic noises and indistinct conversation between familiar voices.

'Jude, stay with us, love,' a woman's voice coaxed.

It was Jude's co-worker, Leah, who greeted her back into the world. For the first time in her adult life, Jude found herself the patient rather than the nurse. Leah's uniform mirrored Jude's; only it didn't display the result of her bloody horrors. Leah was one of the many people Jude had created a fabricated reality for, made of those lies we tell. And now, Jude lay in the most vulnerable and undeniable position she had ever revealed to anyone.

'Help,' Jude managed.

The ambulance carried her through the night and onto a new path of truth.

BLACKNESS

Frazer Ramsden

Blackness.
The night sky is friendless with no moon to keep it company, in a world void of colour and laughter and movement. Mark sits in the gloom and looks at the ground but can't see a thing. His heel traces a circle on a buoyant floor he feels he should be falling through.

Light shines through the stretch of black, making him shield his eyes.

He looks back and finds a streetlamp that illuminates a section of hardwood floor. A wall extends from one side of the light's perimeter to the other. Outside of the light's gleam, darkness completely conceals his surroundings, as if nothing else exists.

The wall's profile is drab, stripped of wallpaper or coloured paint, as it always is. Along the wall, a sliding-door closet has been pried open and in front of it, a storage box lies on its side. Photographs litter the floor, and a large photo frame with dark mahogany edges lies facedown on the strewn pictures. He hasn't seen the frame since he moved in, which was months ago.

He turns and sprints through the blackness, not once turning back to the light.

Mark sits on the living room couch with a dinner plate full of beef and vegetables lying on his lap, and cutlery sits face-up over the food while he crosses his arms. Just like at every meal, his stomach screams, but he can't manage more than a few bites.

The television blares but Mark doesn't hear a word. Instead, his mind wanders to last night's dream. He shakes his head, grabs his beer resting on the coffee table and takes a swig. Some late-night talk show host speaks on the screen in a black and white pinstriped suit, with fabric so sleek it looks like wallpaper. Mark pinches his own work shirt and looks at a stain the size of a tennis ball covering his collar. He has no idea what caused it or how long it's been there.

Glass smashes on tiles.

He jolts and looks down. Beer seeps between his toes while shards of glass twinkle on the white-tiled floor. He stares at his hand where the glass had been. 'Fuck,' he says.

He shoots to his feet, steps over the mess and marches up the stairs, the hardwood floor thudding under him. When he reaches the hallway closet, he throws the sliding door to the side and clasps a broom handle. He rips it from the closet and spins but stops when he hears something thump on the floor behind him.

He turns. Piles of pictures scatter the ground in front of a storage box tipped on its side. Light glimmers off a dark mahogany picture frame lying on its face. He tries to take a step forward to tidy the mess, but he staggers and plants his foot down. He sighs. 'It's just a photo, Mark,' he says and kneels to it, his hand hovering above its back.

As soon as he turns the photo and sees the little girl's auburn hair, the picture slips from his grip. Glass breaks, and Mark spurts to his feet.

He clenches his fists and peers back to the floor where the girl stares up at him, a crack slicing through her smile. A woman with the same shade of auburn hair sits on the girl's left and smooches her head, while a man with long, scraggly locks kisses her from her right. The girl smiles with a clenched face as the man's bushy beard tickles her cheek.

Mark steps over the photo and heaves his bedroom door open. The mattress creaks as he rolls onto his bed. He rips the doona across him and leaves the house a mess.

Blackness.

Mark hums and strides through the darkness. There's no urge to feel out for what's in front of him. He'd be fine with walking off a cliff.

A beam flashes above, followed by a hiss and crackle. He stops as blinding white light fills his vision; he covers his eyes as they strain and shakes his head as his brain aches. When his vision finally adjusts, he sees a streetlamp shining over the base of a pine tree.

The tree towers above the lamp, so Mark can't see its crown. Its body leans to the right. He scans down, following its slanted figure. Chunks of wood have splintered from the bottom of the trunk, revealing white inner bark—a wound that will never heal.

He turns and sprints through the blackness, not once turning back to the light.

Mark tugs his tie loose as he drives home from work. As he travels down the highway, exhaustion sets in, and his eyes flutter. He doesn't battle his slipping consciousness. He'd be fine with falling asleep and running right off the road.

He jolts as the tree from last night's dream springs in his mind. He shakes his head furiously and gapes through the windscreen. A sign for the upcoming exit appears in the distance, so he flicks his left indicator, even though the sign says the offramp is five hundred metres away. His fingers drum on the wheel, and his upper body leans forward as he waits. The exiting lane comes into view, so Mark speeds up. Suddenly, he spots blinking yellow lights on the offramp. Large trucks block the exit, while an LED sign sits on the grass road verge. It reads: ROADWORKS AHEAD—USE ALTERNATIVE ROUTE.

Mark inhales sharply, but his throat seizes mid-breath, and air sputters from his mouth. During the coughing fit, his body stiffens and his vision blurs. All he sees is a stream of black and the lurid flash of yellow lights. After he passes the glow, he shakes his head, refocuses his vision and looks to the right. The pine forest he's been ignoring stands tall and in parallel rows.

He looks at their crowns and grimaces as he notices one treetop leans to the right. His eyes glance down its base. When he sees the white wound where bark has splintered off, visions pierce his mind.

Crunched metal, reflective lighting, blood streaming down pale skin.

He clenches his eyes shut, straightens his arms and leans back. A ringing vibrates through the car as his left tyre drives over rumble strip. He tugs the wheel right and the car swerves to the other side of the road where he runs into the opposite line then rips the wheel back. He counts:

One.

Two.

Three.

The afternoon sun shines through the windscreen. He twists his head up and gazes at the trees' crowns. Each treetop stands sharp and straight.

His fingers tremor along the steering wheel. He speeds away from the pine, but the memory still pulses in his head.

Night-time crickets echo through the open window as Mark hunches forward on the side of his bed. His fingers tremor in his lap as he thinks back to the highway. It's been months since he's travelled down that stretch. He shakes his head, lays into his bed and rips the doona across him. His mind races and his body quivers, but he keeps his eyes clasped shut until he reaches—

Blackness.

Winds blow through the shadows and across Mark's skin, making him shiver. He spins and sprints, cutting left and right to avoid the impending glow.

Brightness shines down from his right, followed by the sound of a hissing ring. He turns to his left and sprints through the blackness, not once turning back to the light. He dashes until his chest heaves and his legs burn. Finally, he stops and doubles over, inhaling large spurts of air. As he looks to the ground, he hears a crackle and a hiss. His body stiffens and he looks forward.

A woman stands underneath the streetlamp with her hands at her hips. Sharp blonde strands flow down her head as she glares with blue eyes. Mark rushes to his feet and readies to turn, but her voice freezes him.

'Why'd you kill them?' she says.

Mark staggers backward. 'Wha—what—'

'You killed them,' she cuts through. 'You killed them.' She chants the phrase, louder each time. Mark turns and tries to run but stumbles to the ground. He rises and runs and each time she repeats the phrase, his shoulders and legs jolt. The words spit through her lips a final time. He clasps his ears and drops, unable to rise again.

Mark dawdles down his driveway in his work suit, wheelie bin in tow. He parks it on the gutter, ready for collection day tomorrow. Evening winds blow into him and remind him of last night's dream.

He jerks as the hum of a car engine sounds on the street. Light beams down the road, and Mark turns away from it as he waits for the car to pass. Brake pads squeak. He stops shivering as he feels the warmth of the car's engine.

'Excuse me, can you help me with directions? I'm new to this neighbourhood,' a soft voice says.

He turns his head to the parked car and bends down. Shadows mask her face.

'Where are you heading?' he asks.

'Georgia Street.'

'You've nearly hit it. It's actually your next left,' he says and points ahead.

'Of course, I was that close. Sorry to bother you. I just get confused in this new area. All the streets and houses look the same, don't they?'

'You get used to it. I've actually come to like it.'

'Oh, really? Might be harder for me,' she laughs. 'My old neighbourhood had much more space between houses. Hey, have we met before? You look very familiar.'

Mark frowns. She flicks her interior light on, revealing sky blue eyes and sharp blonde strands that flow down her head. 'Mark?' she says.

He turns and sprints up his driveway. As he reaches the footpath to his front door, the car door clicks open and slams closed. Mark makes it to the front door and clasps the steel handle, hands shaking as he tries to heave down. His fingers slip and he groans. The chant starts in his head as he readies for the words to spit across the driveway.

You.

Mark reclasps the handle and tugs it downwards.

Killed.

He rips the door open.

'It's ok,' she says.

He freezes.

'It's ok,' she repeats. 'You don't have to run.'

He peers over his shoulder. Her arms are open and outstretched.

'You can come back. You don't have to go inside.'

He gapes at her. She smiles and waves him over. His fingers loosen from the handle, and he totters down the driveway.

When he reaches her, his lips part but he says nothing.

She rushes forward with her arms spread wide. Mark grimaces and steps back, stopping her as she approaches. 'Mark, what's wrong? I'm giving you a hug,' she says.

'Oh, right, I'm sorry,' he says and walks forward, leaving his arms by his side while she embraces him. His back stiffens under her touch.

'How are you, Harley?' he says when they part. His eyes direct towards the road.

'I'm great now. I've missed you.'

'Really?' he says, frowning.

'Of course. Didn't expect to see you here. What did you do with your beard and hair? I barely recognised you.'

He rubs his buzzcut. 'I'm trying a plainer look.'

'You've never been plain. You do look handsome, but I wish you kept your locks. Joyce would never have married you if you looked like this.'

He winces.

Harley steps forward and pats his arm. 'Oh, Mark, I'm sorry. I didn't mean to upset you.'

He tugs his arm away and squares his shoulders, still looking to the road. 'This is a little hard for me.'

'I understand. It's been hard for me too. I'm sorry I didn't reach out after the accident. I couldn't really cope during that time. Took a couple months off work and only really talked to the family. I wish I was there for you. You're family too.'

Mark parts his lips.

She leans forward, waiting for a response that never comes. After a while, she says, 'Do you like it here? In this new house?'

He turns to his home and shrugs. 'It's small. Simple. All I really need. So, you moved as well?'

'Yeah, I did. How's that? We're practically neighbours. You'll have to come visit. The kids miss their uncle.'

He bites his lip and rubs his forehead. 'I probably should.'

'I tried visiting you at your old place about a month ago, because you weren't returning my calls. I was a little sad when I knocked on the door and you weren't there. Even when I peered in from the doorstep, I knew something was wrong, seeing all the new furniture. I wish you had stayed.'

He nods his head.

'So, you're done with all your court troubles?' she says.

'Yeah, I'm done with all that.'

'I was following a lot of it in the paper, and I'll admit, when I first started reading, I hoped you'd go to jail. I'm sure that's hard to hear. I was just angry and felt I needed to blame someone. When I calmed down though, I was so thankful you were found not guilty.'

'Really?'

'Of course.'

Mark breaks his gaze from the ground and stares at Harley. 'You don't have to do this.'

'Do what?'

'You don't have to talk to me. You don't have to apologise. You don't have to invite me to your home. You can just leave me to live in my shitty house, with my shitty haircut and my shitty clothes.' His shoulders slump forward. 'I killed your sister and niece.'

She places her hand on her chest and frowns. 'Why would you say that? You didn't kill them.'

'What would you call it?'

'You fell asleep.'

'It doesn't matter.'

She clutches his arm and steps to him. 'Yes, it does matter. It wasn't your fault. You were asleep. Those girls loved you, Mark.'

He winces and looks back to the road.

'Look at me,' she says.

His lip quivers as he twists his head.

She digs her nails into his arm. 'They loved you,' she says. 'And you loved them. And you never wished them harm. It wasn't your fault.'

Mark feels heat rise to his face. He covers his eyes before the tears break.

'Hey, hey, it's ok,' she says, patting his arm. 'You can cry.'

Mark sighs and tries to turn from Harley, but she grabs his hand and spins him back. 'It's ok. Just cry, Mark; it means you care.'

He breathes in. He breathes out. His head sinks into her shoulder, and he weeps.

'I'm sorry,' he says.

FURTHER DOWN THE PATH

Ethan Turner

Creek water ran through the lush green valley, with rocky ridges running parallel on the left side and dense rainforest enveloping the right. A path concealed by large ferns under tall trees poured shade onto the ground below. A tall, middle-aged man with light stubble along his cheeks and jaw, and frayed hair that was greying on the side, walked through the rainforest. He was wearing a faded olive-green jacket, a backpack filled with camping gear, brown pants and brown hiking boots. Finally, he thrust through the oversized plants shrouding the path.

As he walked, the sounds of water flowed through the man's left ear, while the sounds of birds chirping, calling and singing played in his right ear. He watched the light brown ridges clash with the blue creek while the bank met with the assorted greens of the rainforest. The aromas from the plants and creek water moved into the man's nostrils. Broad leaves ran along the sides of the dirt path the man walked on, extending his right hand to brush the plant leaves and ferns, feeling their paper-like texture.

After some distance he spotted a sign with an arrow pointing in the direction he was heading. A tent was painted on the sign, which was splintered, and the paint faded. The man continued and as he marched the sun set and began hiding behind the ridges; the shadows loomed over the creek and blended with the shade of the rainforest trees. The man found a small, flat grassy area between the creek and the rainforest. He took his backpack off and began to set up his tent.

After he finished preparing his tent, the man sat and reached into his jacket to pull out a photo. The photo displayed two young men with their arms hanging around each other's necks beside a creek with a ridge in the background. The one on the right was taller than the one on the left. Both looked similar to each other. One wore an olive-green jacket and the other wore a currant-red jacket. The man turned the photo around—there was writing on the back, saying, 'Randall and Nathan. Camping, 2000.' He stood and faced the campsite, then held up the photo. It matched with the creek and ridge perfectly. He put the photo back into his pocket and released a deep sigh.

'Where'd you go, Nate?' Randall raised his head to look further down the path.

He looked up and saw stars emerging in a dark purple sky as the sun continued to set. He looked towards the path again and noticed imprints. He walked over and squatted to investigate. They had the shape of a boot print. His expression turned troubled. There shouldn't be anyone else in the vicinity. As far as Randall knew, only he and Nate knew about the path. He stood and scanned the edge of the rainforest. He could only see the green of plants and brown trunks near the path. The plants and tree trunks further into the rainforest were swallowed by the shadows. The longer Randall looked, the more the rainforest's shadows grew and became darker. The sounds of birds and insects stopped, as silence quickly swept through the rainforest; the only sound that broke the silence was of the water from the creek. As Randall looked into the rainforest, he heard a stick snap to his left. He turned to look, but there was nothing.

Randall looked down at the footprints. He marched back towards the camp, grabbed his backpack and a torch then took a deep breath before deciding to follow the footprints. As he followed the footprints, yelps and calls entered his ears, startling him. He turned on his torch and continued to walk down the path while trying to locate the source of the sounds. After a minute, the sounds ended.

Randall continued until he reached a fork in the path. This section of the track was unfamiliar to him. The left ran parallel to the creek and the other led to the right, into the rainforest. The sky had finished its transformation, black with white specks across its canvas. Randall shined his torch over and surveyed the area around him. The only sound that could still be heard was the creek flowing through the valley. Where the path divided, a currant-red jacket caught Randall's eye. His hands shook as he studied it; it was in perfect condition, as if he had bought it that day. He began to sweat as thoughts of finding out what happened to his brother raced through his mind. He pointed the torch down the right path, hoping to see what was ahead, but the overgrown flora only got thicker. After shining the torch down the left path all he saw was a dirt trail that continued along the creek, with stones dotted along its bank. He shined the torch towards the ground and noticed that the footprints split into two sets as well, one going left and one going right.

Confused on which way to go, he squatted to study the footprints, trying to see if there was anything that differentiated them from one another. As he studied them, he heard leaves and sticks crunching and cracking deep within the rainforest. He flicked his torch towards the rainforest but saw nothing. The sounds ceased. He looked back at the footprints and concluded that both sets were identical. More cracks and snaps accompanied by rustling surged from the rainforest. Randall stood and looked down both paths. He stepped to the left, towards the path running along the creek.

'Randy. Come on! It's gonna be dark soon!'

Randall snapped towards the right path, torch pointed in that direction, seeing the same sight as before, overgrowth all over the path.

'Nate! You there? Come on, let's go home! Mum's gonna get worried if we don't get home soon!'

'Come on, Randy! Get a move on! It's gonna be dark soon.'

Randall heard footsteps on the dirt ahead of him, walking farther and farther away. He wiped sweat from his forehead, took a deep breath and stormed down the path to find his brother.

'Nate!'

Randall trudged through the rainforest, pushing leaves and plants out of his way, swiping at bugs that were looking to make a home of various parts of his body. The darkness created a pitch-black wall around Randall. The only source of light that remained was shining from Randall's torch. As he strode through the untamed plants, the sounds of ferns swishing and feet crushing leaves all around him. He stopped to listen, and as he focused, whispers emerged.

'Come on, Randy! Let's go down to the creek!'

'Wait up, Nate! Don't leave me behind!'

Randall stood on the path, his arms shaking. Tears welled in his eyes. Footsteps emanated from further down the path, with each step coming closer. When he raised his torch, he saw the leaves and plants moving to the sides as though there was something pushing through them. Randall could not recognise it.

'Come on, Randy, check this out!' echoed through the rainforest.

The footsteps, the rustling, the voices stopped. Sweat poured down Randall's face. He took a deep breath, then continued down the path.

After trudging for some time in silence, the path ended in a small clearing with the darkness surrounding it. In the middle of the clearing was a tent. Randall shined his torch at it.

'Nate?'

No response. No movement. No cricket or insect made ambient noise. No wind. He was too deep into the rainforest for the sound of the creek to play in his ears. Randall took small steps towards the tent. Sweat intensified with every step. As he moved closer, he noticed red mixed with the dirt and the grass in front of the tent. Randall thought, 'Nate's tent?' He stood in front of the tent, above the red coloured dirt and grass. Could not hear anything. Just silence. He reached for the tent flap and slowly pulled it open. He shined the torch inside and saw a sleeping bag, backpack, and other camping gear all neatly set up. Randall looked at the sleeping bag and saw a photo where the feet would be. He picked it up. The photo depicted Randall walking past the dilapidated camping site sign, sun setting with the creek in the background. He dropped the photo and stomped backwards, away from the tent. Eyes wide, breathing fast. He spun and shined his torch at the rainforest, only to see nothing but plants and tree trunks corralling him in the clearing.

As he inspected the rainforest the sound of running surrounded him. Two, three, four, maybe more pairs of feet sprinted all around him in the rainforest. Plants and leaves rustled; whispers echoed.

'Who are you? What did you do with Nate? Where is my brother?'

The whispers were intelligible, but there was one amongst them that grabbed Randall's attention.

'Where were you? Why did you leave me? Why couldn't you find me?'

'I don't know where you went! You disappeared! There was no sign of you! Tell me where you went and I'll find you!'

'Down the path. Further down the path.'

A strong wind came in from behind the tent and blew it directly onto Randall. The tent tangled him within it, he struggled. Finally, he got an arm free and ripped the tent apart, freeing himself from its stranglehold. He then looked back and saw a path leading deeper into the rainforest.

Randall followed it. It took him through a little canyon, with walls of rock on both sides, and after some time his torch started flickering. He held it closer and hit it, but the flickering didn't stop, then it suddenly shut off. He patted himself down and combed through his pockets for any spare batteries, with no success. He ventured on in complete darkness, walking for a couple of metres before his left foot took another step but there was no ground for him to step on. Forward momentum worked against him as he fell five metres to land on a hard surface. He felt lightheaded and fought to keep his eyes open. As his eyes closed, a man's yell reverberated.

'Randall, come on! We're almost there!'

Upon hearing Nate's voice, his eyes shot open. He pushed himself off the ground and felt a moist, rocky texture beneath him. As he stood, his head stung in pain.

He reached up to the right side of his head and felt wet. He winced in pain. Judging by the rocky ground, he believed that he was in a cave. He extended his left arm, found the wall, and limped through the cave, using it to hold himself up.

Randall was unsure how much time had passed since he first started walking in search of Nate. At this point, he questioned whether he wanted the answer regarding the fate of his brother. He questioned if this was real. Or if it was some sick nightmare. After walking for some time his foot caught on a rock and fell onto his front. He planted his hands down and felt something under his right hand. He fiddled with the item. Then he started to flick it with his thumb and sparks came out before a small flame lit. He continued forward with the lighter showing the way.

'Keep going, Randy. You're almost there.'

Every step Randall took, his eyes closed more and more until he stumbled into an open, circular section of the cave. He saw something on the cave ground in the centre. He staggered into the centre and fell to his knees. He extended his lighter closer to the object to make out what it was. The lighter illuminated a skeleton wearing several items of clothing, including a jacket of a faded currant-red colour. Randall's eyes widened as his body and breathing became shaky. As he stared at the skeleton, wind blew through the cave, carrying a voice with it.

'Check it out, Randy.'

The wind became stronger and stronger, Randall tucked his head down to protect himself from its assault. After a couple of seconds, the cave started to shake. The shaking intensified and rocks fell from the cave's ceiling. Randall stood, and wobbled around as he tried to find his footing. He looked to where he entered the room as several rocks fell from the ceiling, blocking it off.

'You found me, Randy.'

More rocks collapsed around Randall, and as he dodged them, the force of the wind blew him off balance, causing him to fall. He tried to get back up but an enormous rock fell onto his legs, crushing them. He screamed but it was drowned out by the sounds of the cave collapsing. He tried to lift the rock but the effort was futile.

The voice being carried on the wind spoke again. 'I always went on without waiting for you, Randy, but this time I'll wait.'

Randall spent the last of his energy trying to move the boulder off his legs. The shaking and wind stopped with the last of the falling rocks. Other than Randall's grunts of pain, silence filled the room. Then the same voice broke the silence. 'Sleep, Randy. We have a big day tomorrow.' Randall laid back in defeat. His eyes refused to stay open, and his breathing slowed as he was lulled to sleep next to his brother in a welcoming darkness.

FATE'S ORDEAL

Pandella Maultby

Cassandra ran a finger along the glimmering crystal ball before her. As she stroked the surface, a perfect image of her walking hand-in-hand with her mortal enemy appeared. His tall, slender stature and dark waves were unmistakable—though it had been years since she last saw him ... since they had parted ways. She watched, captivated as the foreign version of herself stopped walking and kissed the despicable man.

As rage boiled inside her, she slapped the globe right off the table. A scarlet glow filled the room as the glass connected with the tiles. Entranced by the flash, Cass fell to the ground beside the shards, her tears mixing with the glimmering liquid. She reached for a jar, desperate to save the elixir, but as she touched it, it boiled and turned to steam. With the tiles completely dry, Cass scooped the glass shards into the jar instead. She tried desperately to put the translucent puzzle back together. Hours passed, but every time she let go, the pieces shattered to the table.

Cass had always liked to have a clear idea of her clients before they came. It helped to give a better reading if she already had an idea of who they were. She never expected that habit would get her in so much trouble or cause her so much pain. She held a shard in her palm and squeezed; she squeezed as hard as her heart wrenched. Blood dripped from her hand and stained the colourful picnic rug she used as a table cloth. Once the ache in her hand overpowered the one in her heart, she dropped the glass. She knew better than anyone that you cannot change your destiny, yet still she wanted to try.

Ignoring the ache in her palm, she pulled out every bottle of potion she could find and laid them out on the table along with a glass punch bowl. She spent the next hour mixing every different concoction she could think of, but none reacted to her touch the way the mixture in the crystal ball did. They would sparkle and bubble and steam, but none produced a picture other than her own tired reflection.

The grandfather clock in the hall striking one was the last thing she heard as she passed out on the potion-stained picnic rug.

There she was, perfect blonde curls shaped her youthful face as her midnight blue eyes focused on the tarots laid out across the plastic folding table. The man across from her flipped three cards: the Magician reversed, the World reversed and the Page of Water upright.

'Interesting. The cards are telling me that it may be time to implement some changes in your life, perhaps you have been feeling like an imposter in your own world, you're not feeling connected to others. But, they're also showing that you may be nearing the end of that journey. Someone new is going to enter your life or a new phase is beginning within your existing relationships,' the young Cass explained.

'I've been feeling like I have been living in an illusion; nothing seems quite real. That was until today. Until I saw you.'

'You're too kind. I hope the reading helps you find the connection that you've been missing. I haven't yet got the skills or utensils to give you more direction, but one day ... maybe.'

'Perhaps you could help me find that connection over dinner? Surely I don't need to tell you when or where, surely you know that already.'

'I'm not that good yet, but I can give you my card. That way you can always contact me for a follow up consult. I do home calls and meetings.'

The grandfather clock chimed six times startling Cass. Golden light filtered through the sheer curtains, steering her gaze to the mess she'd left. As her stare focused on the indigo concoction, her mind began to wander.

'That reading was never meant for him, was it, spirit? It was meant for me, wasn't it? The new person, time of change, master of illusion, heightened psychic abilities, end of a journey ... that all happened to me, not him. I can't do it again, spirit.' The liquid began to boil. 'I know, spirit, but look what it cost.'

Her phone chimed from its dock behind her, reminding her of the day's appointments—not that she ever needed reminding, but that day she was glad for her own preparedness. With a long day of readings ahead of her, she knew she had to open her doors, despite the crystal ball mishap. After downing a double shot vanilla latte and doing a quick meditation, she swept up the tiny shards of glass, tipped the indigo liquid down the sink, rearranged the potion bottles on the shelves and changed the soiled picnic rug. And so as not to disappoint her regular clients, she found a glass ornamental ball that could pass as a crystal ball—after all, the clients couldn't see what she saw anyway, she just had to hope the cards would tell her enough to create a convincing read. She had relied so heavily on the ball to do the work for her, the thought of going back to basic tarot readings terrified her.

Cass regained confidence in her abilities as she breezed through every appointment without a hitch—no unexpected walk-ins, no doubting clients and no devil-man. When the grandfather clock chimed four she let out a relieved sigh and started to pack up the deck and sweep out the shop. Just as she was putting the broom away, she heard the doorbell jingle. She knew it could only be one person; his dark aura was unmistakable.

'Hello, Cassie. Long time no see. I've been calling you, but you haven't replied. Why might that be?'

She refused to face him. 'I'm not sure. Maybe you have an old number.'

'Oh, I wasn't calling your phone.'

'I know. I got your message and then I ... I deleted it.'

'You can't delete destiny, my darling.'

'No. You can.' Cass gathered her confidence and turned to face the tall, slender man. 'Despite everything you said, I tell each of my clients this. And I'm not out of business yet ... quite the contrary, actually. I'm the most popular psychic in the city. People don't want to just know their future, they want to know how they can have the best future possible.'

'Still ... you know your best future is by my side. You know I can help you become so much more than this.'

'I'm happy with this.' She gestured around the shop. 'This is all I need. I don't want or need your dark magic.'

'You will.' He opened the door. 'I'll see you tomorrow, when you change your mind.'

Cass gulped down a heavy breath once the door slammed behind him. The rage reignited within her. She hung an 'Out of Business' notice on the door and got to work boarding up the windows and doors. It wasn't the first time she'd started anew, only this time she knew she had to give up her talent once and for all. She pulled out a suitcase and began to pack. Clothes, toiletries, snacks, tarots, and potions all went in, and tarots and potions came back out. With suitcase in hand and a navy cape draped over her head and cascading down her back, she drenched the fire and left.

She walked for hours—no plan, no end destination— until the moon peaked overhead. An encounter with the man in the dark was inevitable at her current pace. Buses waited patiently at each bus stop, but she knew better than to get on—they were all traps set by spirit. The manual readings, meeting with her mortal enemy and the walking left her spent. Still, she couldn't spend the night out in the open by the highway, so she continued.

She finally stopped for the night at the furthest picnic bench in a dimly lit park and laid down her suitcase. Dinner consisted of a granola bar and a bottle of water—it wasn't much but her stomach was too knotted to notice. She sunk down to the cement and stared at the full moon.

'Spirit, I need help. I can't go back to him, you need to help me,' she whispered. Just as a rogue cloud blanketed the moon, she groaned and gave in to her heavy eyelids, allowing the visions to return.

Young Cass sat at the dining table in a very bare version of her shop, a smile etched across her face. The dark-auraed man walked in from the kitchen carrying a beautifully decorated two-layer cake with three candles on top. He sang 'Happy Birthday' as he sat the cake down between them and took a seat opposite her. As soon as he finished singing, she closed her eyes and blew out the candles.

'That's not all I have for you, my darling. I love you so much, and I want to help you take your talent to a new level here.'

He reached under his seat and pulled out a wooden box with a big red bow on top and hearts intricately carved into the sides. He carefully passed the box to her. She smiled wider as she carefully untied the ribbon. As the box fell open, a bright pink flash filled the shop. As the light faded, she ran her fingers over the violet velvet inside of the box. Right in the centre sat a glimmering glass globe on a decorative golden stand.

'Is this?' *she whispered as she hovered her hands over the glass.* 'Show me—'

'Save it for your first client. Let's have some cake.'

She nodded and gently closed the box.

Cass awoke to a raven squawking in her face and pecking at her half-eaten granola bar; she tossed the bar into the garden, startling the raven. She stood up, stretched and admired her surroundings—it had been a long time since she'd woken up in a park. She had to do a double-take as the man from her visions appeared out the corner of her eye on the other side of the park. Unfortunately, she wasn't hallucinating. He ambled towards her. She stood her ground and waited for him.

'Good morning, my darling. You changed your mind yet?'

'No, but I, uh ...' she gathered her composure. 'I do need your help.'

'I knew you'd ask sooner or later.'

'It's not what you think. I just need a new crystal ball. Just tell me where you get them.'

'I will get you a new one, on one condition.'

'No. No conditions. Not this time. Just give me an address or whatever, no strings attached.'

'I just want to buy you breakfast, that's all.' He reached out and took her hand in his, rubbing circles on her palm. 'Then I'll take you to get the ball, I promise.'

'Then I'll never have to see you again?'

'If that is still what you wish.'

'Deal.'

Cass allowed him to keep holding her hand and lead her out of the park to a quaint café about a block away. The longer they sat and drank and ate the more comfortable Cass felt. She began to remember how she fell in love with him in the first place; perhaps he was her destiny.

FLATLINE

Mami Okazaki

Please tell me   the truth about
what is **real** and what   is a **daydream**
in the world. Now I know that even if we wish, it may
not come true. I want to live with you in the dream. Just
you and me. I crave for your warmth every time I miss
you. But your cold body is empty and sorrowful. I know
you will never wake in my world. You know that you
will never take me to your world. Over and over
again, even if we wish. When you chose to go to
your world, you shed tears to teach me this
is reality. The tears are beautiful but
cruel, and tempt me into your
dream. But I haven't gone
yet because I decided
to live in my

world.

13

Chelsea   Cartledge

He is sound asleep, laying against the comfort of the plush blankets and heavy throws. His mop of chocolate brown curls falls in a cascade across the pillow, his wire-framed glasses askew on his face—he fell asleep reading. I still can't believe he's mine, even after so many years. I remember the day we met as though it was yesterday.

I frequented the small coffeehouse around the corner from the university housing. Sitting in the big, red lounges with my head in a book and a hot chocolate in my hand, lost in my world of whirlwind romances and audacious adventures.

I wasn't planning on going that day, as I was getting ready to meet a blind date for lunch. My best friend, Becky, had a habit of setting me up with all her boyfriend's friends—whether I wanted it or not. We'd known each other since kindy, and I couldn't tell her no—not that she'd listen if I did—so I would go along with it. This was the 12th guy she had set me up with, and from what she told me of him, I was hopeful. He was top of his class and, from what I'd heard, a good laugh. I'm a sucker for humour. I put on my nicest sundress—after changing half-a-dozen times—did my makeup—twice—and curled my hair—after straightening it first. I was 22 and never had a boyfriend. I wasn't picky; I just believed the right guy was out there, and I hadn't found him yet. Maybe lucky number 12 would prove me right.

I grabbed my handbag and checked myself twice in the mirror before heading out. Hesitating as I pushed the key into the lock of my dorm room, I kicked myself out of my head and headed down to the lobby. *What could go wrong this time that I hadn't already seen?*

Number 1 was obsessed with how much taller I was than him.

Number 3 already had another date lined up after ours.

Number 5 would not get off his phone the first 30 minutes of our date.

Number 7 kept looking at himself in the window reflection.

Number 9 was swiping right on Tinder as we were eating.

And don't even get me started on number 11. I thought I had seen it all.

Finding a park bench outside the lobby, I sat down; fifteen minutes early, but that was nothing unusual. It drove me crazy if I was ever stuck in traffic on the way to something important or running behind in getting ready. I pulled out the book I always kept in my handbag while I waited. It was a book I had found in an op-shop, an old and battered copy of *A Room with a View*, one of my favourites. The kind of unexpected love story you could only find in older times. Traipsing through early-1900s Italy with no purpose in mind, falling in love with a stranger. What a dream.

I glanced down at my watch: 12.15pm. Being stood up was worse than being late, in my book. And I had thought number 12 would be better than the last 11. I put my book in my purse and was heading back to the lobby when a car pulled up to the curb.

'Casey?' called a voice through the open window.

I bent down and saw a fresh cut of blonde hair and piercing blue eyes.

'Freddie?' I asked back. Becky forgot to mention he was cute. Maybe 12 was a lucky number after all.

Freddie smiled at me and hopped out of the car, heading around to open my door.

'Oh, thank you.' And gentlemanly.

'Sorry I was late. I'm new to this area,' he began, as he got back into the car and pulled out onto the street. 'I've never been on a blind date if I'm completely honest.'

'Really? Well, glad I can pop your blind date virginity.'

Had I really just said that? I wasn't good with surprises, and this date was already turning out to be a pleasant surprise, so of course my foot was already in my mouth.

'Well, I'm glad it is with someone as beautiful as you.' He laughed and looked over at me with a bright smile.

I relaxed into my seat, relieved to dodge that awkward first date bullet. I began to look around his car—nice and expensive. And him—clean, shaven, fancy watch, nice outfit.

We pulled up outside an extravagant restaurant. I'd heard of the place but never imagined ever being able to afford to eat there. But Freddie—with the nice car and fancy watch—I supposed he must come from some money. I always wondered what that was like, and now I guess I was finding out. He opened my door and offered me his arm before heading inside. I quietly gasped as we passed through the doors to reveal lush red carpets underneath cushy armchairs, stark white linen and polished cutlery on each table, glittery lights and sparkly chandeliers adorning the mirrored ceiling. I honestly believed I was dreaming. Especially since I was not dressed for the occasion. A sundress was not the correct attire for a place this nice. I wished we had spoken before, now I just looked out of place.

'Can you tell me a bit more about yourself? Becky didn't tell me much,' I asked, after we were seated at our table. Becky always liked an air of mystery, leaving me in the dark. And this was certainly all very mysterious. How could a uni student afford to even get a booking here?

'Well, there's not a whole lot to say.' He chuckled, pouring us both some champagne from the complimentary bottle. I suppose when you dined at a place as expensive as this, they were nice enough to give you free champagne. 'I grew up in Sydney with my two older sisters and parents, I play basketball for the university team, I'm studying biochemical engineering ...'

'Biochemical engineering, wow. That's intriguing.' Fancy guy, fancy degree. 'That must be a long degree.' I always dreamed of being a teacher, and my diploma was only four years; I couldn't imagine studying for longer than that.

'Yeah, it is.' He chuckled again, so smooth. 'It's six years. I have a long way to go.'

Six years. 'Wow.' I wondered why he would have a long way to go. He seemed old enough to be in his third or fourth year at least. I looked him over carefully. He seemed so mature and put together, he had to be 20-something. I began to wonder how quickly this was set up by Becky; surely she had done her background research. I took a sip of champagne to settle myself.

'Wait. How old are you?' I asked.

'I'm 17.'

I choked on my champagne.

'Are you alright?' he asked, concerned.

'Yeah, yeah, I'm fine.' I said, whacking my chest. '17? How are you in uni?'

'Well,' he laughed nervously, 'I'm not there yet. I graduate high school in a few weeks, but I'm taking all my prerequisites now.'

He was in high school. I, a 22-year-old student, was on a blind date with a high school boy.

'I'm sorry, I just ...' I didn't know what to say. 'How can you even afford to come here? And drink?'

He skulled the champagne, then grimaced. 'Oh, well, my parents have reserved seating ... I'm not meant to drink but come on. Free champagne.' He poured himself another full glass.

'I don't understand. But you play basketball with Alex on the uni team, right?'

'University basketball was lacking so they offered spots to seniors in high school.'

All these questions had come to my mind. I definitely could not stay on a date with a 17-year-old. I wondered if that was even legal.

'Is this not a surprise to you? Did you think I knew you were 17?'

He looked at me blankly. 'That never really came to mind. I mean, age is just a number, right?'

'Wrong. When you're five years older.' I couldn't believe my luck, I had to get out of there. While Freddie had continued to empty the champagne bottle, I slipped my phone out of my purse and typed ooo to Becky. In an instant, my phone rang.

'Oh, sorry. It's my Nan, do you mind?' I pointed to my phone.

'Not at all.'

I answered the phone as I left the table. 'Nan? Is everything alright?' Once I was out of earshot, I turned the tables. 'Are you crazy?'

'I ... what? Is the date not going well?' Becky asked on the other end of the line.

'Is it not going well?' I fumed. 'For starters, he is 17. A minor! And you think it'll be legal to sleep with him? How could you set me up with a baby? He's probably still on his red P plates but hid them when he picked me up. Honestly, Becky. Twelve dates and not even one worth it.'

'Hey, woah, relax,' she jumped in. 'I didn't know he was 17. I thought he was Alex's age because they played basketball together ... but I suppose he could have been younger.'

'Uh-huh,' I growled, but all I was met with was a moment of silence and then laughter.

'You're on a date with a teenager.'

'Becky, I will find you and I will kill you for this. How do I get out?'

'Oh, come on. It's a blind date. What do you expect?'

'For my best friend to take a little more care and not set me up with someone five years younger than me.'

She sighed. 'Okay, I'm Nan, right? So, say I had a fall.'

'Is that believable?'

'Come on, Casey. You've already done this 11 times. You should know how to flee a bad date by now.'

'Oh, shut up. I'm hanging up now.'

'Bye—' I stowed my phone back in my purse. I took a deep breath before heading back to the table, preparing the scene in my head.

'Freddie.'

He looked at me and saw the worried look on my face.

'Is everything alright?'

'I'm so sorry, but my Nan took a bad tumble and needs me to take her to the doctor.' I wondered if he would take the bait.

'Right now?' he asked.

Now I wondered if he was a bit thick.

'Yes, right now. I have to leave, I'm sorry.' I fled, ignoring his request to call him. I felt bad for running out, but that date needed to end.

Becky may be my best friend, but that was just horrific. I debated calling her again for an update, but at that moment I needed cocoa and some alone time. And I knew the perfect place to go.

I headed to my favourite little coffee house and ordered myself a hot chocolate. Looking around, I noticed how many people were sitting down. *Were there any seats left?* After a quick scan, I found the perfect seat in front of the fireplace ... only someone else was sitting in the seat across. Usually, I would pick a seat farthest away from others so I could really focus on my book, but he was cute. He had a curly mop of chocolate brown hair and old-fashioned wire-framed glasses. He was wearing a dark green cardigan with an old-school style number 13 in large block numbers over the left side of his chest, a white button-up shirt peeking out underneath. I stopped undressing him with my eyes and sat down before my hovering was noticed. Opening my book, I felt someone looking at me. I stopped reading and met his gaze, his golden hazel eyes. I looked away before our eye contact became awkward, although I couldn't help but feel he was still looking at me. I knew I seemed out of place in my dress and heels, especially sitting in a large, red armchair with a cosy blanket and a book. I took a chance and looked up again.

'Casey!' The barista came over with my drink. 'I added extra marshmallows for you.'

'Thank you, Emma.' I came here too often, but it was my happy place. I picked up my drink and stirred it, plonking in two marshmallows.

'You ordered a hot chocolate? Over a coffee?' His warm voice startled me.

'I ... well, I don't like coffee.' Most 22-year-olds needed it to function, but I couldn't get past the taste.

He held out his hand after realising his sudden interruption. 'I'm sorry. I'm Jasper.'

'Casey.' I shook it. He had a firm shake.

'I don't mean to intrude on your ... downtime?' He looked pointedly at my book. 'I just haven't met someone who has preferred a hot chocolate to coffee, like myself.'

'You don't like coffee?' And he reads, and is cute, and has nice hair ...

'Can't get past the taste.'

'... Neither.' I wondered who else could possibly not like coffee as much as me, wondered if I had met my match. I went back to my book, and so did he. But I couldn't help myself and looked at him reading. I couldn't believe my eyes. This day was turning out to be a dream all along.

'I'm sorry,' I interrupted. He looked up at me curiously. 'But are you reading *A Room with a View*?'

He looked at his cover. 'Yes, it's one I always seem to go back to. It's just so ...'

'Whimsical?' I interjected, holding up my book.
I wondered if maybe 13 was my lucky number after all.

I reach my hand out to take his glasses off as he sleeps. They were always my favourite, so soft against his masculine features. Remembering the past always made me thankful for what I had. I wonder if he dreamt about those moments as much as I do. The way we met felt like a dream. I only wish we had more time together. The leukemia spread too quickly. It's causing his organs to fail. Sitting in this little hospital room day in and day out definitely puts life into perspective; continuously reading my worn copy of *A Room with a View* and fantasising a perfect ending. The soft beeping of the heart monitor echoes throughout the room. The sunlight reflects off the metal IV pole, highlighting the liquids pumping into his frail body. I look over at him again, hooked up to machines round the clock, but still as handsome as the day I met him. I know he doesn't have long left. My only hope is to meet again, one day, in a new life; a life where illness doesn't exist. And where our dreams can continue together.

MIND OVER MOVEMENT

Nikki Vee

FROM: +61 496 543 79
TODAY 6:04 PM

Hey

FROM: +61 422 142 87

TODAY 6:14 PM

Send pic plz

TODAY 6:15 PM

Hey?

Workin or no?

FROM: +61 421 111 11

TODAY 6:31 PM

I got $50

Ruby scrolls through recent messages on her smart phone, then swipes through her Notes app where a series of pre-prepared responses lay ready. She would have rolled her eyes early in her career and individually responded to each pointless message. Copy and paste are now her two best friends.

FROM +61 422 432 55

TODAY 6:31 PM

You avail?

TODAY 6:44 PM

Hi, for information on my services and pricing,check out my website www.LittleRedRider.com Don't forget to check the 'How To Book' section for hints and tips on contacting Escorts – xxoo

Then there are the texts that don't event warrant a response. She prefers to think the owners of these are harmless, albeit horny, teenage boys with little self-restraint, instead of the more likely 'time wasters', 'fake bookers' and 'address collectors'. Some of the more polite texts she ignores this evening are 'I'm horny', 'you like dick?' and her all-time favourite: 'I'll make you feel so good you'll be paying me'. That's not to say all her clientele are this terrible with first impressions. No, not at all. Genuine clients are terrific at requesting her services and just as Ruby starts dressing for her 7pm session, the phone dings with proof.

FROM **+61 422 979 97**
TODAY 6:49 PM

> Hi, I'm Ted. Looking for a
> 1hr GFE, outcall to South Side.
> Tonight, if possible.

Ruby reads the message again. Critiquing the content. Checking for red-flags; any minor sign that this person may not be genuine. *Complete words, full sentences, and basic grammar with punctuation. It's a good start ... but I'll just check ...*

The LowLife Listings, a sort of underground network if you like, where workers collate information and lock it away in online databases. Access is membership only and Sex Workers guard it fiercely. Had a bad experience?

Log their details. Assaulted in the past? Log their details. Stood up? Time wasted? Log their details. On numerous occasions, Ruby has used this lookup and avoided a serial time waster, or worse, someone with a known history of violence. Ruby taps Ted's number into the search. Nothing. *... and that's a great start.*

TODAY 7:01 PM

> Hi Ted, I have other bookings this evening, but I could do 10PM if that isn't too late? Otherwise, tomorrow evening from 7:30pm is available. 1hr booking is $300 + $50 outcall fee.

Ruby touches up her makeup, a little bronzer and a dash of eyeliner, just in time for the familiar knock on her front door. Her 7pm client has arrived.

Thirty minutes pass and Ruby sees her client off with a lingering kiss and the promise of another rendezvous soon. She returns to the bedroom, collecting a rattan laundry basket along the way, and strips the now crumpled satin sheets. A stray condom wrapper floats to the floor which she promptly places in the little bin before removing the liner and escorting it to the trash. In an ornate box, traditionally reserved for tea bags, condoms of all shapes, sizes and flavours sit on display with a collection of oils and lubricants to the side. Ruby makes her way to the walk-in wardrobe where a stack of crisp sheets waits, ready to be stretched, contorted and spread across her work surface.

With the bed made, the stage is set once more for her next performance and Ruby can take a moment to enter a session note into her Client Management Software.

Luke arrived at 7pm, punctual as always, and requested a shower together. Our shower together was slow, careful, lots of touch. Odd, usually has a quick shower and begins quickly. We easily spent 20 minutes in the shower, then I had to gently remind him of our time together and once we made it to the bedroom things proceeded in his usual fast fashion. I lay with him for the last few minutes and asked, 'rough day, huh?' He just nodded. Text him tomorrow afternoon—'Hey Luke, hope you're having a better day today.'

With admin out of the way, she turns her attention to establishing a new client.

FROM **+61 422 979 97**
TODAY 7:10 PM

> 10PM is fine. I normally work nights. This is my night off. My address is 52 Solemn Avenue, South Side. I do not recommend street parking, but there is space in my driveway.

TODAY 7:47 PM

> Thanks Ted, I'll see you at
> 10pm this evening. If you've not
> yet done so, please review the
> basic Ts&Cs on my website. –
> xxoo

TODAY 9:35 PM

> Hi Ted, leaving my place
> now. See you soon.

Ruby pulls out onto the main road and cranks the stereo. Spotify blasts a random selection of tunes through her VW Mini's speakers. The sound distorts slightly at this volume, but she doesn't care. *The Strongest* is tonight's anthem and it needs to be loud. Loud enough to mute the thoughts that bubble away deep in Ruby's mind where they stay, hidden, in the background: collecting data, adding to the narrative, assessing and reassessing, then calculating risk vs reward. Cancel the booking, or continue on.

I'M STRONG, I'M WILD, I'M FREE.

Is Ted real? Is he going to cancel before I get there? No evidence for that—continue on.

YOU WON'T, BE THE BOSS, OF ME.

I hope he actually lives there. I don't want a repeat of last time. That family had no idea ... continue on.

I'M STRONG, I'M WILD, I'M FREE ...

The music fades mid-song as a robotic voice interrupts.

'You have one new message, would you like to hear it?'

'Yes.'

'Message says—ok I will leave the light on for you see you soon beautiful—would you like to send a reply?'

'No.'

With the interruption complete, music resumes in full force and Ruby hastens to turn it down. YOU WON'T, BE THE BOSS, OF ME ...

It's an unkempt street—typical for this suburb. Chain-link fencing, six-feet high, lines either side. Overgrown hedging has ripped the mesh from its posts creating unofficial gateways between neighbours. A few of the nicer houses have wooden fencing and, yet even these, with the missing planks and faded brown paint, give clear indicators of the residents' lower social and economic status.

No one here can afford my rates ... surely this is a time waster ... or worse ... no, don't think about that ... continue on.

The house she's looking for is right next to a park. With broad-brimmed trees shielding the desolate equipment from the streetlight above, Ruby has no doubt that the deep shadows could harbour danger without once questioning motive.

The park looks deserted. No lone person waiting in the darkness. No mob waiting to take me somewhere. Continue on.

Number 52 has a wooden fence. Unlike the others, it's seen some repairs recently. The double gates are wedged ajar. Ruby pulls in, taking a moment before shutting off the engine.

Only one car in the driveway. My car's blocking the gates so they can't be closed. Porch light is on. House lights are all on. Yard looks tidy. No dogs or people in sight. All green flags, continue on.

Ruby checks her makeup in the mirror and reapplies her trademark Ruby Red lipstick. She tussles her fiery curls forward a little, dons her red leather coat and makes her way up the landing stairs.

Disarray of shoes. Large pair of black tradie boots. Several sandals; same size. Do these shoes belong to one person? Continue on.

With a knock on the door and a warm smile at the ready, Ruby enters work mode. With a bag clutched in her left hand, she reaches across her body to hold the strap with her right, causing an increase in cleavage lift. Ruby is well practiced in the subtle art of looking cutely adorable for a first impression. She cocks her head with a slight downward tilt; a submissive gesture on her part that works wonders for the clients' egos. The door opens widely, they both pause, just for a moment, taking in the sight of the other.

Clean and tidy, neat clothes, open posture, visible hands, middle-aged, mostly fit, not overly muscular—I'd still lose in a tussle, but overall appears safe. Continue on.

'Hi, Ted, I'm Ruby.'

'Thank you for coming out here so late, please come in.'

There's a slight strain to Ted's voice as he steps to the side and waves his arm, motioning for Ruby to enter. Ruby's experienced ears can recognise roughly six different forms of strained welcomes: shy and nervous, hiding something, false bravado (nervous, but doesn't want to show it), disappointed by her appearance, tired, and excitement mixed with general jitters. Ted's voice strained with first meet jitters.

Just the jitters, perfectly normal under these circumstances. Continue on.

'You're welcome. So, how's your day been?' Ruby asks as she enters, her voice light and breezy. Moving further forward into his home, she both listens to his brief account of the day and takes in the surroundings. Ruby's mind takes on a duality of roles. The public, smiling figure that nods and listens, engaging the client in casual conversation—like that of a long-lost friend eager to make up for missing time. Then there's the fast-thinking mind, tracking minor details, cataloguing and marking them for assessment; comparing, contrasting, looking for contradictions, or a sign that something doesn't match the person present before her. In this business, minor discrepancies are rare, but they can matter. They can matter a lot.

'It was a day, that's for sure,' he says.

'Oh? Rough day, huh?'

Open-plan living room and kitchen. Soft music playing—instrumentals. Could be masking the sound of other people. Long curtains—no apparent bulges. Hallway, likely bedrooms, off to the left—no sign of movement. Continue on.

'First day, new job, new town ... well you know how it goes.' Ted begins fixing a variety of cheeses onto a plate in the kitchen.

'New is hard. I read it can take six months to fully appreciate a new town. How are you enjoying it here in South Side so far?'

Clean and tidy kitchen. Knives where knives should be. Lounge—couches in good condition. Big screen TV. Sad looking plant. Empty packing boxes stacked at the back door. Assessment: clean, tidy person, recently moved in. No red flags. Continue on.

'Well,' Ted says, retrieving two bottles of water from the fridge. Ruby takes a sideways glance, checking they still have their seal. 'I moved in last Saturday, so I've not exactly had the time to explore. Looks pleasant enough, people are quite the mix here at least. Shall we sit?'

Ok, everything looks fine here ... except ... is that couch off the wall? That's odd positioning, isn't it? Why is it off the wall? Could a person fit there?

Ted, cheese plate in one hand and bottles in the other, makes the short journey from the kitchen to the lounge room. Watching Ted move past the sofa, Ruby's breath catches in her chest. He's speaking about his recent transfer and the much-needed change of scenery after the divorce, but Ruby isn't listening. Her sole focus: the couch. The sights and sounds from the room fall away, the piano music all but gone, till all that is left in the world is that couch.

Ruby's ears catch a sound. Scuffling? Shifting? Her stomach begins a series of somersaults that would make an Olympic judge proud, and her heart has taken to its new role of lead drummer in earnest. Her subconscious thoughts, having found a clear and immediate red flag, propel themselves forward, pushing through the emergency doors of her mind to bring this news to those in charge.

This is it, there's a second person, a second person is hiding, you're about to get attacked, get out, get out, GET OUT!

The lounge room comes rushing back into focus, knocking Ruby a step sideways. The lights feel brighter than the sun, the sounds of the room deafening as they roll and jumble atop one another, fighting for priority in her ears.

'Ruby, is everything alright?'

Safety call, go. Do it now!

Forcing her eyes to meet his, she cocks her head, forces out a smile and says, 'Yes, yes, it is ... uhm, sorry, I've just got to check in with Camilla and let her know I've arrived. If I forget, she will worry.'

'Yes, of course, that's fine.'

Ruby fumbles her phone as Ted arranges the cheese plate in front of her and returns to the kitchen to rummage around one of the cupboards. Ruby searches her contacts to find Camilla's name.

Shit, I didn't tell Camilla I was going out, or where I'd be.

As the phone begins to ring, Ruby eyes the couch. Watches it move. Just a little. Then a little more.

Come on ... answer ... come on, come on, come on ...

'The person you have dialled is not available ...'

Ruby braces herself and takes a deep breath that feels like inhaling pure courage, absorbing it from the very air that surrounds her.

'Ted, who else is here?'

'What?' Ted's head emerges from the cupboard, his body follows soon after with a box of Jatz in one hand and a tray of assorted crackers in the other. There's a look of confusion on Ted's face, genuinely puzzled. Ruby doesn't notice. Her gaze keeps returning to the couch and whoever lies in wait to join him in the attack.

'Who else is here, Ted?' she asks again with more force and winces at the crack in her voice.

'No one. No one else is here.' He places the boxes on the bench, frowning and moves towards the lounge, glancing around for what has caused her alarm.

'Look, it's fine, ok? No harm, no foul, right? You and your friend can go about having a lovely night and I'll just leave. Ok? NO! Don't ... don't come any closer!'

'Whoa! What the hell? Is this ... what? Yeah ok ... leave if you want.'

Ted holds his palms outstretched and retreats into the kitchen as Ruby takes several tentative backward steps toward the door—then the couch moves again.

'Don't even think about it, mate,' she shouts to the air, her hand raised, finger instinctively pointing towards the invisible assailant. 'You stay behind the couch till I'm gone.'

You're ok, just calmly leave. You've caught them off-guard, use it. You're just leaving.

Ruby fumbles behind her for the door handle, no one else moves, the door opens and she whirls around to make her exit into the cool night air. Then comes a sound that is so disarming it catches her off guard. She stops and looks back. Ted, still in the kitchen, is almost doubled over with one hand holding onto his stomach and the other acting as a brace atop the bench, keeping him upright. This fit of laughter holds Ruby captive, a mix of long and loud howls combining with intermittent periods of wheezing and she watches as he tries to recapture his breath. Ted battles to compose himself, almost succeeds, takes one look at the couch and doubles over once more. Ruby remains frozen in the doorway. So disarming is this turn of events that even her subconscious mind has taken pause.

Finally, Ted finds enough breath to talk. Wiping his eyes, he says, 'I'm sorry, Ruby, but ... God, I'm sorry I shouldn't be laughing ok, but ... Sasha? Sasha, come here, girl ...' Ted taps his open palm against his thigh, twice. Ruby sees the wet nose first.

'Come on, girl. Yeah, I know you were sleeping but you've scared the poor lady. Atta girl. Ruby, this is Sasha.'

An aging German Shepherd eases her way out and moves towards Ruby. She moves on unyielding limbs, limping on just about every paw. Ruby kneels and greets Sasha, with a pet and a scratch behind the ears. Sasha raises a paw to shake hands.

'Sasha was my first partner when I joined the Security Unit. Sasha, go to bed.' Sasha follows Ted's commands and returns, slow and steady, to her space behind the couch.

'So,' Ruby stands, taking a tentative step into the room once more. 'You're a police officer?'

'Private security, not a cop.'

'And to be clear: there aren't any extra people hiding in your house?'

A broad smile doesn't leave his face.

'Just me ... Oh, and Sasha.'

I'm an idiot. How do we continue on?

'I feel like an idiot.'

He nods in agreement but says nothing more. After a few moments, Ruby breaks the silence. 'This is really awkward, so I'm going to go out and knock again, yeah? You don't have to answer.'

With a knock on the door and a warm smile at the ready, Ruby enters work mode. With a bag clutched in her left hand, she reaches across her body to the strap with her right, causing an increase in cleavage lift. The door opens wide.

'Hi, Ted, I'm Ruby.'

'Hi, Ruby, thank you for coming out here so late, please come on in—and just so you know I have an old dog asleep behind the couch.'

MY SERENDIPITY

Betty Sills

The well-kept secret that ultimately ended her marriage. The experience and the temptation showed her the world was more than just merely a backyard of family disposition and fake family exteriors. The mock-up perfect relationship, simulating the perfect family with 2.5 kids to boot. An opportunity existed to change one's current outlook and open her eyes and see the signs of so much possibility.

For her, it was easy. She was a dreamer, an adventurer who had a wild imagination, and above it all she was a hopeless romantic. She married Robby five years ago and in hindsight—it wasn't for love; it was that he had a swagger in his persona which she found attractive at the time.

Reflecting, she was young and naïve, inexperienced at what made up the whole kit and caboodle of the perfect relationship that fits in with family. Maybe she married for stability, to replace the upbringing she was denied, wanting to prove something even. That's not to say she didn't care about Robby. She was sure he loved her and cared for her, but she felt more like the visible void he needed filling and perhaps even a carer, rather than a part player in a relationship destined to improve, evolve, and conquer.

Then he wandered in to shake up her life ... Meet Wade.

From the moment she opened that inbox, she knew something inside of her changed, and she thought he knew too. This was the second time their lives crossed paths, there had to be a reason. There was an unspoken attraction between them, an undeniable chemistry from the outset—and that was just verbal. It took just three weeks for them to make an excuse to find a way to see and meet up with one another. The beauty of friendship. Where there is a will, her girlfriends found a way to make it happen. Both denying the intensity of their feelings and anxious anticipation for the meetup. Both fearing a fizzling outcome once the meet became reality.

That evening was spent reconnecting. It had been a few years since the last day of high school. As they divulged their pasts, tribulations and successes, they became increasingly comfortable with one another's presence it was crazy.

The conversation stopped, like a sudden expectation, that it needed to take a different direction like they could hear and feel each other's thoughts. They both knew time was fleeting. They had less than twelve hours left together if it was to include no sleep before they would part each other's company and return to their uneventful daily life. Neither dared to express just how boring it was.

Moving from her girlfriend's indoor atmosphere of her lounge room, to outside where it felt a little less restricted by the volume of their engagement that appeared to be disturbing the sleeping members of her household. Fifty metres from the house, they found a patch of grass manicured above a retaining wall bordering a garage. She turned to sit when she was spun around to face him. Determination was set in his eyes. With a stronghold grip around her waist, he began kissing her with passion. The rush, she felt her legs go from under her. A surge of newfound emotions flooded throughout.

Overwhelmed—she had never felt this way in her entire life, nor was this something she would have ever partaken in before. She was confused, yet eagerly adaptable at the same time. She was instantly turned on. A switch had just been flicked. Without speaking, their bodies just moved with one another, as he licenced his hands to explore and restrain where necessary. Her reciprocation was welcomed, pleasing, and she could feel how her response heightened his willingness to continue beyond that invisible boundary. The next she knew, her panties were discarded on the gravel floor. They were not removed in the conventional method. Instead, he ripped them off her. His hands now wandered down her trembling torso, hovering above where her virtues once lay. All her inhibitions rushed to her mindset, obscured with new excitement.

She felt her body arch upwards, shaking, feeling his erection, cool and smooth against her belly. Unable to concentrate on all the sensations she felt, she grabbed his arse, permitting him with urgency to draw closer to her bosom. Fingernails still gripped in his butt cheek, their bodies grew hungry and impatient. Their movement paused, then it happened. There were no words to explain it, something so distinctively familiar overcame them both with a heightened sense of knowing. Their gaze locked; smiles arose from their lips. She bit down on his lips, intending to tease him. Sensually, he placed tender kisses to her bare neck and shoulder, then upwards until she felt his breath nearing her lips, that longing and lustful feeling felt just moments before, returned.

Without a word exchanged, their hands paced in slow exploration, wanting to savour each minute in time they dare not wanted to waste.

With her back still firmly pinned to the side of the shed and feet fixed to the edge of the retaining wall, her body was held in support, his hand still firmly grasping the lower of her back.

Unbuttoning the remainder of his collared shirt, exposing his strong masculinity she had so curiously wondered about the whole evening, whilst she was being teased with a mere two-button window open for observation. Dragging his sleeved shirt backward off one arm at a time, she removed his shirt, as he changed support arms around her to allow its removal. Their eyes never redirecting from one another's.

The pace slowed as they became intoxicated by the warmth of bare skin that enveloped them. His shirt fell to the same fate as her panties. Slipping her shoestring straps off her shoulders, he cupped her breasts with gentleness, his eyes still never leaving her gaze.

She took a deep breath, nervous, unsure of his reaction, and initiated further her desire for wanting him by taking his swollen manhood firmly into her left hand, stroking his two masters with her right, until the deep groaning of enjoyment arose from his throat. Eyes still adoringly laid upon one another's for several moments until she reached out with both her hands to him. Lowering her off the retaining wall, she then affectionately drew him to his knees.

Cusping both of his tensed arse cheeks in her hands she examined his manhood, his beating appendage, with the roof of her mouth. Gripping almost a firmer, smoothing hold with a gentle rhythm. The moment her mouth closed, she wanted all of him. She feverishly began to hum in delight, as she rocked back and forth enjoying the taste of his conviction in her mouth. Noticing only the faint sound of his delight pulsing through his body.

His eyes closed; she knew he was dissolved within the experience. There was something of triumph in the knowledge that he was powerless against withdrawal at this point. She pulled his hips closer and swallowed him more longingly, so lost in ecstasy that she felt his swelling bulge in her throat.

His taste was cleaner than she had previously experienced, swallowing rhythmically until there was no more, finding it harder to stop. She didn't want to give him up, her mouth was engaged with his knightly appendage. He began stroking her head hard, with the obvious approval of his satisfaction permitting her to release, but it just encouraged her to pull him closer. With more restraint and increasing the speed in which her mouth was making love with its knight. Thereafter, his body collapsed over her head with multiple climaxes. No longer able to handle the repeat of heightened stimulation.

He gripped her by her shoulders, removing her from his appendage with delicateness and appreciation. Moving his arms under her armpits he pulled her back up to him, lying her on her back on the green. Rolling her skirt up to her waist, he lowered himself on top of her and the gentleness had gone.

She let her muscles tense against him. A storm was brewing overhead, and they were riding this weather out together. The first heavy drop of the heavens fell from above, landing between her exposed breasts. Wade lowered his lips, capturing it sensually, the starting point of trailed kisses that would spark an eruption brewing beneath him.

The breeze cooled their skin, the urgency of their shared pleasure becoming too much to remain patient for it. As his head emerged from below her navel, up to her breasts that he caressed teasingly with his tongue, his hand slipped between her legs, exploring her neglected womb in which he would revitalize.

Taking hold of both her hands, fingers entwined, he placed them up behind her head, feeling the comfortable warmth of his body over hers. She felt him enter her, so lovingly. Eyes still fixed, the desire in his gaze had wilted and was replaced with the need for acceptance, belonging, and yearning. He wanted only to be equally wanted by her, needed by her. The desire to be replaced with passion.

His eyes became the window to his soul for the next hour, as he ravished her intimately with his masculinity inside and out. He left her fulfilled physically, mentally, and emotionally in every conceivable way. A wave of euphoria and surrender had become of her.

The rain fell hard, like a second wave of adrenalin, caused by the sudden drop of temperature—their passion rose again to a feverish pitch. He pulled her to her feet. Tenderly kissing her, committing himself to her, overwhelmed by the feelings she had for him. Like their language of love was well understood between them. He was an open book of emotion as if their souls were communicating. No longer did it feel wrong or of betrayal.

He made repetitive love to her; she became increasingly engaged within the moments. Their bodies fell into complete surrender to one another as they felt the overdue complexity of their meet and knew nothing would ever return to normal.

He turned her around, bending her over to where her hands just reached the shed sheeting and her toes met with the edge of the retaining wall. He whispered, 'Hold on,' as he entered her with hunger again.

Cradling her securely with his arm around her mid-waist as he drove longingly and deep within her, she thought her ovaries would take no more. Maintaining the strength in one hand, she held the wall firm, holding the weight whilst she flung her right arm up around his neck. Pulling his face closer to hers as she panted heavily into his ear. As she began to climax, she bit down on his lobe, causing him to moan out, increasing the speed at which he drove in and out of her. Peaking in equal climax, she clenched her muscles tighter around his knighthood for the next few seconds as a wave of euphoria flushed over them as they orgasmed with intensity. Buckling their weary legs beneath them, falling back onto the grassy knoll with the greatest feeling of divine intoxication. He was insatiable, but so was she. Looking back, she was amazed at how it happened.

They could feel one another's body quivering with sensations. Blanketed by one another's flesh, their heartbeats falling and rising in alignment. She knew at that exact moment this was her serendipitous encounter, her moment had come—that she had forever longed for.

'Will you want to see me again?' he asked. His blue eyes were besotted with desperation from a much-wanted response, as he tenderly brushed strands of blonde locks matted to her cheekbone by the rain. He tucked the stray hair behind her ear and stroked her cheek with his thumb, returning her to his trance.

She smiled enigmatically, raising her forefinger to his bruised lips, brushing across them decidedly, maintaining restraint from not following through with her need to devour them again.

'I am only yours if you want me, or I am now nobody's. You've now wrecked me for any other,' she said, playfully pushing him off his resting elbow.

He smirked at her wit. Just the smell and thought of her turned his insides into covetous longing. She laughed out loud with the joy of awakening; she was no longer the woman she thought she always was.

HE LOVES ME,
HE LOVES ME NOT

K.S.

His dream was simple,
To be betrothed;
To have a woman in white.
Yearning for paper that connects them together,
yet he couldn't see the truth in her eyes.

Her reality was tortured, disturbed.
Complexities that were masked behind pain,
Destruction where once left was hope.
Tell him the truth. She wants forever;
However, her heart lives way beneath in caverns.

He's caught within a daydream as frustrations build.
Simply fed up, he bellows, demands
'If *you* won't do this, *I'll* find another woman.'
Blind to her sensitivities, says he doesn't understand;
Epiphany in waiting, but will it change the man?

It's become her nightmare,

She just wanted love,

But his blind ambition is tearing her apart.

She says she's sorry, but the paper is weighted;

Please love me as I am, because even I don't understand...

DARK PARADISE

Ainsley Botterell

S he'd known the moment he walked through the door, fifteen minutes late.

For the past three years, Jennifer had lived and breathed for this man—for his love, for his dream, for his schedule. Vincent had been entirely driven to reclaim the company his father had established from the moment they'd met. Years prior, when Vincent had still been in high school, his father had sold more than half of his company to a promising investor—business hadn't been going so well and he'd felt the need to bring in some extra support. But shortly after the contracts had been finalised, the investor turned and ripped the company right out from underneath him. Vincent and his family had been left with nothing and the investor had grown the small start-up into an absolute powerhouse within the scientific research industry.

Jennifer had found his determination to 'avenge' his family endearing. She'd fallen for him almost too quickly. They'd met during her final year of university and after only six months together, she'd given up her entire life— left her parents and siblings behind on the other side of the country and dropped her entire degree two months from the finishing date—to help him achieve his goal.

Not once had Vincent ever come home late from work, even during the busier times of the year when his colleagues would spend days at a time in the office, scrambling to meet their deadlines. He hated that place— vehemently—and outright refused to spend any more time than what was required of him stooped behind his desk.

Jennifer often had to remind him that he only hated his job because of how much work the senior executives dumped onto him. Yes, they made him fret over missing documents and fabricated numbers, but if he wanted to surpass them and take back what was rightfully his, it was work he had to put up with. He was more than capable of doing so.

And besides, it wasn't like he was tackling it all on his own.

They'd both studied business—Vincent having graduated the year before they met. So, when his workload got too heavy, he'd bring his computer and all his paperwork home and Jennifer would take over. She'd become an expert at forging his signature on reports and adjustments, and the senior executives had yet to realise that more than half of the work they dumped on Vincent had been completed by her. Her help on his annual performance review had even gotten him a promotion—another step closer to taking back what was rightfully his.

After all she'd done for him, he should at least have the decency not to cheat on her.

While his lateness had been the first indicator, the way he'd stuttered in response to her greeting had been the second. Jennifer could recall every little flaw and quirk her husband possessed without even trying; the way his eyebrows twitched when he was annoyed at something, the backhanded compliments he'd give when he felt that the people around him were lesser, the way he tied his shoes. She'd seen right through him. Vincent's typically low toned voice had pitched a little higher and his ears had been red underneath his unusually messy hair.

He'd claimed it was stress and calmed down shortly after, Jennifer masking her realisation and feigning ignorance as she took the work he'd brought home for her.

But she knew.

And if things went her way, Vincent would remain blissfully ignorant to the fact.

She felt no need to disrupt the absolute dream that was their marriage and continued to behave normally around her husband, spending her days at his beck and call like usual. He'd never kept secrets from her before—perhaps he'd come clean without her having to confront him?

Two weeks later, she learnt that Vincent *definitely* wasn't making plans to admit his wrongs anytime soon and that this—her husband having a *mistress*—was apparently her new reality.

The woman he'd been seeing was a colleague from his office.

There was a new number in his contacts list labelled 'New PA'.

Jennifer had seen a missed call on his phone from the woman late at night when Vincent was showering, followed by a text message thanking him for 'such a fun day' that concluded with a cute 'miss you already!'. Jennifer narrowed her eyes at the text, turned the phone over and went back to bed. She wouldn't get upset. There was no need to be angry. The fury she was feeling was unwarranted, really. He'd tell her all about it when he was ready, and she was willing to be patient for that.

Jennifer couldn't recall having ever met any of the assistants—even at the end of the year office party Vincent and by association, Jennifer, had been forced to attend the year before. Nobody she'd been introduced to had worked in the role and her conversation with the office receptionist—who liked to gossip more than anything else in the world—hadn't revealed anything of the like either. Jennifer had figured they hadn't been allowed to attend the party and forgotten all about it.

Deciding to give Vincent another chance to fess up, Jennifer had visited the company building during his lunch break, bringing with her the bank card that she'd discreetly removed from his wallet before he left for work that morning. She'd feigned ignorance as he'd flailed about looking for it and sent him a text after claiming she'd found it in the pocket of his pants in their bathroom.

Without it—and with her bringing it to him—he wouldn't be able to buy himself, or anyone else for that matter, lunch. And that was exactly how Jennifer wanted it.

Stepping into his office later that day, she flashed him a grin. 'Missing something?' she asked casually, brandishing the bank card between her fingers.

His relief had been palpable. 'Oh, thank god. You found it.'

Jennifer retrieved his wallet from his desk and returned the card to its slot. 'You left it on the counter—I don't know how you managed to miss it on your way out. Lucky you have me around, right?'

'Yeah. Absolutely.'

Then, *she* had appeared in the doorway.

Jennifer had known straight away that this was the woman he'd been seeing behind her back. Vincent's shoulders had become impossibly tense underneath her hands, his voice strained with underlying panic when he asked the woman what she needed. He'd fumbled with the pen and the woman's question—or proposition, Jennifer didn't know—had died on her lips upon noticing Jennifer in the room. She'd gone white in the face and hurriedly apologised for the interruption before slamming the door shut and fleeing down the hall.

Holding back her laughter, Jennifer had slid herself into Vincent's lap. It was comical really, the pure panic on their expressions. 'Who was that?' she asked, tracing a finger across the lapel of his jacket.

'No one—a new hire. Naomi, I think. Probably needed help with the program or something.'

Naomi. 'Oh? How long ago did she start?'

'Uh ... she's been here two months.'

'Ah,' Jennifer quipped, sliding her hand further down his chest. 'She was cute.'

He'd had no response to that, but the tick in his jaw had given everything away even as he'd pushed her onto his desk and put an end to her questions with his hands.

She'd left his office an hour later with a pep in her step and a smug smile thrown in Naomi's direction as they passed by each other at the reception desk.

Jennifer arrived home entirely convinced that after today, Vincent would come clean the second he stepped through the door. She'd practically caught him—he'd be foolish not to.

But he didn't, entering their home a whopping 53 minutes late (she hadn't looked away from the clock all afternoon) and smelling of perfume—perfume that wasn't her own.

Jennifer's decision to let him admit everything himself had died, then and there. He wouldn't make a fool of her.

William had been so easy to break—it was almost disappointing.

If Vincent wasn't going to be honest, maybe he would.

A resident doctor at the local hospital, William and Vincent had been best friends since childhood and had spent their entire lives together—he'd been Vincent's best man at their wedding. There wasn't a secret between them.

But Jennifer knew that William had always found her attractive. He'd told her so himself on many occasions— sometimes when he was drunk and sometimes when he wasn't. Despite his close bond with her husband, she wouldn't put it past him to betray Vincent in a second, given the right motive.

And she'd been right.

'Jen,' he breathed in her ear, standing between her legs after she'd arrived at his office and sat herself down on his examination table.

Fighting back a bored sigh, Jennifer had sifted her fingers through his shaggy brown hair. 'Will,' she returned, trying her best to feign breathlessness. 'If I asked you a difficult question, would you tell me the truth?'

'Of course,' he confessed reverently, panting against her neck. 'Anything.'

She curled her fingers a little tighter in his silky locks and pushed her lips against his ear. 'Is Vince cheating on me?'

The movement of his hips stuttered to a stop as he struggled to respond, lips forming words but no sound coming out.

Jennifer pursed her lips and twined both of her arms around his neck. 'It's ok,' she soothed, pressing her chest closer to his. 'You can tell me.'

'He is,' William finally replied, sounding ashamed.

Jennifer felt satisfaction at his admission fill her chest. While she hadn't doubted her suspicions at all, the confirmation that she'd been right felt better than anything Jennifer had ever experienced before.

'Naomi?' she queried.

'... You're not angry?'

Of course not—that wasn't who she was as a person.

But that wasn't normal ... was it?

By the time he drew back to look at her face, Jennifer already had the tears rolling. A moment thinking about her grandmother's death and having to miss the funeral due to a project Vincent had had due was enough to bring them on.

'I tried to tell him it was wrong, but he wouldn't listen,' he soothed, wiping at her cheeks with his thumbs. Jennifer barely repressed a roll of her eyes. 'I don't know why he'd ever do that to you, Jen ... you're phenomenal.'

'Thank you for telling me,' she returned, forcing her tone to waver and hooking her chin over his shoulder. 'I know you're close to him; I'd hate to be the reason you drifted apart.'

'I don't care about him.'

Jennifer grinned wickedly at his words, tears drying by now. 'I knew I could count on you.'

Will gathered himself then and picked up where he left off, professing to her over and over again that he'd always be there whenever she needed him, utterly oblivious to the murderous expression that had overtaken her features even as she pretended to moan.

That night at dinner, when Vincent had asked her how her appointment with William had gone and if he'd given her anything to ease the pesky migraine she'd been struggling with, she'd graced him with her brightest smile and rattled off the name of the low-dose painkiller William had prescribed.

Vincent only proceeded to assume her obliviousness in the month that followed.

They continued to maintain the image of their perfect, paradisial marriage even as they attended William's 28th birthday party and Vincent had disappeared to attend to 'an emergency at work'. He'd returned an hour later in a different shirt and spent the remainder of the night gushing over Jennifer to anybody that would listen, while she fumed.

Jennifer reached her breaking point the day she climbed into Vincent's car and found a pair of high heels sitting on the floor of the passenger side. He'd brushed off her question with a laugh and tried to convince her they must have been hers from years ago.

Oh. Vincent didn't think she was oblivious—he thought she was *stupid*.

They weren't even her size.

If Jennifer was going to confront him, she was going to make sure he knew exactly how he'd made her feel. Screw the 'till death do us part' they'd vowed to each other at their wedding all those years ago—he'd ruined their lives.

She was going to be the *reckoning* he deserved.

'Vince ... do you have something you need to tell me?' she questioned as soon as he'd returned home from work, not even giving him a chance to put down his things.

She'd been waiting by the door all afternoon, watching for his car in the driveway.

'What? No, Jen—why would you think that?'

Jennifer narrowed her eyes at him. 'Why would I think that?' she mocked his tone, flipping her hair over her shoulder, 'I don't know, Vince, you tell me.'

Never in their entire time as a couple had she spoken to him like this. Her parents had raised her under the idea that people needed to be treated with respect, no matter the circumstance. No exceptions.

Jennifer had never really thought much of it, but the lesson has seemingly integrated itself into her very being anyway. Now, she was going to destroy it.

'What's going on, Jen? What's wrong? Why are you wearing gloves?'

'What's wrong?!' she screamed, finally revealing the knife she'd been hiding behind her back. 'What's wrong is that my husband is an unfaithful *arsehole* with the complete inability to hide it!'

Vincent's face paled. 'What are you talking about?'

'Don't play dumb! You know exactly what I'm talking about!'

Vincent faltered. '... You knew?'

'Of course I knew! I'm not an idiot, you bastard!'

'Jen ... I can explain. Just ... just put the knife down.'

'No!' she seethed, thrusting it in his direction. 'I gave you multiple chances to admit everything and you didn't! You're past the opportunity for a confession—you don't fucking deserve it!'

'I'm sorry! I didn't mean for it to—'

She lurched forward and plunged the knife into his stomach, a giddy feeling bubbling up into her chest. Blood began to seep through the fabric of his white dress shirt and onto Jennifer's hands. Jennifer pulled it out with a gleeful grin and drove it forward into his skin again and again before twisting it in her hand.

Vincent collapsed to the floor with a pained moan and moments later, he'd stopped breathing.

Jennifer had already removed the gloves and picked up her phone.

'Will?' she spoke into the receiver, easily slipping into an act of hysterics. 'I need help!'

'Jen? What's wrong—are you ok?'

'These men—they just broke into our house. I don't—I don't think they were expecting we'd be home and they attacked Vince! Th ... they stabbed him! He's bleeding really badly! Please—I need your help!'

'What? Oh my god. Shit. You need to apply pressure to the wound, ok? Try and slow the bleeding—get a cloth or something and press really hard.'

'O ... ok,' she returned, running across the floorboards and opening the drawer they kept their tea-towels in. She closed it a little more forcefully than necessary after grabbing one, knowing William would hear and assume she was doing precisely what he'd told her to. 'Please hurry!'

'I'm on my way. Is he breathing? Did you call an ambulance?'

'I don't know! You're the first person I th ... thought of...' she paused to heave in a deep breath, 'I'm scared that they'll come back!'

'Ok. It's ok. I'm on my way. I'm going to hang up and call an ambulance, ok? Just sit tight.'

'Ok,' she breathed before he'd hung up, already on her feet and moving about the house.

By the time the ambulance and William had arrived, she'd already disposed of the knife in the neighbours' trash, flushed her gloves down the toilet and knelt by Vincent's side like a good little wife, hands squelching in the cooling blood that had seeped into the fabric of the towel.

'God,' William whispered after the paramedics had pried her away from Vincent's side and he'd gathered her into his arms, convincing, heart-wrenching sobs spilling over her lips. One of the paramedics had passed him an insulated blanket and he hurried to wrap it around her. 'You've had a rough year, haven't you, Jen?'

She nodded her agreement and purposely feigned rapid breaths, chest heaving. Then, reaching a bloody hand forward, she pointed at the paramedics still bustling around Vincent. 'Is he going to be ok?'

'It'll be ok. I've got you. It's going to be ok.'

With one last choked sob, Jennifer hid her smile in his chest.

BROKEN BUTTON

Amy Henderson

The weather provides no breeze to ease my sweat glands from spewing. It's 12.04am on my first day at the new school and my eyelids refuse to shut. My uniform sits on the desk, reminding me of how I should be asleep. I attempt to imagine sheep jumping over my bed one by one, however, my eyes meet with my doll, Bree. My grandmother made Bree from scratch like she does with everything. She even refuses to buy bread. Bree is a hand-embroidered rag doll with one black button for an eye, down from two, incidentally after moving house. I check my phone and suddenly, it's 12.19am. *Maybe scrolling will help me fall asleep,* I ask myself.

The clock strikes 12.52am and I come across a past acquaintance's profile. Her name is Anna Rogers, we played dolls together in grade seven. Looking at her account, she has a lot of friends, wears the latest trends and has over six-thousand followers. There are no dolls in sight. *I wonder how she got so popular*, I ponder.

After checking out Anna's life, I check out my own. I have two pictures: one is a selfie with my grandmother and one with Bree. I decide to delete all of them and post a picture of a friend and I from a few weeks ago and tag her, captioning, 'This was one of the best days of my life! I can't believe how fun it was lol #bestday #bestfriends'. I hope she doesn't comment on anything about what we did because we both complained how boring that day was. I barely even know her, but I can't let people think I'm boring.

Sleep has left the chat and it's time to research how to be the most popular girl at this new school. I type 'how to be popular' straight into Google. I see keywords such as 'confident', 'smart', and 'mature', which makes me realise how immature I am to still have a doll. I know Anna Rogers wouldn't have one, or else how would she be so popular?

I jump out of bed to grab Bree. I hug her one last time and chuck her in my bin. I hope it didn't wake Grandmother up. *It's time to grow up.*

'Have a lovely first day, darling,' Grandmother says as she waves goodbye.

'I will,' I reply, quickly leaving her yellow VW Beetle— how embarrassing for a popular girl.

As soon as Grandmother turns the corner, I adjust my skirt to show off my knees, I rip out my hair tie and undo the top button of my shirt.

My nerves are wrapped tightly around my windpipe. I resent crossing my arms and I constantly remind myself to smile. I don't want to show I'm nervous; popular people don't get nervous; they're confident. My sweat glands' accomplice is the Australian humidity; it doesn't do the white uniform shirt any favours. *Act confident, so people can like you.*

Before entering maths, I shower in Katy Perry perfume and morph my spine into a pole. Located in the middle of the class is a collection of popular-looking people. I lock onto my target and move in.

'Are you the new girl?' one boy asks. 'I'm Jacob.'

'I am, my name—'

A girl, who gives off leader vibes, interrupts me. 'Hey new girl, you are so beautiful and oh my god I love your hair!'

'Oh thanks! My name is Abby.' I meet eyes with her and realise it's Anna Rogers. 'I remember you from our old school. You used to like to play with dolls and—'

She interrupts again. 'Do you have Instagram, new girl, or do you even have a phone?'

'Of course, I have Instagram, Snapchat, Twitter and—'

Anna cuts me off again. 'Then you should follow me. Don't get too obsessed with me though!' she laughs.

After an uncomfortable first half of the day, I make my way to the bathroom to eat lunch; a tradition created at my old school.

When I hear no one else in the room, I sneak out of the stall. My cover is blown when Anna enters.

'Hey, new girl, I heard you mentioning my dolls. If you bring that up again, I will ruin your entire reputation. You are just a stupid, immature, wannabe popular girl.' A random enters. 'Thanks, beautiful! I love you so much! Enjoy your first day!' Before she leaves, she quickly touches up on eye liner.

I look at the mirror. I roll my skirt up higher, I pop on some eye liner and I undo the next top button. I follow the same footsteps as Anna and I see her near my locker on her phone. I sneak up behind her to see what she is doing on her phone and find her viewing my Twitter profile.

I don't bite my tongue. 'Are you obsessed with me or something?'

Anna looks back at me in shock. 'What are you talking about?'

'You are at my locker, I saw you stalking my profile, and earlier you were saying how much you love me!' I turn and begin to walk away. I keep looking forward, hoping that she feels the way I felt earlier.

'Hi, can you pick me up?'

'Excuse me. Manners, Abby?' I feel her brows frown.

'My first day was great, thanks! I'll see you soon, Granny.'

'Granny? Who even are you? You can walk home, dear.' Then she hangs up, shocking me in the moment. She has never hung up on me and I didn't think she'd make me walk home.

I spot Anna exiting the school gate. Her arms are crossed, her second button done up and her hair tied up in a neat bun.

She approaches me and I put my hands on my hips.

'Don't do it, Abby.'

'Excuse me?'

'Don't fall in the trap. It's not worth it.'

Knowing exactly what she is talking about, I say, 'Are you scared to lose your throne?'

'I am scared that you will be like me. Do you understand how lonely this life is? I wish I could be myself.'

Through the phone, in her snaps and selfies, she looked so happy being popular. I feel a sudden urge to be honest.

'I play with dolls too ...' I cross my arms.

'Let's not feel embarrassed anymore.'

I uncross my arms. 'Come to my house. I have someone for you to meet.'

As I go to grab Bree back out of the trash, I notice she isn't there. It's Monday, meaning the bin man hasn't come yet.

'Wait here, Anna.' I skip every second stair and check the wheelie bin near the garden for dearest Bree. Since it's only Grandmother and I, there is only one bag, thankfully.

The bag search is complete. Bree isn't there and my nerves begin to scratch out of my skin. My tendons tighten.

Colours lose their vividness. I feel I've lost permission to smell Grandmother's flowers.

Avoiding Grandmother's room, I investigate the house. I check the washing machine, drawers, cupboards.

It's official: I murdered Bree. I do a walk of shame to my bed and lie in silence.

'Are you ok?' Anna asks.

'Knock, knock. May I come in?' Grandmother says.

'Yes.'

'What was up your bottom today?' Then she realises our visitor. 'Oh, who is this?'

'Hi, I'm Anna.'

'Hi, Grandmother,' I say. 'I am sorry about earlier.'

'It's ok, darling. I assumed that you had a bad day, so I did something to cheer you up.' Grandmother hands me Bree and I squeeze her tightly.

'I thought I lost Bree and I didn't want to tell you because I didn't want to upset you.'

'Look. Her vision is fixed now.' Grandmother points to Bree's mended button eye.

'OMG, she is so cool!' Anna exclaims.

A QUILL TO
THE HEART

Nathan Pennington

You want to know the full story?

Fine. Let's see if you're disturbed by your curiosity. What do I know about this? I'll tell you what I know. The Quills were a very famous aristocratic family headed by Alexander's parents ... but he didn't really remember them as they were tragically killed when he was about a year old. Had they not been taken from him so soon, things would've turned out very differently. Their lives of luxury, status, and comfort would've all been his ... should have been his.

After his parents' deaths, the rest of the family took notice and fought over every penny. None of them cared about Alex, crying over the deaths of those who cherished him most. When I knew him in school it was sickening to hear him describe their attitudes. Then again, maybe the family deserved each other—none of them wanted him. He was sent to an orphanage where he wasn't treated great, but it wasn't torturous. Lucky for him, though, his parents had paid for tuition at a private boarding school, the same one I attended when I was 16: Luxembourg Private School. All his problems should've been solved ... he was going to a better place, right?

Wrong.

I remember that first day. Mrs Price was our English teacher. She was shorter than most of us, very austere, and one of the most tenured teachers there, but was just like all the others.

'Welcome to the Luxembourg Private School. I am Mrs Price and I will be your English teacher during your first year here. You are only here because you are among the best of the best ... I would like you to introduce and tell us a little bit about yourselves.'

One by one the kids introduced themselves, until it was my turn.

'Hello, my name is Charlotte Denvers.'

'Denvers ... as in the daughter of Richard Denvers of the Denvers and Winters Innovations?'

'... Yes ...'

'Interesting ... Next.'

Then, he stood up. His waist-length, silky, dark-brown hair covered half his face, and he answered with insecurities lacing his quiet voice.

'Alexander Quill.'

'Quill ... where have I heard that name? Oh, right, son of the late head of Quill Architecture Limited.'

'Y-yes ...'

'Do you still have contact with any of your family?'

'No ...'

'Such a shame ... Well, that wraps up introductions ...'

Later at lunch, I noticed that he was sitting by himself, so I sat across from him, but he didn't seem to notice.

'You're Alexander, right?'

'Hm? Oh ... yeah.'

'You seem down, are you alright?'

'Do I even belong here?'

'Does that matter?'

'You saw her attitude change when I told them that I don't have ... connections ... That's all these people see.'

'That ... Well, I can't disagree. But I don't see things like that.'

He was sceptical, about to ask another question when we were approached by a group of five. One was the clear leader, and the others followed him in a cult-like fashion. They looked funny and were a mixed group. The only girl was average height, another was tall and thin, and one of them was fairly short. Despite the comical variety of appearances, they all projected sinister intentions.

The clear leader of the group asked Alexander a simple question.

'So, you are a famous Quill, then?'

'What do you want?'

'You don't look like much ... especially with that haircut!'

Knowing what kind of person he was, I tried to distract him.

'You're Eugene, right? Eugene Simmons, son of ...' Pretending to be confident, I told what I knew was a boldfaced lie. 'I don't care who your parents are. They mean nothing here.'

'Oh, but it does. Without any rich family connections ... you are ... alone,' he smirked. 'Right, Brutus, bring our new "friend" with us. Let's give him the rundown of how things work around here.'

They grabbed Alexander and jerked him out of his seat. He struggled against them, but he soon resigned himself to whatever they had in store. I tried to help him, but another lackey stopped me from following.

As you can tell, this group was built upon the shoulders of each other, but without Eugene, the group would have dissolved. Despite that he himself was weak. That was where it all began ...

Alexander tried to avoid them. He studied the halls of the school better than anyone, but they'd find him. They seemed to have a mental compass which guided them to him. Other students learned of this, and they began to cheer them on in sickening displays. When they caught him, they'd rip his clothes, take his bag. On the bad days

they'd destroy his work or bash him. I tried to help him—
getting him spare uniforms, repairing his books and bag.
Patching him up. I learned a lot about medicine that way,
and I think that inspired my studies, even if it was against
my father's wishes.

Even on field trips Alexander wasn't safe. The teachers
changed plans all the time, but they didn't stop it. We
couldn't go to the zoo, since the bullies had nearly thrown
him in the alligator pit. We couldn't go to the museum
either after they locked him in a sarcophagus. So, teachers
planned field trips so they could see what the 'common
man did' and what their future workers would be like. It
was a pretentious show of ignorance on the part of the
teachers, clueless of anything below their pay grade. They
went to factories, office workplaces, processing plants,
and more, all in the name of 'exploring the working
environments of blue-collar workers'. Nine years of living
through that school, and the staff still believed that they
could take us all to a lumberyard without any 'accidents'
happening. Absolute idiots.

The lumberyard field trip went relatively well, at first.
Everyone was fascinated by the equipment and tools—
especially the industrial bandsaw. Oh yes, the bandsaw.
The blade was a foot wide, with jagged, alternating teeth,
looped through an advanced system. It raced downward
at high speed, splitting logs like tissue paper. Everyone
was amazed by the demonstration, the clean cuts, and
the raw power of the machine. Workers tried to discuss
general safety practices but fell on deaf ears. I tried to stay
with Alexander. This place was a lot more dangerous than

anywhere else we'd been, but we got separated. I regret not trying harder.

I can tell by your eyes ... You know where this is going, right?

Alexander wandered off by himself. He didn't like the other students or teachers as they all showed disdain toward him like Mrs Price. I'm not sure if he considered me a friend at the time, but he sure as hell didn't consider anyone else a friend.

He found a solitary room, one which contained the other part of the bandsaw. The upward moving blade. We learned the bandsaw works by having the blade on a continuous band with the part that goes down used for cutting, while the rest loops back through the system, with a portion going up. The door was open so if there was anything blocking the blade, workers could check it easily. It was loud, and a dangerous place to try to find some solitude.

I had no clue what happened back there. I was worried when we left without him. The bullies were their usual selves, but I could tell something had happened. Eugene had a broken nose. Alexander must've fought back, and they did something terrible to him in return.

They would regret that decision.

A worker noticed the blood. It had seeped into the machine, staining the blade crimson. The room with Alexander was drenched in it, and that meant signs of the incident wouldn't remain unnoticed. When I heard about what had happened, I came back the next day. By that time, all the workers were clearing the debris left by the bullies. I had a horrible feeling of what I would find ...

When the room was finally opened, we found him. He was on the floor, covered in injuries, and the most distinctive was on his face. His cheek was cut open at such an angle it made an inhuman smile. We were horrified, but realised he was still alive. They drove us to a nearby hospital.

The doctors stabilised him and his recovery was slow. I wasn't allowed to stay long, as I had to focus on my increased studies. My free time dwindled. I was told that they wanted to stitch him back together, calling in the best plastic surgeons, but all that cost money he didn't have. He refused treatment, arguing, 'I will be hated with or without stitches. No need to spend more energy on me.' He spent a month in the hospital.

He was cleared on Friday, the 1st of January, 2003, released from the hospital in his freshly clean school uniform. Before he left, though, he stole a 12" chef's knife from a nearby store. None of us knew what had been unleashed.

Alexander died that day, and what came back was something else. A metaphorical revenant. I hadn't seen this side of him, because I wasn't able to talk with him, but apparently, he was more energetic, and showing signs of trauma and the starting traits of psychosis. He had a drive, a thirst he never had before.

For revenge.

Alexander strode through the grand portcullis of his private school. The repurposed ancient castle welcomed his presence. His air of gloom was replaced with another, more sinister aura. The time was 8.05am. Class started at 8am. He moved at his own pace to the first class of the day: English.

The class was boring Eugene, but Mrs Price didn't notice, or, more accurately, didn't care. She taught the others, regardless. Most of the students were paying attention to the lesson. Only one desk was empty, but that was because everyone thought he was dead. They didn't care to remember his name. Only I did. Alexander. They thought he had died or gone missing. Either way, they continued without him. Today, they were discussing the book we were reading, the Count of Monte Cristo by Alexandre Dumas. They were interrupted by the door opening with a soft creak. In walked a ghost, one they all thought was dead, his uniform covered in blood. I was the only one to be happy with his return, but a looming sense of dread quickly covered the room.

It was fun to see Eugene's eyes nearly popping out of his head when he saw that familiar, long hair.

'You ... we all thought you died ...' His voice was soft as it cut through the silence.

'What ... have you seen a ghost, Eugene?'

'But ...'

'You're actually reading? That's a new one ...' He noticed the cover. 'Ah ... how ironic. If you and your cohorts are the Danglars, Villeforts and Morrels, then what does that make me?'

Leaning over, he stabbed the blade he'd been holding through Eugene's hand, causing him to scream in pain.

'Well? Do you know?'

He was almost as pale as Alex, and stiff with pain. Tears streamed down his face.

'I ... I ...'

Hearing the movement of Brutus approaching behind him, he dodged under a punch ... and proceeded to gut him before the class. He smiled and laughed maniacally as Brutus bled out.

'You've no idea how long I've wanted to do that!'

Mrs Price was horrified.

'M-Mr Quill ... Do you know what your family would think of this?'

'I don't give a damn about what they think. They abandoned me! And you! You. Never. Helped!'

He picked up Eugene's book and stalked closer to her, everyone terrified in their seats.

'Of course I did!'

'Liar! You left me behind! All of you did! Left me to die ... and you don't even learn from what you teach!'

He slammed it on her desk, looking down at her. Alexander was 6'5". He leaned down to her eye level, at 5'4". Stabilising his left hand on the desk, he used the knife to show her what was behind his hair. She was petrified at the sight. Everyone saw the permanent half-smile which mutilated the right side of his face.

'This is what they did to me. You did nothing to stop them!'

A fatal mistake left her lips.

'You probably deserved it ...' He silenced her with a swift slash across her throat. She collapsed to the floor in a noisy gurgle.

'Maybe now you'll listen to me ... ha ...'

He straightened and looked back at the rest of us.

'Who's next?'

The silence was heavy, punctured only by the sound of Mrs Price's final convulsions.

'You're no fun ... didn't you like to see others being beaten up? I mean, you loved it when I was nearly fed to alligators!'

One girl in the front row was nearly on the verge of tears. Alexander immediately noticed and walked slowly over to her, the loyal blade at his side.

'Aw ... are you really going to cry, Jennifer? I put on a show for you! And here I thought you loved to insult her!'

'I ...'

That broke her and she started sobbing.

'I never wanted her to get hurt!'

'But then why did you laugh when your friends beat me and set my hair on fire?'

'Please ...'

'Please ... what?'

'D-don't hurt me,' she whimpered as he leaned down to her.

'You think begging will change my mind? If it didn't change yours, then why the hell would it change mine?'

He stabbed her through the side of the neck and watched as she fell to the floor.

The room erupted into chaos, everyone bolting from the room. Even me. I was terrified! This wasn't Alexander! Where was the kind, gloomy boy I was friends with? This is a madman who just killed three people! I ran. Not to any place the others would, but to hide in an empty classroom on the second floor. Throughout the day, I heard the screams. Boys, girls, teachers ... He went after everyone. Fewer of them could be heard towards the end of the day. Many hid like I did, but he was thorough.

In the end, I could hear nothing but the crows circling the sky, lucky enough to have found an unexpected feast. Dusk started to settle, and the sunset stained the sky. Before I could move, I heard footsteps. Not rushed, panicked footsteps ... but the methodical, quiet footsteps of a killer.

'I have a feeling that there is a person nearby ... where are you?'

I heard him go into the room across from mine.

'Not there ... hm ... how about ... here?'

He surveyed the room. The lights were off, and I was hidden inside one of the cabinets next to the door.

'Hm ...'

Alexander walked to the window and looked over the grounds. He appreciated the view before turning and leaving the room ... before suddenly leaping and violently wrenching the cabinet open, putting the blade to my neck.

'Found ... you ...'

He didn't really want to find me. I could tell from his voice.

'W-well, you did ...' I tried to smile, but he could clearly see fear in my eyes.

A single tear streaked down his left cheek. Lowering the blade, he started to cry in earnest.

'I'm ... sorry ... I'm sorry ... I ... I can't. Not you ...'

I comforted him with a hug, staining my uniform with blood in the process.

'I'm sorry, Alex ... I wasn't there for you ...'

'You were my only friend ... Here—' He took a set keys out of his pocket. 'Go to security, raise the gate.'

'Why?'

His manic smile combined with the gentle stream of tears told me everything I needed to know. I didn't ask again as I turned and left.

I wandered to security in a daze. I saw the blood-soaked, mangled corpses of people I knew and those I didn't. I watched the ravens fight over pieces as I passed. There was one plucking out an eye from what used to be Eugene. The sickly scent of iron hung heavy in the air. When I entered the security office, the man's neck had been carved open, his tongue severed. I choked back the urge to puke and called for the police. The gate opened and I walked to it. Outside, police officers had lined vehicles up in a barricade, and pointed guns at the entrance. I was a little bloody myself, having given Alex that hug. I turned to look back, and saw him there, for a moment, before an evening fog rolled in and obscured him from sight. Later, when the police asked what the hell happened inside those gates, I couldn't bring myself to talk. They would never see it, but it was karma.

Alex was lonely, dejected. All he wanted was a friend, since he'd never had one before me. Someone to appreciate him. I know he's still out there, somewhere. I haven't seen him since, and they never found him. I don't know if they ever will.

WAKING TO A NIGHTMARE

Kyle Mackenzie

M y REM pod opened for the first time in three weeks, and I stepped out to find darkness and the complete absence of sound. The pod's vitality and preservation system had malfunctioned, causing an emergency eject when my reserves dropped to zero percent.

My feet stumbled through the darkness toward my bedroom window and I pulled the curtains open. I lived on the fifth floor of an apartment building with my brother; the view from my bedroom window was the reason I paid more rent than he did. Before REM pods were distributed,

I'd wake up and watch the sunrise while steam from a fresh cup of coffee slowly fogged the window.

I stood in shock until long after the curtains stopped swaying. The urban plain of rooftops, roads, and glowing neon I was used to had become a jungle of green moss and sprawling trees. The buildings and roads were still there, some cracked and falling apart, others toppled and overgrown.

I rushed through my apartment, calling out for my brother and flicking every light switch I passed. None of the lights worked and I couldn't find my brother anywhere. I made my way into the kitchen and reached for the cupboard above the stove, taking out a flashlight and the last four batteries from their open packaging.

I loaded the flashlight and flicked it on. A beam of light reflected off the stainless-steel door of the refrigerator, highlighting a swaying piece of paper that was taped at eye level.

Will, I hope you get this. I tried to get your pod open, but it wouldn't budge. I've gone to Detroit City. If I'm still alive, you will find me there. Love you, please stay safe.

I opened my apartment door to the dim corridor. The flashlight beamed down the hallway as I stepped out and walked past the elevator. I pushed the button and listened, but the elevator never came. It was a long shot considering that the power in the rest of the building seemed to be out. So, I took the stairs to the ground floor.

Pools of swampy-green water were scattered around the lobby and the street-side windows were smashed—although there was no glass on the ground anywhere nearby. I moved through the lobby and onto the street and walked with my brother's note folded in one hand, flashlight in the other.

Streams of the morning sun squeezed through the canopy of leaves and branches several storeys above my head. It wasn't much, but it was enough light for me to turn off the flashlight and save as much battery time as I could.

I walked for a couple of hours, hopping over large cracks in the unlevelled asphalt on my way to downtown Detroit. The sun had risen over the horizon, and I could see its light in the sky through the trees.

At the edge of the Detroit River, my first option into the city was across the Ambassador Bridge. But, from afar, I could see that the bridge was no longer standing. The collapsed middle section grew slightly larger as I observed it; small pieces of rubble splashed into the flowing water beneath.

I was left with two options: the Underground Railway and the Detroit Windsor Tunnel. I passed the Railway entrance as I headed east, down Riverside Drive. Unfortunately, the entrance to the tunnel was partially collapsed. I could hear the echoing of gushing water, so I continued down Riverside to the Detroit Windsor.

When I arrived, the entrance was in a similar state as the Railway, without the threatening sound of violently flowing water.

I didn't go into the city much, but I remembered travelling through the tunnel with my parents when I was younger, so I knew it would take roughly half an hour to cross on-foot. The flashlight was still working well, despite the intermittent usage from earlier. Luckily, considering the state of everything else. I was surprised the flashlight worked at all.

I started down the tunnel and the partial sunlight, which I had only just become comfortable with, grew dimmer with each step. Soon, the flashlight's narrow beam was the only light I had to guide me through the tunnel. I ducked between and climbed over the sea of rusted vehicles and rubble.

After ten minutes of walking, the darkness began to toll on my sanity. Scratching noises and deep, hoarse grunting echoed through the opaque void, with no real point of origin. Another two minutes had passed, and I had crossed the Canada–United States border, marked by a cracked line between two faded flags.

The noises only grew louder the further I travelled until they abruptly stopped.

I froze, dead in my tracks, and rapidly scanned the blackness with my flashlight. The beam of light instinctively snapped to the hood of a decaying sedan as a scratchy rustling noise thudded from the vehicle behind me. The noise repeated as the sound bounced around the open darkness and eventually faded out.

I stood with the light trained on the hood of the rusty car as the heavy thud turned to quick, light taps. Eight round black orbs, each the size of golf balls, appeared from the darkness.

Eight legs followed and pulled the creature up and onto the hood of the car. It was covered in rough, patchy chitin with gaps at the joints of its legs and torso. The legs were bent and seemed to cradle the bulk of its weight from below its body. Just below its eyes, pincers tapped each other as it lowered itself and its legs grew closer to each other.

The pincers opened wide, and it launched at me. I ducked as it flew by and landed on the wall of the tunnel. The spider turned to face me and lowered once more. Similar scratchy noises erupted behind me and I shifted to a full sprint for the remaining kilometre of the tunnel. The tapping of pincers and thudding of legs across the field of decaying metal followed me the entire way. The giant spider relentlessly pounced at me from atop the vehicles as I sprinted, each time, narrowly missing me and smashing into my surroundings.

The light at the end of the tunnel did almost nothing to calm my violent heartbeat. I ran out of breath minutes before and was only still running because of the pure adrenaline pumping through my veins. Luckily, the pod's vitality and preservation systems kept me in good physical shape while it was still functioning.

The sunlight brushed across my face as I emerged from the tunnel. The arthropod followed me out but retreated into the shadowed darkness when the sunlight touched its chitin shell. The spider squealed at me from the entrance of the tunnel, spitting a thick, mint-green liquid.

'Get clear!' a voice called out from above the entrance.

I looked up, shielding my eyes from the sun, to see the silhouette of a woman sitting in a rust-covered, faded yellow excavator. She operated the machine like an extension of her body, pulling levers and pushing pedals seamlessly. The bucket of the excavator pushed a van off the road above the tunnel's entrance. The giant spider kept all eight of its unblinking eyes trained on me while the van, twice its size, flattened the oversized arthropod.

I dropped to my knees and held my chest while it burned viciously. I struggled for my breath for a few minutes while the woman made her way down to me. She walked nonchalantly past the spider's corpse, stepping over its guts splayed across the hot asphalt. She tossed a bottle of water on the ground in front of me.

'I've been trying to get that creepy crawler for weeks. Thanks for baiting it out,' she said as she clipped her machete into the holster on her hip.

'What the fuck is going on?' I said, struggling to speak between exhausted breaths.

The woman laughed. 'The world's gone to shit and everyone disappeared.' She extended an open hand and gestured toward the direction she came from with a slight nod.

I took her hand and she pulled me to my feet.

'Oh, and I don't know about the spider. Just evolution at work I guess?' She started climbing up the mound of rubble by the tunnel.

I followed closely behind her.

'So, how long have you been doing this?' I said.

'Since I woke up from my REM pod. Which reminds me,' she reached the top and helped me over the edge once I caught up. 'Did you wake from REM?'

'Yeah, about six hours ago,' I said, still trying to catch my breath.

'Ouch, so you're seeing all this for the first time?' She started walking toward the downtown area, the morning silhouette of the Detroit skyline in front of her.

'Talking about the giant spiders? Yeah, nobody told me when I got in the pod I'd be waking to a nightmare,' I said, choosing to follow her because she was my best chance of surviving and, eventually, finding my brother. Plus... I had no idea what I was doing.

'I don't think they knew what they were getting themselves into either,' she said, glancing in my direction as I walked beside her. 'Sorry, I'm Bec,' she said, extending her arm into the gap between us.

'Will,' I reached out in return and shook her hand.

'Will,' Bec said to herself quietly. She nodded gently and the slight curve of a smile formed on her cheek. 'It's been a quiet six months, good to have some company again,' she said, shaking her head.

'Six months? It feels like I only got into the pod three weeks ago.' I stopped walking, and my mind started racing.

Bec stopped walking as well and laughed. 'Three weeks?' she said. 'You think all this happened in three weeks? You think it took three weeks for spiders to evolve to be that big?' She pointed back toward the tunnel we had just climbed out of.

'No. I don't know. I just figured that those spiders were a one-off,' I said as Bec continued walking.

'Ok. It's better to show you. You'll see when we get there anyway.'

'Oh yeah, where *are* we going?'

'The city. Despite what you've seen—even if it looks like it—not everything in this world wants to kill you. It's probably the only safe place around,' she said as we stepped over cracks and journeyed into the concrete jungle ahead of us.

There was no way for me to know precisely what the time was, but I could tell from how the sun perched in the sky above us it was around midday. Bec strolled through the decaying, abandoned streets of Detroit without a care in the world. It threw me off because she had kept her hand resting on the butt of her machete the entire time we walked together.

'I live just over there.' Bec pointed toward one of the high-rise buildings through the skyline.

'You still live in an apartment?' I said, expecting to hear that she had built a hut somewhere in the trees, like the movies I'd watched before the world went to shit.

'Why not? The building is still sturdy. It has solid walls and insulation to keep me cool in the summer and warm in the winter.'

'Ok, that's fair.'

Rustling noises and growls shook me to my core as we walked through the downtown streets of Detroit. The occasional aluminium can skipped along the ground behind us and echoed through the open spaces. Urine and a wet dog smell engulfed the city, which somehow still felt alive despite the absence of humans.

'How are you so calm, even with all of these noises?' I said, cautiously watching behind, beside and in front of us.

'Don't worry about them. They just aren't familiar with you yet,' she said, walking with her hands by her side and her head facing down.

'They?'

'Think of them as small gorillas that evolved, like the spiders, to survive this environment. Just don't let the claws frighten you; they can be kinda scary at first.' Bec pushed open the French doors into one of the apartment buildings. 'We're here,' she said, holding one of the doors open for me as I followed her inside. We walked up the stairs to the seventh floor and down the hallway to Bec's apartment.

The building was clean. The carpets in the hallway were free of trash and mould, and the walls were only minimally damaged.

'This place actually looks nice,' I said as Bec approached the door at the end of the hall, beside the window.

'Yeah, I cleaned it up when I woke from REM. Were you expecting me to live like a savage?' she said in a playful, but accusatory tone.

'No, no, I was just—'

'I'm kidding, relax,' she interrupted, laughing as she stepped into her apartment.

I followed her inside and waited as she removed all of her weapons and gear and stored it in a large wooden wardrobe by the door.

'So, what happened before you woke up?' she said as she moved over toward the living room and collapsed on the couch.

'I got a notification for a VPS malfunction. Then the system ejected me, and I woke up.' I dropped my backpack on the floor by the wardrobe and moved over toward the living room.

'You got anyone still in pods at home?' she asked, kicking her feet up over the couch's armrest as she lay back.

'Nah, my brother John got out before me. He left a note, told me to come to the city when I woke up.' I sat on the single-seater couch opposite where Bec was seated.

She sat up in a panic. 'Your brother's name is John?'

Confused, I stared back and nodded.

She jumped up and ran over toward the wardrobe with her gear inside. The doors swung open and she reached into her travel pack. She pulled a small black picture frame from her bag and walked back to me, handing me the frame. I was shocked to see my brother's face cuddled next to hers.

'That's my brother! When was this taken?'

'A month or so after I woke up. John found me. We survived together for a few months. I took that with a polaroid camera I found not long before—' She paused, staring at the ground, unable to look at me. 'I'm so sorry, Will.' Small puddles started building on her lower eyelids and she couldn't lift her gaze from the floor.

Tears of my own splashed onto my brother's face.

STRANDED

Jai Thompson-Roach

Why *is the roof upside down?* To Colonel Henry Stewart, the roof being upside down meant one hell of a bender the night before. But that hadn't been the case in years. Klaxon sounds filled his ears as his face pressed against the glass of his cryopod. Opening with a hiss, it dropped him to the metal below with an unceremonious thud. Smoke and the acrid scent of burning rubber assaulted his nose as he struggled to his feet in the dark. The only source of illumination in the hall were the tiny red emergency lights, flashing in short bursts.

What the hell is that? Low, feral rumbles reverberated through the air, dulling the sharp noise of the alarms.

Primal fear filled Henry as he stumbled backwards. A hand reached out of the darkness and pulled him through the doorway.

A diminutive figure held her finger over her lips to silence him. They both watched as shadows moved past the door, the rumble louder than before. Henry's breath froze in his lungs. An elongated snout, dripping slime, traced the edge of the door, not quite entering but leaving thick trails behind it as it explored. Several explosions blasted over the alarms, rocking the ship, almost pitching the pair into the creature's sight but Henry hung on to wall. The snout retracted, disappearing into the ship. Breath seeped into Henry's lungs.

He removed Major Bit-Bug's hand from his mouth. She was a smart and savvy soldier who he had served with him in countless battles. 'Major, what was—'

She waved to silence him, mouthed the word armoury, and pushed a pistol into his palm. Taking point, Henry moved slowly but alertly as he shifted through the shadows. *What in the blue fuck was that? How the hell did it get on the ship?* Questions swam through his head, threatening to overwhelm him. He rounded the corner and froze. The creature was hunched underneath a destroyed cryopod. Exsanguinated corpses littered the floor, one victim locked in a silent scream as the colour drained from his body.

The alien was a hideous mix of wolf and lamprey. The canid mouth distended and latched on to the poor bastard's torso. Corkscrew teeth pierced his flesh as an interior set of jaws chewed a hole through his ribcage and his juices were sucked out. Black fur spread down its flank, giving way to mottled grey leather atop unnaturally long, gangly legs, as two bulbous yellow eyes retracted into the beast's skull to increase suction of the victim. With a sickening wrench, it ripped its jaws out of the man and began to sniff the air.

Bit pulled Henry out of sight just in time, saving his life for a second time. She peered around the corner. They had to pass the beast to get to the armoury. Bit picked up a loose piece of metal and threw it down the hallway. The cascading clangs drew the attention of the creature. It skulked away, growling as it passed.

'Is it gone?' Bit asked.

'I don't hear anything,' Henry replied. He peeked around the corner. An empty hallway greeted him, and he sighed in relief. 'It's gone, Major,' he whispered.

'What the hell was that?'

'I don't know, but I have a bad feeling.'

The pair sneaked into the corridor where the creature had been feeding. Drained, mutilated corpses lay about, each with the same horrified death mask. One cryopod at the far end of the row was untouched.

'Check to see if there's anyone in that, Major,' Henry ordered, as he stood watch, pistol raised.

'On it, Colonel.' Bit moved swiftly to the pod and examined it.

Inside the pod was the sole survivor of the feeding. Major Bit keyed several prompts into the machine's console and, with a pneumatic hiss, it dropped a figure onto the floor. Henry approached with his back to them, eyes trained on where the creature had disappeared.

'Name and rank, soldier,' he said softly.

'Captain Christine Baxter, R&D,' she replied groggily, the effects of cryo still evident.

'Colonel Stewart and this is Major Bit,' Henry said as the Major helped Baxter to her feet. 'We have a bit of a crisis here, Captain. Hostiles on board. You would have been next on the menu.' Henry gestured to the pile of bodies.

The captain, unable to stomach the sight and the effects of cryo at once, vomited to the side. Once she finished expelling bile, she stood upright. 'What's the plan?' she said as she wiped her mouth.

'Get to the armoury, get the heavy artillery and search for survivors while blowing shit up,' Bit said with a half-smile, looking almost psychotic in the red light.

'Easy, Major. Until we know how many of those things there are, we do not engage unless spotted. Understood?' Henry said.

'Yes, Sir,' Bit replied sarcastically.

The three inched down the remainder of the corridor. Shadows seemed to flicker and dance on their own. The end of the corridor split into two paths.

'It's left to the armoury,' Bit said.

'The ship is upside down, Major. We have to go right,' Henry said.

'Why the hell is the ship upside down?'

'I don't know. We have gravity but it's flipped.'

'That shouldn't be possible. The G-Drive can't just flip, Sir,' Christine interjected.

'We can figure it out later. Right now, we need weapons,' Henry said.

Thumping echoed down the corridor as a shadow stalked behind them.

'Oh, I wish I had on more than my skivvies right now,' Henry muttered.

'You and me both, Colonel. Your hairy legs are scarier than that thing,' Bit said.

'You're not above a court martial, Major.'

'Well, you have to admit that it's a little scary, Sir. I'm sure the captain agrees.'

'Don't bring me into this,' Christine said.

'Look, it's the armoury,' Henry said, cutting off the banter. He stepped over the lip in the doorway. Racks that once held weapons lay smashed all around the room. 'Son of a bitch,' he muttered. 'Alright, see what is salvageable. Captain, help me seal the door.'

'Yes, Sir,' Christine replied.

Grunting with effort, the pair got the door moving and it began to close. Until the slime-covered snout of the alien jammed its way inside. Fangs latched on to the colonel's shoulder and began to drag him through the gap.

'Get off me, you ugly fuck!'

The retort of Henry's pistol deafened them in the enclosed space as he fired it point blank at the creature's throat, spraying neon blue blood over the colonel. With an unearthly, wet shriek it let go and disappeared through the door. As Henry fell back into the armoury, Bit and Christine forced the doors shut.

'Where are you hurt, Sir?' Christine said as she crouched down to examine the torn clothing.

'Shoulder—but it didn't get enough of a grip to do much damage,' Henry said. He pulled his shirt down to show small punctures and a trickle of blood. 'There should be a first aid kit in here. Somewhere.'

He pulled himself up and helped search the room. It was large, spacious and usually held racks of neatly stored weapons and armour. *What the hell has happened to this damn ship?*

Several hours had passed since the armoury door was sealed. The crash had damaged much of the equipment beyond use. Outside, the alien lurked in the corridors, its wounded throat dripping a trail of neon ichor. It snuffled around before leaping into the darkness. Screams filled the ship. Silence followed, only punctured by the sounds of feeding.

Inside the armoury, the trio were still salvaging gear.

'I've managed to find several sets of fatigues that fit, combat boots and other gear. Specifically, six pulse rifles and three pistols.' Bit pointed to some intact crates. 'Several cases of ammunition survived, two blades and only a couple pieces of undamaged armour, Colonel,' Bit reported.

'More than I was expecting, Major,' Henry said.

'Goddamnit, can't we catch a break? This whole situation is like a fever dream,' Bit said. She yelled and kicked a crate over.

'Easy, Major. We managed our first objective. Now our priority is to find survivors and eliminate any hostiles we encounter if safe to do so.'

'Yeah, yeah, I know the rules. We're not to engage if the odds aren't in our favour.'

'Well, it is a smart tactic,' Christine said.

'No one asked you, Captain. Did you even see battle in the war?' Bit said.

'Sit on a cactus and rotate,' Christine said, extending her middle finger.

'Give it a rest, you two,' Henry said as he pinched the bridge of his nose and closed his eyes.

As Bit went to interject, a loud clang in the back of the room silenced them. Henry signalled a command gesture and the trio approached the noise with weapons raised. Half hanging out of a vent in the wall was a dishevelled man, older than even Henry.

'It's General Grant, help me get him down,' Henry said.

When Henry grabbed his shoulder, the general hollered like an angry bull and swung outwards. His fist caught Henry in the jaw and sent him to the floor with a loud thump. Bit and Christine jumped in and hauled the bellowing man out of the vent.

'Will you shut up?! You're going to bring god knows what down on us,' Bit said angrily.

The general blinked several times as he fell silent. With a grunt, he sat up and looked at Henry who was rubbing his jaw while still flat on his back.

'I thought you were one of those things,' Grant said.

'I don't blame you. We saw firsthand what the fugly bastards can do,' Henry said.

'We've managed to secure the room and rustle up some usable weapons from the destruction,' Christine added. General Grant looked around the room, assessing the situation.

'You've done well given all that's happened. What was your plan after taking here?' Grant asked.

'To arm up and look for survivors, Sir. And maybe in the process find out what the hell happened,' Henry said.

'Fatigues are over there, Sir,' Bit said, pointing at a pile of clothing.

Once the group was dressed and armed, they approached the door that the alien had attacked them through. Henry stood behind Bit as the general opened it slowly. The hall was empty, a trail of bright blue blood disappearing around the corner.

'Those things are terrifying,' Christine said.

'There's four of us, we'll be ok,' Bit reassured her. 'And we have some big honking guns now.'

'I guess you're right.'

'Yep. Right up until we get sucked dry,' Bit said

'You really like messing with people, don't you?'

'Yep.'

'Can the chatter,' Grant said. 'Eyes forwards, mouths shut.'

The group continued in silence with Henry in the lead and Grant covering the rear. The flashlight on Henry's rifle illuminated the empty hallway as they crept onwards.

The alarm had fallen silent, and its absence suffocated their senses. Henry felt the pounding of his heart in his ears as he rounded the corner at the end of the hallway. A howl ripped out of the darkness and the canid alien, bleeding neon everywhere, loped through a doorway ahead. It barrelled Henry over and pounced on Christine before she could fire.

She fought back, jamming the pulse rifle between its distended mouth and her. Bit dropped her gun, drew her blades, and charged the alien. Screaming, she leapt at the alien. Her momentum drove the blades into the thing's head. It relinquished Christine and began to thrash about.

'How do you like it, huh?!' Bit screamed. She began to bite the alien's hide like a wild thing, savaging the creature in a bizarre reversal of predator and prey.

'Let go of the damn thing,' Henry shouted as he and the general pulled Christine out of the way.

Bit ignored Henry's order and twisted the blades in the creature's flesh. It spun around and slammed its head into a support beam with a loud crack and crashed to the floor, limp. The major pulled herself out from under the alien and spat on its body before extracting her blades. She slit its throat.

'Don't you ever do that again, Major,' Henry said. He approached the alien and gave it a swift kick. 'Well, at least it's good to see time hasn't dulled your psychotic edge, Major.'

'You know me, Colonel. Jump in teeth first and all.'

'What the hell is wrong with you?' Christine said.

'The major is a trained berserker. She excels at hand to hand,' Henry said. He kicked the alien again. 'Usually not with something so big though.'

'Major, you are crazy. Normally I'd reprimand such recklessness but, given our circumstances, good job,' Grant said as he knelt next to the alien. 'Good god, these things are ugly, look at the teeth on it.'

'We're lucky the Major took it down then,' Henry said.

'Yeah, you're right,' Grant said before turning to look up the hall. 'Right up ahead should take us toward the command deck. We can find out what happened.'

The command deck's door was hanging ajar as the group approached. Henry pressed up against the wall and leaned around to scan the room with his flashlight. They entered the room and looked about, but it was empty, the equipment totalled beyond use.

'Oh, come on, this is bullshit!' Henry said.

The general stood in the doorway and sighed. As he opened his mouth to speak, a wet crunch emanated from his torso. Grant looked down at a thin fleshy tube that had punched through his stomach, vicious barbs hooking into his flesh. The major and Captain watched, stunned, as Henry grabbed the general. The colonel was ripped off his feet and lost his hold as the general was yanked into the shadows. His screams pierced the darkness, curdling their blood. They heard the wet, viscous sound of snapping bones over the general's screams before they mercifully stopped. The ravaged skull of the general rolled out of the shadows, flesh destroyed, bone cracked. A single eyeball remained in the skull, burst and leaking.

The colonel retched and crawled backwards as Christine and Bit let loose into the shadows. A honking bellow responded as a large mass retreated.

'It ... It ate him whole,' Christine said as she took several steps away from the door.

'I'm done. This place can go to hell and take its monsters with it,' Bit said.

An explosion rocked the ship, pitching Christine into the colonel, cracking the blast shields over the cockpit's windows open in front of them.

'Breach!' Bit yelled.

Nothing happened.

'So why aren't we getting sucked into space yet?' Henry mused as he sat up.

The colonel picked himself up and helped Christine to her feet. Then he approached the door at the far end of the room.

'What are you doing? Don't open that emergency hatch,' Bit said.

Henry ignored her and forced the door open. Bright light filled the room and a breeze swept in, assaulting them with the smell of saltwater. Almost completely blinded, the colonel squinted into the light, letting his eyes adjust before taking the first steps outside.

A lush green landscape, bordering cerulean waters, greeted him. The door exited onto the ledge of a short cliff, where the ground was rocky and sparse. Henry stood at the edge and looked out as Bit and Christine joined him.

'It's beautiful ...' Christine said, trailing off.

'And deadly,' Henry said. He pointed down to the beach just below where two more of the canid aliens stalked along the sand. Something poked out of the sand ahead of the aliens. They approached cautiously before the first one dives on it. Sand erupted as a black shape snatched the alien up and disappeared into the ground.

'Fuck me,' Bit exclaimed.

'Maybe later,' Christine retorted.

The major cracked a smile as the tension broke. 'Don't forget your cactus then.'

'You really are twisted, you know that?'

Henry looked up to the sky. Through the blue he could see the shape of a gas giant that neighboured the planet they had crashed on.

How do I get us home now?

A large shape flew overhead, leathery wings outstretched as it dived, scooping water into its mouth. It soared back up, expelling the water in a shower, drenching the sand. Several hidden aliens thrashed in reaction.

'So, what do we do now, Colonel?' Bit asked.

'We survive, Major. We'll find a way home. Somehow.'

'We'd better, I don't need to be stuck here with you and your hairy legs.'

The colonel laughed for the first time in what felt like a lifetime. He placed his hand on her shoulder. 'We will, Major. That's a promise.'

MADNESS BLOOMS IN SOMNIUM

Juliette Sauvage

Fluffy clouds drift through the cerulean sky as my skin soaks up the summer sun's warmth. My breaths are deep and uninhibited by my loosened corset, the skin of my legs prickling with heat from where I've rolled up the hem of my dress. Sybil lazes in her chemise beside me, having ditched the thick overskirt. Her dark hair splays around her head, her blue eyes and sun-kissed skin shining in the afternoon light.

The field is carpeted with wildflowers, stretching from the horizon all the way to the edges of the village; the small, grouped cottages perch at the outskirts of the forest, the mountains looming behind. A brook bubbles over the crest of the hill, sparrows twitter from the orchard to the left, and a gentle breeze cools our heated skin.

I run my fingers through the wildflowers around me, petals tickling my palms. I pluck one, bringing it to my nose to inhale its sweet perfume. Rolling over to face Sybil, I laugh at her blissed-out expression. 'Did you get the ale?'

She faces me with a cheeky grin. 'How else would I celebrate reuniting with my oldest friend?'

'Well, of course.'

Giggling, she reaches for her overskirt and retrieves the bottle she pilfered from her mother's stash.

'Only one?' I pout.

'Pity your magic can't stretch this a little further, if you know what I mean.' She waggles her eyebrows at me.

Rolling my eyes, I snatch the bottle and crack it open, taking a quick swig before passing it back. 'You were the one who always used to tell me I was supposed to do 'great things' with it. Now you want cheap tricks?'

'Well, it would be—' Her face pales, and her irises swirl with silver. She jerks to sitting and then yanks us both to our feet. 'We have to go.'

'What? Why?'

'Now.' She snatches up her overskirt and grabs my hand, tugging me to a run as we head back towards the village.

'Did you have a vision? What did you see?'

'The last witch, born of blood and storm to save us all,' she gets out between panted breaths.

The words echo in my mind, a half-formed memory from our childhood. 'What?'

Thunder rumbles, and I frown up at the clear sky.

'They're coming for you. To take you back. I hoped we'd have more time.' Sybil pushes us harder, ignoring my questions.

The cottages are only a few hundred metres away.

The thunder booms, sounding even closer now. I turn to look behind me, but my hand is ripped from Sybil's and I'm shoved to the ground.

A man on horseback gallops past me, swinging around and doubling back.

My gaze flies to Sybil, prone on the grass in front of me. Her eyes are closed and there's a gash bleeding steadily on her forehead. 'Sybil!'

I scramble to my feet, eyes darting around for a weapon. I dive for the nearest sharp rock. *It'll have to do.*

I grip it until it cuts into my skin. *Good.*

Breathing deeply, I plant my feet and crouch slightly as he nears.

Twenty metres. Ten. Five.

When I can see my reflection in the horse's sable coat, I dive to the side, dodging his sword and lashing out with the rock.

A flash of gold blinds me. I blink to clear my fuzzy vision and stare down at my glowing hands. *What the hell?*

The man lies a few metres away. Unmoving. His sword, a serpent carved into the blade, lies in his loosened grip. I'm too fixated on the blood pooling beneath him to notice his horse running past me. *Did I do that? I can't have. Is he de—*

'Sybil!' My heart beats a panicked staccato as I fall to my knees at her side. Cradling her head in my lap, I jostle her shoulders and pray she'll open her eyes. 'Wake up, Sybil. You have to wake up.'

Her eyelids flicker open, silver still leeching into her irises. My breath whooshes out, and I thank whatever god was listening.

'You have to go, Aislinn,' she whispers. 'Run.'

Hooves pound the grass, and two armoured men approach us.

'I'm not leaving you.'

I wake with a start, the violence of my dream fading rapidly as I stare at the cream ceiling. I dig my palms into my eyes.

Inhale. Car horns. Sirens. Dogs barking.

Exhale. Vanilla candle. Sweaty sheets.

I lean over to my bedside and grab the bottle, the capsules rattling inside. Squinting in the early morning light, I read the label: One tablet, once a day. It's been a few days, at least, since my last one. *God, no wonder I dreamt about her.*

Mum always dismissed my vivid dreams as the overactive imagination of a child. When I insisted Sybil was real, weekly visits began with a woman who spent an hour frowning at me and writing copious notes. Words like delusion and schizophrenia were exchanged in hushed conversations when they thought I wasn't listening (because apparently giving a kid a colouring book and telling them to 'sit quietly over there' made them deaf) and they started me on medication; it sometimes made me a bit hazy, but the dreams stopped. Until last night.

With shaking hands, I uncap the bottle and take the pill. *Do better, Gallagher.*

I groan at the time. *Who wants to wake up at 5am?*

Me, apparently. It's as good a time as any to get ready for work. I really should go to the gym, but not a single bone in my body has the motivation for it.

I flick the sheets back and swing my legs over the side of the bed, frowning when something tickles the sole of my foot. Reaching down, I scoop up a slightly squashed daisy. As I bring it closer to my face to sniff, my world blurs as I recall the field. The blood.

No. Nope. Uh-uh. Pull yourself together.

Screwing my eyes shut, I take a deep breath before opening my eyes again.

The flower is gone.

I sit at the breakfast bar, showered, hair perfectly coifed and makeup subtle and professional. My stomach churns, but I force mouthfuls of muesli down between gulps of tea.

My phone rings, breaking the eerie silence as I try to shake off my dream.

'Hello, Mother.'

'Don't take that tone with me, Aislinn.'

I roll my eyes to the ceiling. It's too early for this.

She clears her throat. 'I'm just calling to say I hope you're prepared for this presentation. This is not a time to be slacking off. Your father didn't get you that job for you to waste opportunities like this.'

I got myself this job, I want to scream. 'Yes, Mother, I'm prepared. I'm leaving for the office soon.' *Even though it's barely past six thirty.*

She hums noncommittally. My mother is one of those insanely hard workers who expects nothing but the best from everyone around her. Impossible standards defined my childhood. Hence, a call at an ungodly hour in the morning to ensure I'm ready for a presentation I hadn't told her about. My father and Greg Leighton of Marks, Leighton & Spencer are old friends.

I yawn, and she jumps on the involuntary sound. 'Have you been sleeping, Aislinn? You know exhaustion is a trigger for you. Are you taking your pills?'

'I'm just tired. I've been working long hours. I'm fine,' I lie.

Stress, that's all it is. No way would I tell her what happened last night.

'Hmm. Well, make sure you're sleeping ok.'

This coming from the woman who'd once told me I could sleep after the work was done.

'Your concern is noted.'

She responds with, 'Don't mess this up.'

Thanks, Mum.

'Let's get started.' Valerie's voice rings through the boardroom, and everyone snaps to attention. Valerie Marks (yes, *that* Marks of Marks, Leighton & Spencer) is a fearsome attorney who takes no nonsense. And although she isn't exactly the nurturing mentor I hoped for, she's everything I want to be: cunning, relentless and determined. Ok, so maybe I'd dial up the warmth a bit, but other than that she's my idol.

'Gallagher, where are we at with the Bakers?'

Our firm has taken on a case against one of the big developers in the city for harassing and abusing residents, causing them to forfeit their land. Their underhanded and barbaric tactics had left families frightened and temporarily homeless. I've compiled all the interview notes, and I pass them around now as I give a rundown of their statements.

Valerie is composed and stony throughout my presentation, but she gives a tiny nod at the end. Practically a glowing review from her. Coming off that high, I start my wrap-up.

'So, all that's left now is—' The words dry in my throat, cut off as a woman appears on the other side of the desk. Her chemise and soft blue skirt, embroidered with flowers but ripped and muddied, is a stark contrast to the suits and pressed blouses of the people sitting in the boardroom. Her turquoise eyes call to me as the scent of wildflowers drifts through the room.

'Aislinn, wake up.' Her voice is soft but tinged with desperation. 'I need you to wake up. You need to come back.'

My heart pounds, the room around me fading as I focus on her. *Sybil.* 'What?'

She reaches out a hand towards me. 'I've been trying to reach you for so long.'

A throat clearing jerks my attention away from her to a frowning Valerie. She flicks a barely discernible glance across the table—*at Sybil?*—before she looks back at me, tapping red-tipped nails on the glass tabletop. The light glints off the golden ring on her pinkie. 'You were saying?'

When I look back, the woman is gone, as is the sweet scent that had lingered in the air.

Clearing my throat, I say, 'Yes, sorry. The deposition will be...'

Sybil haunts me for the rest of the day. My work lies practically untouched, my mind drifting again and again to the blood-drenched field and silver-filled irises. My fingers hover over Dr Albert's number, but I never go through with it. My gaze strays to my purse and the pills I know are there, but I decide to ride the wave for a few days and hope it kicks back in.

She's waiting for me again that night.

Cold chains encircle my wrists, attached to a wall opposite Sybil, who mirrors my position. The dank cell is carpeted in hay, reeking of mould and barely staving off the chill of the concrete beneath us.

She sighs when I open my eyes. 'Thank the goddess you're here. We won't have much time before they're back. You need to free us.'

'What are you talking about?' The chains rattle around my wrists as I shift, trying to pull away from the wall only to meet the very short end of my tether. 'What happened?'

'I know it's hard to remember, and I'm sorry to do this but we don't have time.' She reaches as far as she can, stopping short a few centimetres from touching my hands. 'We were captured because they're after you—your gifts. And now you need to use them to get us out of here.'

'What?' I scowl as I look around. 'Where are we? Seriously, let's go back to the field ... although that didn't end so well last night.'

The clanking of her chains cuts off my mumbling as she tries to reach me again. 'This isn't a dream, Aislinn. This is your home. Your real one. She's been keeping you from us—everyone there has. I don't have time to explain. I know it sounds crazy after everything they did to make you forget, but you need to hold your chains and whisper these words.'

The chant falls off her tongue, flat and wrong to my ears. When she just stares expectantly, I sigh and, deciding to forget everything for the moment, recite the words myself. They wrap around my mouth and flow from my lips. The chains glow, rattle, and groan as they fall to a useless heap on the ground. Visions of a blood-drenched field and my golden hands fill my head.

Wide-eyed and gaping like an idiot, I look up at Sybil's pleased expression.

'Now mine,' she says.

The words taste like the most decadent chocolate on my tongue, and they have the same effect. Sybil kicks her chains away and tugs me to my feet. 'The door.'

We both focus on the lock in the middle of the cell door. The square of worn metal has serpents and strange symbols carved around the keyhole. Something tingles at the back of my skull, a memory aching to burst free.

Sybil swears. 'They're better prepared than I thought.'

I open my mouth but snap it shut again at the resounding clang of a gate opening.

Sybil shoves me to the ground, pressing a hand over my eyes and hushing me when I struggle. 'You need to go back to sleep. They can't ask you anything if you're asleep.'

I fight to throw off her hand but the darkness seeps in.

'I'll see you soon, Aislinn.'

The pill sticks in my throat that morning, chalky and gargantuan.

Get it together, Gallagher.

It felt so real. Even now, I can perfectly recall the cool kiss of steel wrapped around my wrists, the stench of the hay, the sweat beading on Sybil's forehead despite the chill of the concrete. Her voice echoes in my mind, hounding me in my apartment, haunting me on the subway. Her eyes stare back at me in the elevator.

My hands jitter from excessive coffee consumption, and I jump in my chair when Valerie calls out to me.

'Gallagher. How are the notes coming along?'

I swivel in my chair to face her. 'Really well, Ms Marks. I'm just finishing up the last of them. They'll be ready for the depositions next week.'

'Good work.' She nods and eyes me for a moment, crossing her arms. My eyes land on her signet ring, and I frown at the serpent engraved where initials should be. *Why does that look so familiar?*

'We need your focus on this, Gallagher. You're doing good work, but don't let yourself get distracted. Yes?'

'Of course, Ms Marks. I'm completely committed. You can count on me.'

'Mhm. Good to hear.' As she turns to leave, her critical gaze snags on my wrists. 'What happened? That looks nasty.'

Nasty? I look down at the irritated flesh of my wrists, rubbed raw from chains I've never been locked in. Static fills my head, but I manage to spit out, 'Oh, um, I got rope burn from my dog's leash when I walked him yesterday.'

She raises a perfectly sculpted eyebrow, but something lurks behind her gaze.

I retreat to the bathroom as soon as she leaves. *It's just like the flower—the marks will go away.*

Turning on the tap, I splash my wrists with water, wincing as the initial burn dissipates and the cool water soothes the enflamed sores. I hang my head and screw my eyes shut. Tap my fingers to my thumb one at a time. Focus on slowing my heartbeat.

In. Hold for three. Out. Hold for three. Repeat.

I slump against the sink. Reaching into the pocket of my blazer, I withdraw the bottle I stashed there earlier. The label says once a day, but ... I shake the pill into my hand. As it rolls into my palm, the stamped symbol catches my eye: a tiny serpent. It can't be.

I look up at my reflection, but something entirely different greets me in the mirror. Sybil crouches in that dank cell, chin up and defiance in her gaze as she glares at the soldiers in front of her. I can't hear what they're saying, but whatever it is, the men aren't happy about it. One of them reaches out and backhands Sybil. She slumps, cradling her bleeding cheek. Every inch of her visible flesh is covered in scabs and bruises, her tattered clothing barely protecting her from the chill of the cell.

I have to do something.

'Gallagher, we were supposed to meet five minutes ago.' Frenzied knocks land on the door as Valerie rattles the doorhandle. I picture that serpent on her finger hissing at me as she calls, 'What are you doing? Open the door!'

I chuck the pill down the sink. If what Sybil said was true, they want me. It's my fault she's there, my fault she's being tortured. I'll never forgive myself if anything happens to her, dream or not.

I whisper those strange words that fit so comfortably on my tongue. My hand lifts to the mirror, and instead of the harsh resistance of glass, my fingers begin to sink in, like plunging them into water. I meet Sybil's gaze, shushing her as I gesture to the guards. She blinks twice, stony-faced.

Screwing my eyes shut, I push once more with my hands, sinking further, then—

I open my eyes.